The Great Interlude

Books by Francis Russell

THE GREAT INTERLUDE

TRAGEDY IN DEDHAM

THREE STUDIES IN
20TH-CENTURY OBSCURITY

THE AMERICAN HERITAGE BOOK
OF THE PIONEER SPIRIT (*co-author*)

THE GREAT INTERLUDE

Neglected Events and Persons from the First World War to the Depression

by FRANCIS RUSSELL

McGRAW-HILL BOOK COMPANY

New York Toronto London

The Great Interlude

Library of Congress Catalog Card Number: 63-22157

First Edition

54339

Für
Karin
im Osten
und
Irmhild
im Westen

Contents

Introduction

The Hill was really Wellington Hill in the Mattapan section of Dorchester, five miles from Boston's City Hall. I have called it by the more inclusive name of Dorchester Hill because it dominated the area, giving a unity and a perspective to the amorphous district named so incongruously after a Dorset market town. Dorchester without the Hill would have lost its character.

Though I am more distant from Dorchester Hill in time than in space, that rounded drumlin is still for me the panoramic summit from which I view the events of the First World War and the twenties, and even those occurrences that came after seem to fall into its green perspective. When the war broke out I was four years old. One of my first cohesive hill memories is of a hot August afternoon in 1914, a concrete walk just wetted by a hose and smelling faintly of lime as warm damp concrete does, and my father in a stiff straw hat coming up the steps carrying the evening paper. Although I could not read I was struck by the huge black lettering of the headlines, and for the first time I heard the word "war." "It will only last six weeks," my father said. I remember it exactly, with a vividness that has grown more poignant with the years. It was on the Hill that my Uncle Amos, graduate of the second Plattsburg camp, visited us after he was commissioned, splendidly martial in mahogany-colored riding boots and chain spurs that clinked as he walked. The next year, on a bright and windy

October afternoon, I came back from flying a kite on the slope facing Boston Harbor to learn that he had died of influenza at Camp Meade, Maryland. On the Hill I lived through the police strike, the suddenness of Harding's death, and first heard Coolidge's nasal voice over my homemade crystal set. For four years I took the Mattapan streetcar at the foot of the Hill on my way to the old Roxbury Latin School on Kearsarge Avenue, and then—after the headmaster temporarily banished me—spent a lost and lonely year at Boston Latin before I left Dorchester for good. At the self-conscious age of sixteen I was glad to turn my back on such an out-of-the-mode place, for all the Hill's wind and sunshine and glimpses of the sea, little thinking that a third of a century later I should meet myself there again in my mind's eye.

Most of the persons and events I have written about here have impinged on my own life, and my life itself intrudes when I write of them. Yet—quite apart from any personal point of view—they deserve recording and recalling, these neglected facets of post-1914 American history. No draftee reporting at his local draft board, no ROTC student standing uneasily at ease in his new green uniform on the floor of the college gymnasium but has his antecedents in the Plattsburg volunteers. The Boston police strike took an obscure governor and made him President. The influenza epidemic of 1918 killed four times as many as did the First World War. Harding has been so disregarded that no standard biography of him has been written. After the transvaluations of the Roosevelt Era it is scarcely remembered that there was once a Coolidge Era. The medium Margery is forgotten; Jim Curley, the last of the bosses, who vowed he would live to be one hundred and twenty-five, is almost forgotten; Honey Fitz is remembered only artificially as the grandfather of the Kennedy dynasty. The Joyce cult has long since conquered literary Harvard, with no one to recall the fire of its beginnings when S. Foster Damon from the gazebos of the new Harvard houses proclaimed the revised gospel that Bloom was Christ.

Although he affected me least personally, I have written about Carlo Tresca as the last of the anarchist leaders, the last of the romantic revolutionaries in the tradition of Malatesta. Until I began my book on the Sacco-Vanzetti case I had barely heard of him. But as my work progressed and the references to him piled up, he became more and more a living person to me, the most outrageously attractive character involved in that world-shaking affair.

With the belated exception of Margery, the only persons I actually saw are the Boston mayors, Honey Fitz and Gentleman Jim Curley. Honey Fitz I met when I was five years old, a little over a year after Curley had driven him from public life. My father had taken me to some political reception in Dorchester Lower Mills with the promise that if I behaved myself I should meet the "ex-Mayor." "Ex-Mayor" had a magic sound. Brought up as I was on English children's books with their illustrations of "Turn again Whittington, thrice Lord Mayor of London," I pictured an ex-mayor as a stately being in a sweeping velvet gown and with a gold chain of office round his neck. "Where is the ex-Mayor?" I kept badgering my father, until finally I saw before my disbelieving eyes the brusque, dumpy, pot-bellied figure in a brown-striped suit that was ex-Mayor John F. Fitzgerald. Honey Fitz may have been a ladies' man, but he obviously had no great liking for children. He exchanged a few words with my father, gave me a perfunctory pat on the head and turned away. I was too disappointed to speak.

I did not meet Curley until his last years, just before he moved away from that politician's landmark, his house with the shamrock shutters on Jamaicaway. My friend Paul from the Irish delegation to the United Nations had come to Boston for the first time, and when I asked him what he would like to see locally, he said, "Concord and Curley." Any politician would have used Curley's unlisted telephone number to make an appointment, but I did not know that number. The simplest way seemed best. We merely walked up to the shamrock-fringed front door on a Sunday afternoon and rang the bell. Curley himself came to the door. I'm afraid we interrupted his Sunday dinner, for he was still chewing slightly, although he gave a quick swallow and showed nothing but geniality as he welcomed us in.

The whole downstairs was crowded, almost enveloped, with expensively inappropriate gewgaws. In the vestibule was a marble statue of St. Joseph holding his arm out as if to take one's hat or umbrella. A graceful double stairway curved into the reception hall, and from the ceiling hung a vast Waterford glass chandelier. Before taking us into his study, Curley led us through the downstairs labyrinth to his celebrated paneled dining room. What I remember most sharply is the sideboard with a massive silver service under cellophane.

"Which chair will you have, the mayor's or the governor's?" Curley asked us as we entered the study. Mayors of Boston and governors of Massachusetts are given such commemorative chairs when they leave office. I took the mayor's chair. Curley then spoke a few words in Gaelic, which he said he had learned as a child from his mother. Those in the Irish foreign service have to know Gaelic, so Paul was able to answer him.

There was a crude charm about Curley that Honey Fitz never had. Whatever my private thoughts about him, I couldn't help but like him, couldn't hold myself apart from the hypnotic effect of that resonant voice. The diction was uneven but the timber was magnificent. Curley's original voice had been harsh and high-pitched. But as a young man at a Faneuil Hall rally for Grover Cleveland, he had heard the eloquent bass of the Democratic Speaker of the House of Representatives, Champ Clark. After the rally he had sought out the elderly Speaker and asked him how to talk that way. "Breath deep and speak from your guts," Clark told him—and ever afterward Curley did just that. Paul was less impressed by the sonorities than I, and when Curley boomed vibrantly: "You have no doubt heard of the great Irish pote, Yeets," I saw my friend wince. When we left, Curley gave us each a photograph of himself and a record album of his speeches. That was my only meeting with him. The next time I saw him he lay in state, a primped and painted corpse, under the dome of the Hall of Flags in the Massachusetts State House.

Wilfred Doyle, the Assistant City Clerk of Boston, was one of my childhood neighbors on Dorchester Hill, and he had known Fitzgerald and Curley from the beginnings of their political careers. His memory went back as far as the eighties, to Hugh O'Brien, the first Irish-born mayor of the city. O'Brien, Patrick Collins, John Boyle O'Reilly—those men who within their parochial limits held to the eighteenth-century Irish parliamentary tradition of Grattan—were the men he admired. He liked Curley; did not like Fitzgerald—but admired neither of them.

I remember Mr. Doyle's cranelike figure striding down the Hill to the Norfolk Street station, his wide-brimmed black hat flopping, a curved-stem pipe with a meerschaum bowl wedged in the side of his mouth. He had been Assistant City Clerk for a generation, and would be for almost another generation. The actual city clerk was invariably a political appointee who considered his job a sinecure, with the administrative work to be left to his assistant. While mayors came and went, Mr. Doyle administered—and said nothing. For fifty years he lived on the crest of Dorchester Hill in the modest shingle house that he had bought there in 1908. The only money he ever had came from his City Hall salary.

Not until after the Second World War, when he had at last retired, would he ever talk about City Hall. From time to time, after his wife died, I used to visit him in his isolation. "I could have made a half million," he told me once, taking the pipe out of his mouth that seemed to be the same one I had seen forty years before. "Quite honestly, too. I've often thought that all I'd need to do would be to threaten to write my autobiography. There would easily be enough people to pay me that much not to."

Once we happened to get talking about Curley and Fitzgerald, and graft at City Hall. "Yes," he said. "I know what you think—that the Irish started it. When Curley was mayor they all paid him—the banks and the utilities and the rest. But who were the ones who did the paying? All of them, old Yankees. Tell me, who is more venal, the man who pays off or the man who gets paid?

"Whatever he took, I liked Curley," he went on. "If he asked me to do something I couldn't approve of, I said 'no' and that ended it. Another thing: Curley never took from the little people. He was never mean that way. When Fitzgerald was mayor everybody had to pay, from the scrubwomen to the elevator man. Curley wasn't like that."

Mr. Doyle concluded all those I had known on the Hill. He died there, and when he passed away, my last link with the twenties was broken, that period since glibly labelled "roaring," although its echo today more nearly resembles the reflected murmurings of a seashell. "The Roaring Twenties" is a retrospective cliché that most of the interpretations of the period merely underline. Fundamentally it was the twentieth century starting out twenty years late. In fashions, habits, clothes and manners it marked a much sharper break with the pre-war world than did the decade after World War II. Many aspects of it still make scandalous or exciting reading. Yet, seen from the perspective of a vanished hill, it seems—with the scattered war years preceding it—merely a period like other periods, where people, mostly anonymous, live out their uncertain lives in love and sorrow and wonder and some hope.

Plattsburg: The Camp by the Lake

Few recall now those Plattsburg training camps of 1915 and 1916 where, during the dog days, at a sleepy army post on the shores of Lake Champlain, several thousand sweaty, earnest businessmen-volunteers in unaccustomed khakis learned the manual of arms and how to form fours. The memory of their amateur soldiering—existing still in the minds of a scattering of elderly men—has been overlaid and obscured by the mass levies of three intervening wars. Yet the Plattsburg idea, as it came to be called, was, for all its naivety, the beginning in the United States of the modern conception of the citizen soldier, the genesis of the officers' training camps of the two World Wars, a psychological preparation for the drafts that were to follow. Plattsburg was a portent. As late as the summer of 1940, just after the fall of France, there was a brief revival of the Plattsburg idea, when another generation of businessmen-volunteers, impatient at their country's laggard preparations, spent a month of basic military training at their own expense at Plattsburg.

In 1914 the Plattsburg idea would have been inconceivable. For if there was one general reaction in the United States to the European war that broke out in midsummer of that year, it was that Americans wanted to have no part in it. President Wilson appealed to his countrymen to be "impartial in thought as well as in action . . . neutral in fact as well as in name." Even ex-President Theodore Roosevelt, who never believed in keeping his belligerence under a bushel, felt at the outbreak that the United States should remain entirely neutral.

The invasion of Belgium soon made impartiality of thought impossible. To most Americans, the complicated military issues involved reduced themselves to the simple imagery of *Punch*'s cartoon showing Belgium as a small boy, stick in hand, defiantly blocking the pasture gate against a cudgel-swinging German. A chain of additional factors turned American sympathy toward the Allies—the ties of English language and literature, the Anglophilism of the upperclass East, Allied skill and German ineptness in propaganda. Sympathy for the Allies, however, was a far cry from any wish to join the slaughter. Although the torpedoing of the *Lusitania* in May, 1915, was probably the culminating event that determined the entry of the United States into the war, yet eighteen months after her sinking Wilson could still be re-elected on the slogan: "He kept us out of war!"

A few American leaders felt from the war's outbreak that United States participation was inevitable. Most authoritative of these was the Army's Commander of the Department of the East and former Chief of Staff, Major General Leonard Wood. For years Wood had been preaching preparedness to an indifferent public and an uninterested government. And to his dismay, as the millions mobilized in Europe, the strength—if one could call it that—of the United States Army was only 80,000 men.

Wood—without whose zeal the Plattsburg idea would never have taken form—was the Army's senior general. His career was the more extraordinary in that he had come to the Army from the Harvard Medical School rather than the generals' way from West Point. As a young medical lieutenant he had first served in Arizona with an army detachment that captured Chief Geronimo and ended the Apache War. During this campaign he had shown so much courage, military skill, and readiness to take command in emergencies that he was awarded the Medal of Honor. His capacity did not get a chance to prove itself on a more expanded stage, however, until the Spanish-American War. Although only a medical captain at the outset, he was soon appointed colonel of one of the three volunteer regiments of frontiersmen—the Rough Riders—with his friend, Theodore Roosevelt, as second in command. It was like releasing a powerful spring. By the war's end Wood's energy and ability had made him a major general.

Subsequently, while Governor of Cuba's Santiago City and then Santiago Province, he ruled as America's first proconsul, becoming as popular with the Cubans as he was with his own men. In 1899 President McKinley appointed him Military Governor of the whole island, and some months later raised him to the permanent rank of Brigadier General. No such rapid advance by a nonprofessional had ever before been known in the regular army. His success in Cuba was followed by equal success in the Philippines, where he became Governor of the Moro Province and, in 1906, Commanding General of the Philippines Division. In 1908 he returned to the United States to take command of the Department of the East. The following year found him Chief of Staff and ranking officer of the army he had joined twenty-four years before as a contract surgeon.

With his imperious yet somehow gentle face and hawk nose, Wood looked every inch the general, from his chain spurs to the dog-headed riding crop that he always carried with him and that became his tag of identity. Something in the person of this austere father figure seemed to command obedience. There was no bombast about him, nothing of the martinet. He did not need to assert an authority that was innate. What has been said falsely of many generals could be said truly of him, that he was loved by his men.

It was in Germany in 1902 that he began to reflect on the need for American preparedness, when, as a military observer, he stood beside the Kaiser and watched the field maneuvers of the German Army. That magnificently formidable machine might yet become a threat to the world, as his fellow observer, the old English marshal, Lord Roberts, remarked to him. But Wood knew the absurd impossibility of trying to create any American equivalent. What he conceived of was the formation of a citizen-army, a vast trained reserve on the Swiss model, militarily efficient yet not militaristic. For years he tried to make his countrymen aware of the need of increased national defense. He talked preparedness night and day. He wrote articles and gave interviews. He spoke to clubs and colleges all over the country. He encouraged the formation of preparedness groups like the National Security League and the American Defense Society. In 1913, when clouds were gathering over Mexico, and German officers in their messes were drinking toasts to the Day, he took a first practical step by setting up two small summer camps for college students. Through such camps, he felt, young men would not only receive an introduction to army life, but—more to the point—would become concerned with the national defense problem. At Gettysburg, Pennsylvania, and Monterey, California, 222 students from ninety colleges spent five weeks at their own expense, drilling, parading, firing on the range, and finally—after a sham battle lasting a week—making a sixty-five-mile forced march. The camps were endorsed by educators as well-known as ex-President Eliot and President Lowell of Harvard, President Hibben of Princeton, and President Hadley of Yale. Even the pacific Wilson gave his approval. In 1914, three times as many students enrolled, and additional camps were held at Luddington, Michigan; Asheville, North Carolina; and Burlington, Vermont.

By the time of the sinking of the *Lusitania* most Americans had begun to reconcile themselves to the need for increased military preparedness, and an articulate minority demanded the entry of the United States on the side of the Allies. Sternly voluble spokesman for the war-hawks was Theodore Roosevelt, who felt that after the loss of so many American lives on the *Lusitania* it was "inconceivable we should refrain from action." Increasing numbers of venturesome Americans drifted north to join the Canadian Army. Others were paying their passage across the ocean to serve as volunteer ambulance drivers with the French.

Two days after the *Lusitania* went down, a group of fifteen romantically indignant Harvard graduates—among them, Theodore Roosevelt, Jr., Hamilton Fish, Jr., Elihu Root, Jr., and

United States Ambassador to France Robert L. Bacon—met in New York and sent a telegram to President Wilson demanding that adequate military measures, "however serious," be taken. The fifteen then drew up a plan of action. But Wilson, engaged in dispatching notes to the Imperial German Government, still did not consider preparedness a pressing question. Young Ted Roosevelt and two others then approached General Wood to ask if he would hold a summer camp along the lines of the student camps for business and professional men who wanted military training. They thought that they could produce at least a hundred volunteers. Wood was enthusiastic. He promised to hold such a camp at Plattsburg in August if even as few as twenty-five men should enroll.

The informal fifteen—later to become formalized and expanded as the Military Training Camps Association—sent out over 15,000 application forms to a selected group of businessmen, bankers, lawyers, doctors, college professors, and sportsmen. At first the response was slow, with only two or three applications a day coming in, but after Wood addressed a large group at the Harvard Club in June, there was a rush to apply. By August, over a thousand had enrolled, and 1,300 were on hand for the camp's opening on the tenth of the month.

No funds for the new venture were forthcoming from the War Department. The recruits paid their own way—thirty dollars—which included the cost of the cotton uniform. Wood had to raise extra money to take care of such amenities as screens for the mess hall windows. Bernard Baruch gave $10,000 and persuaded others to contribute. Wood took particular pains in the selection of his training officers. All of them were West Pointers, under the command of Major Halstead Dorey. The sergeants and the corporals were old-line army noncoms.

Early on the morning of August 9, the Business Men's Camp Special pulled out of Grand Central Station for Plattsburg. About half those aboard had optimistically bought their uniforms in advance and were already wearing them with all the awkward self-consciousness of recruits. Officially these somewhat overweight men, mostly in their late thirties and early forties, were motivated by undiluted patriotism and the spirit of self-sacrifice. Actually they felt they were off on a great adventure. To them the ponderously styled United States Military Instruction Camp—known more familiarly and readily as the Business Men's Camp—was a chance to learn man's oldest trade, to say nothing of allowing them to leave the world of banks and offices behind with full public approval. Also, there was the latent understanding that if America should enter the war, camp attendance would be the first step toward a commission.

The 1,300 men who signed the Plattsburg roster on that rainy August day were a well-advertised élite. Among the political figures were John Purroy Mitchel, the mayor of New York, Arthur Woods, New York's Police Commissioner, Dudley Field Malone, the Collector of the Port of New York and Pennsylvania's United States senator-to-be, George Wharton Pepper. Percy Haughton, Harvard's football coach, was matched by Yale's greatest fullback, Frank Butterworth. Bishop Perry of Rhode Island led the clerical contingent. Among the younger recruits were four Roosevelts: Ted, Quentin, Archie, and their cousin Philip, the tallest man in camp. From the newspaper references to "millionaire rookies"—like Alexander Smith Cochran, owner of the cup challenger *Vanitie*—it seemed as if the *Social Register* had gone into khaki for the summer. Richard Harding Davis noted that in his squad there were "two fox-hunting squires from Maryland, a master of foxhounds, a gentleman jockey from Boston, and two steeplechase riders who divide between them about all the cups this country offers." The still glamorous, if no longer youthful, Davis, fresh from his experiences as a war correspondent in France and Belgium, was the most noted notable at Plattsburg. Although by his own request, no mention was made of him in the press, everyone was aware of the martial presence. He was then fifty-one years old, six years above the age limit that could no more apply to him than it could to Mayor Mitchel. Indeed the limit was elastic enough to include one Andrew Pickering of Boston who was just short of three score and ten.

The rain was beginning to lift as the Business Men's Special pulled into a siding beyond the permanent brick buildings.

Plattsburg, which seemed so strange a world to the new arrivals, was commonplace enough: an Army post in the standardized pattern of all such built since the Civil War. Ever since the War of 1812 there had been a small infantry outpost here, and this had been expanded to a regimental post in 1890.

As the men piled off the train in the drizzle, they found themselves facing a long uneven drill field edged with tansy and melilot. Beyond the field, a brown tent-city waited for them —long rows of pyramid tents extending as far as mist-shrouded Lake Champlain, and large open-sided buildings that looked to be no more than tarred roofs on posts, and turned out to be the mess shelters. A sergeant led them to the adjutant's tent where each man paid his thirty dollars—five of which he would receive back if he did no damage to government property during the month. At the adjoining quartermaster's he received a rifle and bayonet well smeared with cosmoline, a mess kit, water bottle and cup, a web belt and pack. The supply sergeant in the tent beyond issued him three blankets, a sweater, a poncho, half a pup tent, and five aluminum tent pegs. Those without uniforms were now given two pairs of olive-drab breeches, two olive-drab shirts, a pair of leggings, a cotton blouse, and a felt campaign hat with a braided cord. With this overflowing collection in his arms the recruit stumbled across the field to the orderly tent of the company assigned him. Here the officer in charge measured his height, and, as a result of this measurement, sent him to one of the pyramid tents that extended like giant mushrooms down both sides of the company street. Sixteen such streets made up the two battalions of what was now known as the Business Men's Regiment. The forty regular officers assigned to the camp referred to their recruits as TBMs (Tired Business Men). The two hundred or so enlisted-men instructors, unable to suppress their profane amazement that anyone would pay to serve in the Army even for a month, called the eager civilians in uniform "tourists."

There were eight men to a dirt-floored tent, furnished with collapsible canvas cots, a lantern, a water bucket, and several tin wash basins. After the newcomers had set up their cots, sorted out their equipment as best they could, and tentatively essayed their uniforms, they were summoned outside by the sergeant's whistle and marched to the mess shelters where in a clatter of tin plates they ate their first army meal. Later, in the clearing evening, they were free to explore the camp and the post beyond. Although men of affairs in their ordinary lives, now, in their temporarily adopted military life, they felt something of the uncertainty of all recruits. The regulars, in their close-fitting uniforms and campaign hats with faded cords, looked so very regular. The businessmen soldiers-to-be, wandering in groups past the post parade ground, were uncertain whether to salute the officers they passed or not, were uncertain as to just who were officers.

Along one side of the trim parade ground stood the heavy brick lumps of the officers' quarters, duplex for the lieutenants and captains, solidly single for field officers, each marked with name and rank. In the middle distance were the equally solid two-storied enlisted men's barracks with iron-railed porches running the length of the fronts. Behind lay the stables and workshops. As these most unmilitary recruits sauntered along the macadam walks they could see the placid lake on the other side of the parade ground, the curve of Cumberland Bay, and through a lifting cloud-rack fugitive glimpses of the Green Mountains across the water to the east. It was a remarkably peaceful setting in which to prepare for war.

The recruits' first day began at the unnatural hour of 5:55 A.M. with the staccato notes of reveille. That day was the muster pattern of the days to follow. Assembly at 6 and thirty minutes of calisthenics gave way relievingly to breakfast. After breakfast came tent-keeping and policing of grounds, rifle cleaning, and with first call at 7:25 the long morning of the school of the soldier. Like all recruits, the TBMs began with the elementals—the position of the soldier at attention; saluting; left, right, and about face. Then came their first fumbling attempts at the manual of arms, soft hands slapping the stocks and slings as the noncoms repeated the ancient "Hit 'em! You won't hurt the rifle!" Philip Roosevelt remarked that learning the manual of arms was like learning to tango—you kept on, and all of a sudden you found you could do it.

After forty minutes off for lunch, the newcomers slogged the hardening miles of a route march at the old army pace of three miles an hour. As time went on, such marches were varied by cross-country skirmishes, over fences and ditches, past abandoned cemeteries, and through swamps, with the unwary tangling themselves in poison ivy. Sometimes, with luck, there was time for an afternoon swim. At 5:15 P.M., in blouse and belt, they stood in formation to the martial melancholy of the bugles sounding retreat as the flag fluttered down the mast. That daily ceremony, so taken for granted by the old sweats, was to the recruits solemnly new and impressive. They were then given three quarters of an hour free until mess call. After supper there were lectures on various aspects of the military. Tattoo came at 9 P.M., call to quarters at 9:45, and taps at 10 P.M.

The Business Men's Camp was bounded by a thick grove of oaks and maples. At the edge of the grove, separated from the camp by a rail fence, stood a solitary pyramid tent with a flagstaff in front of it. This was the temporary quarters of the Commanding General of the East, who had come to Plattsburg for the month to observe his preparedness idea take tangible form. Every day General Wood could be seen leaning on the top fence rail watching his civilian volunteers at their drill. Often, as a substitute for their evening lectures, he talked to them informally around a campfire at a natural amphitheater near the lake. Facing them in a semicircle as the twilight faded, he spoke quietly, without rhetoric, of the military history of the United States, of preparedness, of citizens as soldiers, of the imminence of war. What he said was plain, stirring, and above all true. Those who attended the camps never forgot that austerely genial man with his dog's-head riding crop tucked under his arm and the lines of his face etched deep by the blaze of the logs.

For the first few days the TBMs drilled as individuals and squads, then as platoons. By the end of the first week they were drilling as companies. The next week saw them parading in battalion formation, and by its end they were ready to appear for the first time on the post parade ground as a regiment. It had taken them only days to absorb what the ordinary recruits took weeks and months to learn. With them, will and intelligence more than made up for the handicap of their years. Astonishingly—as much to themselves as to their regular army instructors—they actually began to march and look and feel like soldiers. Suddenly their ordinary life of only a few days back seemed infinitely remote, the only reality that of the khaki present. From his rail fence, General Wood looked at them approvingly.

To review the regimental parade, scheduled for August 25, Wood invited President Wilson, ex-Presidents Taft and Roosevelt, Secretary of War Lindley Garrison, and a number of labor leaders and university presidents. Wilson regretted that "public matters" prevented him from coming. Taft and Garrison made their different excuses. Nothing could have kept Roosevelt from Plattsburg. He at once accepted in a telegram in which he announced that he was going to make a speech to the "rookies," and asking if he might make it when the men were off duty and preferably outside the camp.

If Wood was the chief military advocate of preparedness, Theodore Roosevelt's was the civilian voice that carried farthest. Those who had enrolled in the camp acknowledged two leaders, the Colonel and the General—and it was as the Rough Rider, not as the ex-President, that Roosevelt came to Plattsburg. After the invasion of Belgium, Roosevelt had turned vociferously pro-Ally. After the sinking of the *Lusitania,* he was for the immediate entry of the United States into the war against Germany. Anything less was for him the coward's part. Words did not fail him when he thought of the deedless academician in the White House penning his futile notes to Berlin. Wilson's phrase about "being too proud to fight," made only three days after the *Lusitania* went down, was for Roosevelt as contemptible as Henry Ford's recent remark that anyone who chose to be a soldier was either "lazy or crazy."

The ex-President disliked the President with all the scorn of a man of action for a man of the libraries. Wood, aware that his old friend was not likely to err on the side of tact, asked to see an advance copy of the other's speech and eliminated most of the derogatory references to the professorial Wilson. Roosevelt arrived at camp the morning of the twenty-fifth every inch the Rough Rider, wearing a wide-brimmed hat, a riding jacket of military cut, breeches, and leather leggings. He watched with field glasses while the second TBM battalion worked out a tactical problem on the drill ground. Then in the afternoon he observed a sham battle between the first battalion and the regulars, where the TBMs drove the enemy into the Saranac River and ended the maneuver with a bayonet charge. At the glint of steel, the Colonel showed most of his thirty-two teeth and shouted "Bully!" He was moved almost to tears at retreat when the recruits paraded as a regiment. "I have never seen a more inspiring sight," he told Wood.

At supper, Roosevelt joined the rookies, many of whom he knew personally, for an old-time army meal of beans and brown bread. Afterward, the whole regiment moved down to the amphitheater by the lake to hear the Colonel's speech. The TBMs were joined there by six hundred regulars of the post and several thousand men and women from the countryside. Colonel Roosevelt was introduced by General Wood.

Seeing the row on row of citizen soldiers squatting attentively on the ground in front of him in the fading light, the old Rough Rider felt himself inspired. He sneered at the ignoble part the United States had played in the world for the last thirteen months. He told them resoundingly that no man was fit to be free unless he was not merely willing but eager to fit himself to fight for freedom; and he denounced all "professional pacifists, poltroons and college sissies."

As the light dimmed across the lake and the Green Mountains turned to gray, a lantern was fixed on a photographer's tripod and the uneven rays illuminated the Colonel's martial features. None of his hearers could possibly miss the Wilsonian reference when he told them that "to treat elocution as a substitute for action, to rely upon high-sounding words unbacked by deeds, is proof of a mind that dwells only in the realm of shadow and shame." Just as he was concluding, a half-grown

Airedale wandered into the fringe of light, nudged against him, and then rolled over on its back—amidst much laughter from the uniformed audience—its paws in the air. "That is a very nice dog," Roosevelt remarked, "and I like him. His present attitude is one of strict neutrality."

Although Wood had edited out the saltier parts of the Roosevelt speech, unedited copies had been sent to the press earlier and the text was printed intact in the next day's papers. Roosevelt, while waiting for the train after he had left the camp and the reservation, talked with reporters and felt free then to attack Wilson in much blunter language. On reading the accounts of the Plattsburg day, Wilson was as furious with Wood as he was with his perennial critic, Roosevelt. By the President's order the Commanding General received a sharp rebuke from Secretary Garrison to which was added a warning against providing any further opportunity for such "unfortunate consequences," at Plattsburg or any other camp. Wood accepted the rebuke in soldierly silence. But Roosevelt's speech and Garrison's reply echoed from coast to coast. The incident stirred the public and raised preparedness to a portentous national issue.

During the latter part of their course, the TBMs divided according to aptitude or physical condition into infantry, cavalry, artillery, and signals. Mornings they still drilled together, but mimic warfare more and more supplanted drill. Companies marching outside camp learned to send out cossack posts, combat patrols, and advance rear guards. Each man spent two days firing on the range, found out the bone-shaking way about tightening slings and squeezing triggers, came to recognize the sight of a white disk as indicating a bull's eye, and the dismal red flag ("Maggie's drawers," in newly acquired army lingo) waved across the target's face as a clean miss. In the evening, after lectures, most of the recruits would gather in their company tents to listen to the company commander elucidate the tactics laid down in Drill Regulations. At taps, when the lanterns were extinguished and the camp, except for the brown glow of General Wood's tent, lay dark, the sergeants making bed-checks from tent to tent down each company street never found an AWOL. The TBMs were too serious—and too tired.

The climax of the Business Men's Camp came when the regiment spent nine days of war games in the field matched against regulars. Their mock battles ranged over the Adirondack country, west as far as Dannemora, north to Chazy and Coopersville and the Canadian border. Each night the recruits pitched their pup tents at some new site. They learned to make up their packs, roll their blankets in the dark, cook a meal in a mess tin, break camp in five minutes. Their rifles loaded with blanks, they tramped through the browning countryside, over stone walls and across fields now bright with goldenrod, always on the alert for enemy scouts and patrols identifiable by their white hat bands. Already there was the first hint of scarlet in the maples, the crickets were shrill at night, and mornings the dew lay heavily on tent and poncho. In this roughing-it the men found a curious happiness, a feeling of being old campaigners at last. Richard Harding Davis—naturally in a cavalry troop—described one of their evening bivouacs:

> Back of us was a forest of magnificent pines and overhead a harvest moon. When the work was done and each man began to cook, and the hundreds of tiny fires burned red in the moonlight and were reflected in the lake, the picture was one of great beauty. Nor did the odors of frying bacon and steaming coffee in any degree spoil it.

Many of the men kept diaries and notebooks. One of them sitting in a clump of joe-pye weed and jotting down a few lines at the edge of a field just before a bayonet charge, remarked on the serenity of the blue Adirondacks and the hard puffs of cumulus moving across the sky. "Ahead of me an officer with field glasses," he penciled in his book. "Three brown figures beyond wearing cartridge belts and carrying slung rifles. A whistle blows, there is a shout—and from every bush and hollow a khaki jack-in-the-box springs up rifle in hand until the long field swarms with them."

Camp ended on Saturday, September 4, at the beginning of the Labor Day weekend, the same day that Henry Ford gave a million dollars to a campaign "for peace and against preparedness." From New York had come rumors of a mustering-out parade of the Business Men's Regiment down Fifth Avenue—a gesture that would have appealed to Roosevelt but that Wood quietly and quickly shelved. When reveille sounded on the last morning there were a few moments of silence in the tent city. Suddenly the post band, assembled in secret near the camp flagpole, crashed forth with "Hail! Hail! The gang's all here!" With yells and cheers the TBMs swarmed out of their tents to snake-dance after the band as it marched in and out of the company streets. The gang was all there—for the last line-up, the last mess, the last packing, and then the last look at Plattsburg.

A second course was held two days after Labor Day, but this off-season camp drew only 600 recruits. By the following summer, however, there were nine additional camps on the Plattsburg model attended by 16,000 men. Some of the original Plattsburgers who re-enrolled in 1916 received reserve commissions at the end of their course. Ted Roosevelt became a major, his brother Archie, a first lieutenant. By the war summer of 1917, Plattsburg had evolved into an officers' training camp where the "ninety-day wonders" emerged from a three months' course with gold second-lieutenants' bars on their shoulders. In the sterner light of that training the TBMs seemed play-soldiers.

Looked at in a strict military sense, the effect of the initial 1915 Plattsburg camp was negligible, the lessons learned there almost useless to the minority of TBMs who later saw active service in the war. Nevertheless Plattsburg as an idea was large and compelling, surviving long after the war in the Citizens' Military Training Camps and the summer encampments of the Reserve Officers' Training Corps. In a time of confusion it clarified the issues by visibly bringing home to America the idea of preparedness. It helped prod a reluctant President into a more active defense policy. It did much in laying the groundwork for willing acceptance of the draft in 1917 that was so riotously resisted in 1863. Welcomed by most, dreaded by some, the Plattsburg idea was twentieth-century America's first tentative step toward universal military service.

A Journal of the Plague: The 1918 Influenza

Though it now seems merely an episode in the last year of the First World War, the influenza of the autumn of 1918 was one of the three greatest outbreaks of disease in history. Only the Plague of Justinian and the Black Death can compare with it. A quarter of the world's population was affected. All in all it killed 22 million people, almost twice as many as the war itself. More were dead in India in a few months than in twenty years of cholera. In the United States, half a million died.

Unlike the Black Death, which killed nine out of ten, and cholera, which took four out of five, the 1918 influenza was fatal to only about three or four percent of those who came down with it. It was the tremendous sweep of the disease that made the death totals so large. By the end of October it had spread all over Europe and North America and many parts of South America. India, China, Persia, and South Africa were infected earlier. In two months it covered the globe.

Through centuries the course of epidemics has run from East to West. The 1918 influenza followed this pattern, reaching America last. Traditionally, Asia has been the matrix of disease, as if there were a permanent focus of infection that existed in the vastness of Mongolia, from where it would erupt periodically into the rest of the world. Some doctors maintained that the influenza was introduced into Europe by Chinese labor battalions that landed on the coast of France. Some attributed it to Russian soldiers arriving from Vladivostok. Others thought it might have developed among the troops from an earlier bronchitis so prevalent in Spain in the spring that it gave the name "Spanish" to the autumn influenza. There was even one tenuous theory that the disease sprang into being in an isolated Georgia training camp during the winter of 1917, and that from there it migrated until it had circumnavigated the earth.

Influenza is still a mysterious disease. No one yet knows whether it is caused by one virus or several, why it occurs in cycles, or how and where it stays dormant between epidemics. There are theories of weather, theories of the wearing off of group immunity, even a theory of determination by economic circumstances. However, the most generally held explanation is that a pandemic like that of 1918 is brought about when a new and explosive strain of virus develops through a spontaneous process of mutation or renewal.

In its milder forms, influenza has sometimes been known as the three-day fever, accompanied by headache, congestion, soreness of the joints, and languor. Although it is transmitted by contact, its incubation period is less than two days. Few other diseases are able to spread so far in so short a time. Yet it is brief as it is sudden. The word *influenza* comes from a misunderstanding of the Italian phrase *influenza di freddo*—influence of cold. English writers of the eighteenth century took *influenza* to be the name of a disease.

Influenza pandemics have recurred with each generation in modern times. Similar waves developed in 1857, 1874, 1890, 1936, and 1957. What distinguished the 1918 outbreak was its lethal undercurrent. Influenza had been equally widespread and equally swift before, infecting millions but killing few. The Spanish influenza was different. In addition to the usual transitory symptoms, it had the ominous tendency of developing into pneumonia. When the lungs were affected a quick deterioration set in. This is what gave this influenza its unique character, for over a third of those who came down with the pneumonia died.

As the influenza swept over the cities of the world, it did not create the panics of earlier plagues. For one thing, disease was no longer a portentous and inscrutable affliction. Now it was publicized in advance. One could trace its westward course in the daily papers, and the death percentages were insufficient to disrupt contemporary city organisms. Then again, in four years much of the world had become used to sudden death, and the influenza, as compared to the war, was a silent and unspectacular killer.

Yet there were overtones of the Black Death and the Sweating Sickness that persisted even into the Machine Age. Many left the cities. Numbers of those who stayed, especially in the poorer sections, died alone. Movements of conscripts to the training camps had to be halted. In many places undertakers and coffin makers could not keep up. Through the slum streets where the disease struck heaviest, mothers and infants were found sharing rooms with corpses. In one city a furniture van that had been commandeered to transport influenza dead overturned, spilling the uncoffined bodies over the street. Nothing like this had been seen before in modern Western cities.

That autumn I was eight years old and in the third grade of the Martha Baker School in the Mattapan section of Dorchester. From the summit of Dorchester Hill where I lived, Boston's serrated outline loomed up forebodingly five miles away. Under the gray sky, it seemed both threatening and threatened, the obelisk point of the Custom House itself a kind of mausoleum. Bulfinch's gilt State House dome dimmed to dirty yellow in the line storms, and the ships heading down the harbor for Europe, their hulls zigzagged with zebra-striped camouflage, were a visible part of the uneasy years.

As I try to recall those autumn months, they are fragmented in my mind. I find myself with impressions of events as sharp and vivid as if they happened last week, yet lacking a cohesive pattern—unless the heterogeneous memories cohere within the war itself. That was the stupendous and embracing fact, even to us in Miss Sykes' third-grade room—the war to end wars, to make the world safe for democracy. It was the struggle of good against evil, light against darkness, symbolized indeed by the visions in the sky (so we had been told) at the Battle of the Marne. Never a doubt as to who would triumph, especially now that our boys were there. Like the wicked stepmother or the witch of the fairy tales, the Germans, the Huns, with their lustful Kaiser Bill and the ridiculous Crown Prince would meet the fate of all dark spirits.

For this, for the victory of our boys, we ate peaches and baked the stones dry to be used for gas masks. On Boston Common there were peachstone collection barrels. How they were used we didn't know, but the newspapers showed a boy in Roxbury who had saved 2,000. We joined the Junior Red Cross and wore the rectangular celluloid pins in our buttonholes. Then there were the Thrift Stamps at twenty-five cents each for us to buy from Mr. Gibney, the postman. Mr. Gibney gave us a little book to paste the stamps in. Each space to be filled had a motto like "A Penny Saved Is a Penny Earned" or "Great Oaks from Little Acorns Grow." When we had twenty stamps we exchanged them with Mr. Gibney for a War Savings Certificate. Instead of sugar we used Karo Corn Syrup. The red Karo cans had yellow syrup and the blue ones, white syrup. Neither tasted very good, and there was no frosting any more even for birthday cakes because the sugar had to go to the starving Belgians.

"Beat the Hun!" Those barbarians we were fighting had started it all by attacking brave little Belgium and torturing women and children there—the poor suffering Belgians, most crucified of people. "Beat the Hun!" The Third Liberty Loan poster showed a porcine German with heavy, carnal moustache and spiked helmet silhouetted against the background of a flaming town as he dragged a trembling long-haired girl with him toward the shadows. What was going to happen to her, we knew, shouldn't even happen to Jeanette Galvin, the dirtiest girl in the class, who never cared if she gave a free show of her drawers, swinging on the railing at recess.

The next spring my cousin Ernest came over from England, wearing his Royal Flying Corps tunic, and I was astonished to discover how much he disliked the Belgians. When I asked about them expectantly, he said they were twisters, liars, half of them spies, always stealing petrol, and he wished he could have shot one or two. Next to the Belgians he most disliked the French. The Huns he didn't seem to mind. He didn't call them Huns or Boches, but Jerries. When I asked him about the Miracle of the Marne, he merely laughed.

Though the city on the horizon sickened as September passed, our segment of Dorchester was scarcely affected. No one on the Hill died of influenza, none of us in the third grade so much as caught it. To our confident immortality it seemed no threat at all, rather one more incident in the excitement of the war's climax. At recess time the girls jumped rope on their side of the yard and sang:

I had a little bird and his name was Enza,
I opened the window and
In-flu-enza.

Gradually we became aware of the epidemic as the Boston death rate rose at the end of the month. Our one-storied stucco school building verged on Walk Hill Street, which half a mile farther on branched off to Mount Hope and New Calvary cemeteries. Before this we had scarcely paid any attention to the funeral processions that passed at the rate of one or two a day, as we dawdled along the footway going to and from school or played in the yard at recess. But with the spread of the influenza the processions became almost continuous, and we began to notice. Most of the carriages were still horse-drawn, the familiar black hacks with black horses and solemn silk-hatted coachmen. But now more and more high-topped limousines were appearing, with their long shiny hoods and polished lamps.

In the line-storm days as we sat at attention with folded hands while Miss Sykes read the Bible lesson under the fly-spotted silk flag, or as we followed through the morning routine of reading, multiplication tables, and the push-pull penmanship of the Palmer Method, we could hear the carriages passing outside, the clop of horses' hooves in the wet leaves, or the swish of vacuum-cup tires above the rain trickling in the gutters. The odor of that room on a wet day was an unforgettable compound of damp leather, damp woolens, chalk dust, floor oil, paste, buckram, and a faint but pervading essence of coal dust and ammonia that seeped up from the basement. I can see Miss Sykes glowering at her desk, beside her the brass bell which she used to ring to call us in from recess. Behind her is the blackboard and above it a steel engraving of Longfellow. The wainscotting is covered with a coarse brown buckram, the woodwork painted mud color. Over the door is W. Strutt's picture, "And a Little Child Shall Lead Them," reproduced in sepia and hung in a golden oak frame. The mild-eyed child with the palm—so different from the children of the Mulvey Street gang—is leading a lion. Next to the lion is a lamb and beyond the lamb an amiable wolf. In the foreground a leopard lies asleep, and there are also a camel and a calf.

The Miss Sykes of my recollection is a dun crone with loose under lip and mean voice who had outlived time. Old Lady Sykes, we called her. Jeanette Galvin and the Mulvey Streeters called her Sykesy Spikesy. It never occurred to any of us that she could have feelings. Her hair had begun to turn. I suppose she was really in her middle thirties. Twenty-five years later, when I went back to pay her a visit, I found a kindly white-haired woman, vastly younger in appearance than when I was in her third grade.

Yet I think my recollection is not wholly at fault, for in those weeks the plague had stretched out its fingertips toward Miss Sykes and she could feel that substanceless touch each day. Trying as best as she could to conceal it from us, she became sharp and tense-voiced. The rattle of the hacks and the hiss of the vacuum-cup tires had broken her nerve. In the afternoon the sun's rays would strike against the glass of a passing carriage and reflect waveringly across the ceiling of our room, and we, distracted by light and sound, would crane toward the row of windows. "Eyes front!" she would shriek at us. "Edmund MacDonald, if you look out the window once more I shall send you to the dressing room." Her last resort when she had trouble controlling her voice was to set us to writing Palmer Method exercises. First we had to make a row of interlacing circles across the top of a page, then a similar row of parallel lines about an inch high. All the motion—according to the Method—should come from the elbow, and neither wrist nor fingers were allowed to move. "Push-pull, push-pull," Miss Sykes would call out, walking up and down the aisles with her oak ferule in her hand. We made infinities of circles and grubby parallel lines. "Don't move your wrist. Don't! Don't!" And the ferule would flick out at some guilty moving knuckle. For the fear was on her.

Overseas, the great attack on the Hindenburg Line had begun. Our own Yankee Division was at St. Mihiel. Eliot Dodds came to school with a pin that said To H-LL WITH THE KAISER, but Miss Sykes made him take it off. The Lynch boys' father, who was in the Navy, was torpedoed and rescued, a fact that impressed even the Mulvey Streeters. Always when the time came for singing, Miss Sykes would step forward on the platform and sound the pitch on her harmonica before she waved her arm for us to begin. But now, instead of "The Harp that Once" and "Loch Lomond," we sang "Pack up Your Troubles," "Keep the Home Fires Burning," and "Over There." One afternoon we had a Liberty Pageant at the Tileston School a mile away, and Mr. Beveridge, the headmaster, told us of the song "The Long, Long Trail" and how an English soldier sang it one night in the trenches and it was so beautiful that even the Huns stopped firing to listen. Then someone played the melody on the hall piano, and after that we all sang it together.

October came, and still the black carriages joggled on over the ruts of Walk Hill Street under the leafless elm vista. There were not enough gravediggers, and coffins were beginning to pile up in the yard behind the disintegrating mansard-roofed house that served as a chapel. Finally Pigeye John Mulvey, who owned the land, set up a secondhand circus tent next to the chapel, and the coffins were stacked inside. After the gravediggers had put up the tent, most of them got drunk for several days, and still more coffins accumulated. The tent stood there, white and billowing, like some grotesque autumn carnival among the withered leaves, with the somber line of vehicles trailing through New Calvary gate. Even the undertakers fell behind. Sometimes we would see a touring car with the top down headed for New Calvary, an unboxed coffin stacked on the rear seat.

Then the weather cleared at last, but in spite of predictions, the bright Indian summer had no effect on the course of the disease. At the end of the first week in October, all the Boston schools closed.

As I look back, the 1918 influenza becomes a minor interlude in that climactic year, a ghostly aside, to be almost forgotten in the war's ending in November. Over forty years later, trying to bring some coherence to those third-grade memories, I began going through the newspaper files of the Boston Public Library. Formerly one had to turn over the stacks of brittle yellowed newsprint that seemed as dusty as age itself. Now those old papers were microfilmed, and one could look at them through table projectors set up in the Records and Patents Room. The room, dark and slightly rancid, is beyond the court next to the men's lavatory. Behind the attendant's desk the film reels are stacked in small boxes taking up only a few shelves. The rest of the shelves are filled with city directories from all over the United States, telephone books, and business encyclopedias. What the room has to do with patents I have never been able to discover.

Through several winter days I sat in the corner turning the projector dials, watching the procession of filmed pages. At the end of each three-week cycle I would have to get the attendant to change the reel. When my eyes could stand the pull no longer I would go out to the corner cafeteria for a cup of coffee. I soon felt myself one of the anonymous crew that hangs out in the Records and Patents Room—middle-aged unemployables thumbing endlessly through city directories, indeterminately seedy men copying lists of addresses out of telephone books, crackpots of local history or genealogy peering at the pages of the *Transcript* on the screens, adolescents on some high-school assignment, a lawyer checking death notices, an old man asleep.

It was strange to find the past embalmed in the pages of the

Globe and the *Herald*, the printed records that were once as alive and pulsating as the immediate bustle of Copley Square outside. The papers seemed naive and stilted. It wasn't because the autumn moment of 1918 was any less vital than the moment that encompassed me. But the idiom had changed. Reading the files, it was hard to realize how intense life had been then, perhaps even at its maximum intensity for us in the third grade when the past and the future were irrelevant. The First World War ensigns and lieutenants whose engagements were being announced in the society columns were on the retired list now. And the girls of the rotogravure with the arch smiles and hair in side buns known as "cootie garages"—it didn't seem comical then when they did their bit by dressing up in Red Cross or Salvation Army outfits and handing out doughnuts to the men in uniform.

Time-past, with all its irrelevancies, was controlled by my finger on a dial. On September 1, 1918, someone had raised a three-pound cucumber in Maine. Tilden was beaten in tennis by R. Lindley Murray. Debs had just received a ten-year sentence. One Beatrice Creek, aged twenty-one, appeared in court for trigamy, having at various times married three sailors. Mutt and Jeff were in uniform peeling spuds at Camp Yaphank. Thousands of G.A.R. veterans, undeterred—or perhaps stimulated—by the war, held their annual encampment at Portland, Oregon. Automobiles of vanished names were pictured in the advertisements—Locomobile, Marmon, Haynes, Kisselkar, Metz Master Six, Paige-Detroit. At Tremont Temple the film version of Ambassador Gerard's "My Four Years in Germany" was being shown. "The Kaiser, the Beast of Berlin" held over at the Bowdoin Square. To relax from war tension one could see William S. Hart at the Bijou in "Staking His Life."

Early in September the influenza first crept into Boston through the waterfront when several hundred sailors docked at Commonwealth Pier. On September 10, a few paragraphs on the inside page of the *Herald* announced that thirty sailors suffering from so-called Spanish influenza had been taken off their training ships and placed in hospital tents on Corey Hill. There were seven deaths. On September 13, the *Globe* reported briefly that physicians had the Spanish influenza pretty well in hand. That afternoon the Navy announced 163 new cases.

On September 14, Rear Admiral Wood of the First Naval District declared that the Spanish influenza was simply grippe, and there was no reason for the public to be alarmed. On Sunday, September 15, twenty people died and the next day the number rose to thirty-five. News of the influenza, slowly advancing through advertising and feature articles and comics and sports, finally reached the front pages on September 16.

GRIPPE MAKING GREAT HEADWAY, the headlines announced on Tuesday. But on Wednesday the influenza was off page one, dwarfed by the cracking of the Hindenburg Line. Proper precautions would soon stamp out the 'flu, the *Herald* predicted, and the Homely Physician listed six rules for avoiding it:

1. Spray nose and throat with dichlorium.
2. Get plenty of rest in bed.
3. Keep windows wide open.
4. Eat meals regularly.
5. Beware of persons shaking hands.
6. Don't use common towels, cups and other articles.

From Boston the disease had moved inland forty miles, now to the troops at Camp Devens.

On September 22, the influenza again became front page news. There were fifty-seven deaths in Boston and twenty at Camp Devens. On Monday the twenty-second there were sixty-three deaths, though physicians felt the worst was over. Next day, eighty-seven died in the city. That same day Congress passed the War Prohibition Bill. The British trapped a Turkish army, capturing 18,202 prisoners. HUNS LIVE IN TERROR OF YANKEE DIVISION, said the *Globe*. But the influenza was elbowing the war news from the front page.

INFLUENZA ADDS 109 TO DEATH LIST IN DAY was the eight-column headline on September 25. There were 10,000 cases at Camp Devens now, and soldiers were dying off at the rate of seventy a day. The next day 157 more Bostonians died, and Governor McCall issued a proclamation closing theaters and churches. Salicon Tablets were recommended for the 'flu; the "Spanish" had been forgotten.

By the month's end, a period of clear weather inspired the hopeful belief that the influenza might be dispelled like so much low-hanging fog. IMPROVED WEATHER RESPONSIBLE FOR OPTIMISM, said the *Herald*. The *Post* reported, FINE WEATHER CHECKS GRIPPE. But on October 1, the epidemic reached its height in the city with 202 deaths. Reluctantly, Acting Governor Calvin Coolidge appealed for help to Democratic Washington.

After October 1, barely perceptibly, the influenza turned. The ripple passed on, spreading westward, reaching now into forty-three states. A week later the Boston death roll had fallen to a daily 150. But on Corey Hill where there had earlier been over 200 tents of sick sailors, there were now only ten.

On October 11, 124 died in Boston, the lowest figure since September 25. By now the influenza had expanded to all forty-eight states. On October 13 for the first time that month an influenza story no longer appeared on the *Herald's* front page. The main interest became again France, where American troops were smashing through, putting the Hun on the run.

By November the influenza had passed, and in the turbulence of the war's ending it tended to be forgotten quickly. So many had died since 1914; but it was over now, all the killing and the dying, and better to start again and put death out of mind. For all its deaths the influenza did not last long enough to stamp itself permanently on the popular imagination. And in any case, like the war, it was part of the past. The present was what mattered.

Blue high-winded days followed the line storms after the schools closed. By now the autumn colors had faded, and from the top of the Hill we looked out over Canterbury Hollow to Great Blue Hill over a tawny landscape. Down in the Hollow itself the tent in New Calvary stood out lividly against the russet leaves, and the slanting light as it flashed from the windows of the carriages at the cemetery gate winked like a heliograph. On the opposite horizon the Custom House was dolphin-gray against the sky, and the State House dome glittered again. Far to the right beyond the yellow brick bulk of the Dorchester

High School lay the harbor islands outlined two-dimensionally against the limpid background of the Atlantic. For us it was pure joy in that abounding weather to be free of the third grade and Palmer Method and the multiplication tables and Miss Sykes and her harmonica and ferule. The early mornings turned frosty, blackening the marigolds, but the afternoons were warm and sun-drenched and golden, heavy with cricket sounds, light as milkweed down. By Collins' Pond the witch hazel was in bloom, the lemon-yellow filaments crisscrossed against the bare branches. On the Hill, on such bright days, we lost ourselves in the immediacy of the timeless present, as free to wander as any coma of milkweed.

Every afternoon of those weeks Everett Nudd would sidle down the back road to the Hollow that ended at the monument shop on the corner and disappear in the dip by New Calvary gate. Everett never played with the rest of us. He always wore short trousers of tweed with buttons on the sides and gray woolen socks instead of the corduroy knickerbockers and black cotton stockings that we wore to school. We used to call him Shortpants and Sissy, and he would skulk in the corner of the yard at recess until at some final taunt he would flail out with his thin arms, kick with his copper-toed storm boots, and even bite. Then Miss Sykes would have to drag him away.

Eliot Dodds noticed him first. Eliot and I had been sitting in the grass by the old oak waiting for the others to come out so that we could get up a game of relievo.

"That sissy Everett Nudd," he said as Everett cut across the field in his gray vizored cap and Norfolk jacket and short trousers. "I see him always going down the Hollow." Deliberately he stood up and walked over to the road. I followed along behind. Everett, crossing over, pretended not to see us.

"Hey, Ev, where you going?" Eliot called out with false geniality.

"Nowheres," he muttered.

"You going down the Hollow?"

"I guess I can if I want to."

We fell in with him and the three of us walked along in

silence, our feet plodding in the scrabbled clay, until we had almost reached the monument shop.

"I know you. You're in with Eddie MacDonald." We sensed, gloatingly, that he was afraid of us, but Everett's voice still had challenge in it.

"No I'm not," Eliot protested with the same false note. "He thinks he's too wise."

"Where you going then?"

"Just down the Li'l." Eliot turned to me. "Aren't we?" *Li'l* was short for Little Store. "Where are you?"

With a quick change of mood Everett became confidential. "Eddie MacDonald and his gang don't know what I do, they don't know anyways. I go down to Calvary to watch."

"To funerals?" Eliot asked him in an altered tone.

"Sure," said Everett, his voice now tinged with boastfulness. "I watch them. You want to come?"

I felt the sudden coldness of the air on my face. Never in my life had I been to a funeral. I did not want to go now, and yet at the same time I knew I could not turn back.

When we came to the monument shop we could see the rows of granite stones lined up precisely in the yard, polished to mirror smoothness, the blank surfaces waiting only for names and dates. From the door of the shed came the sound of the stone-cutter's drill, an iterant buzzing like that of a locust.

There was a funeral procession at the New Calvary gate where a line of shiny limousines had stopped at the chapel. Through the plate glass and stylized black draperies of the front coach I could see a coffin banked with sprays of flowers. Following it was a touring car also heaped with flowers, then several limousines with their curtains drawn.

We edged through the gate, skirting the carriages and the clapboard chapel. The yard in front, dotted with plantains, had been tramped to a mire that was beginning to solidify. Just beyond lay the tent, its poles out of line, the guy ropes straining and cracking with each breath of air. The canvas fly had been looped back, and as we came nearer I caught the sick-sweet rotting scent of flowers.

"It's full of caskets," Everett said.

Eliot peered inside. I could see the gap in the canvas, but I did not dare look through the open triangle, and though my legs continued to move I felt a kind of paralysis creep through the rest of my body. Something in me nevertheless wanted to see, dared me to see what was separated from me by that patch of cloth.

"They got a lot of new ones, twice as many as last week," Everett's voice went on.

With a final wrench of will I looked in.

It was nothing. Only piled-up boxes stacked like drawers, with here and there a wreath. Nothing at all. I could feel the warm blood pushing back into my veins again. Only an old tent full of old boxes with handles on them.

"Did you see them?" he asked me.

"It's nothing," I said.

We wandered down the main path past the brown-and gray-stone monuments, past carved crosses and sacred hearts and triumphant stone angels with impassive granite wings. Then the path ended at a dump, and Everett turned right through a thicket of ground oak and speckled alder, holding up his hand in warning. We followed him, inching our way slowly through the matted vegetation to the edge of a bowl-like declivity littered with shale and lumps of puddingstone. Beyond lay another wing of the cemetery, a poorer section with the headstones small and closer together, stretching away over undulations of ground until the stones coalesced in a neutral mass against the background shadow of Blue Hill.

A funeral was going on directly below us. Around the raw earth of an open grave a group of mourners were huddled together like a flock of bedraggled starlings. The fumed oak coffin had been set beside the grave, and a priest in a biretta stood at its head, even as we looked down, making the sign of the cross over it. Then the others began to file past and some of them stopped to pick up a bit of earth which they scattered on the coffin. Just behind them two workmen appeared with ropes fastened in a sling. A heavy-built man with white hair and florid features stopped at the grave's edge, shook the damp clay from his fingers, then glanced up to see us peering through the alder bushes.

"Get out of here, you!" he shouted, his face turning scarlet. "Get out!" And he started up the slope after us. The priest had taken off his biretta and replaced it with a felt hat. Neither he nor the others paid any attention.

As the man started toward us we ran. Even so we could hear his heavy footsteps on the yielding earth. We bolted through the close underbrush, oak roots and brambles tripping us, the speckled alder branches slashing across our faces, our boots stumbling over the shale and broken puddingstone.

Finally, when we could run no more, we threw ourselves down on the ground in the hollow by Collins' Pond, sucking in the cool air with great relieving gasps. There was no more sound of following footsteps. A light wind fluttered the water and hissed among the cattail stalks. Juncoes were darting and swooping, their high-pitched trill audible even after they had settled in the marsh grass.

We lay there on our backs watching the color drain from the sky. Then, deliberately, but without speaking, we stood up, Everett pulled his cap visor over his eyes, we looked about and started back. Keeping to the line of the alder thicket we worked our way along still hesitantly until we came to the gravel walk. The three of us must have seemed lost under the enormous sky. We had not recovered our breath fully, and our cheeks were still flushed, but we were safe again. Everett began to swagger, and kicked the pebbles as he walked.

"Lookit," he said, pointing to a towering granite shaft by the stone wall. "That's where John L. Sullivan is buried, right over there. Oney they never buried him deep enough."

"Why?" Eliot asked. I had the sick sense that I already knew the answer.

"Sometimes they don't bury them deep. There's others under them, that's why. Last spring you could see John L. Sullivan's casket coming up through the ground again. I seen it. They take off all the plates too and sell them. I know." His voice dropped lower. "In that tent they use the caskets over again. They take dead people out and bury them just in their clothes when no one's looking, and then they send the caskets back and use them over."

"You don't know," I said, aware numbly of the late afternoon chill.

"Yes I do too," he said triumphantly. "I guess I know what they do. I know everything in this cemetery." We had come to a stained marble monument with a broken urn lying at its base. "You see that," he told us. "I knocked that off. I pushed over the little ones over there too, and that one with the sheep on the top. When I come round here I push them over. That's what I do. You see that angel without the arm. I did that! I'm not ascared of anybody."

At the crossing we passed an open grave. A gravedigger had just climbed out and stood with his shovel beside him, lighting his pipe. He was an old Italian with a drooping mustache, wearing a shapeless felt hat with a turned-down brim. His gnarled monkey face illuminated briefly as he held the match above the rim of his pipe and sucked on the stem. Then he snubbed out the match and spat into the earth. I think it was seeing the man standing there so casual and familiar that overwhelmed Eliot and me. Now we knew how Everett Nudd spent his afternoons, sneaking down the back road, peering through the bushes at funerals or into the dimness of the chapel tent, racing by himself along the gravel walks and shouting and tipping over monuments, his face shining. With one quick motion Eliot pinioned Everett's arms to his sides.

"Here he is, mister," he gasped at the gravedigger. "You want him? He's the kid that tips over all the stones. He broke the monument over there. He comes here all the time!"

Everett made no attempt to struggle. "No I never," he said in a queer pleading voice. "Honest I didn't mister."

The gravedigger stared at us with shrewd uncomprehending eyes, then took his pipe out of his mouth and spat again. "Ah, you boys-a go-onna home," he said thickly. "You no playa here. Go-onna home."

Uncertain, Eliot relaxed his grip, and with a bound Everett was away, his thin figure with the skinny legs receding, bobbing up among the lines of headstones, smaller at each turn. Only once did he look back. "You wait! I'll get you!" he shouted.

Eliot and I trudged along the gravel, scuffing the chestnut burrs. The sky had turned to slate, and in the west a planet glowed above Canterbury Hollow. At the corner the arc lamp shone down on the monument shop, the light snaking thinly along the stone surfaces. There wasn't a sound in the twilight. Even the wind had died down. But as we crossed Walk Hill Street a stone flicked through the air some ten feet to our left, and then another struck against the curb—and we knew that Everett Nudd was there somewhere in the shadows. Suddenly, a kind of fury seized us both and we dropped to the gutter, snatching up stones with both hands, hurling them without aim into the dark, pelting the bushes again and again until weariness brought us a kind of relief.

Still breathing hard, we stuffed our pockets with stones and started up the back road. I left Eliot by the footway. The windows of the houses on the Hill were square patches of friendly brightness. I could see the lights in the Dodges' house, in Mrs. Clarke's and the Sands's, and in the kitchen of the lower floor where my mother was getting the evening meal ready.

Seeing the lights, thinking of the afternoon, in that bare instant I became aware of time. And I knew then that life was not a perpetual present, and that even tomorrow would be part of the past, and that for all my days and years to come I too must one day die. I pushed the relentless thought aside, knowing even as I did so that I should never again be wholly free of it. As I climbed the slope toward the warm intimacy of those windows, each step seemed a comforting barrier between me and what I had left. But even as my tired legs carried me along I could hear behind me a jeering cry, trailing far off into that vague darkness below the monument shop.

The Strike That Made a President

If it had not been for the Boston Police Strike of September, 1919, Calvin Coolidge would no doubt have ended as just another in the succession of Republican governors of Massachusetts, his name no more remembered than that of his predecessor, Samuel McCall, or Channing Cox, who succeeded him. But that particular set of curious chances made him known all over America. From the blurred perspective of the rest of the country he seemed a courageous Yankee figure of the minuteman stamp who had defied and defeated the violence that had threatened the seventh city of the United States.

For two days Boston's urban core with its more than 700,000 inhabitants was without police protection, and the mob ruled the streets. The city had seen nothing like it even in the draft riots of the Civil War. To find a parallel the historian would have had to go back to Sam Adams' Mohawks. Ordinary Bostonians did not reckon so far. They were shocked by this savagery and dismayed in sensing how thin was the veneer of legal forms by which they had ordered their lives. Conservatives like Henry Cabot Lodge saw the strike as a first step toward sovietizing the country.

The striking policemen, who by descent were for the most part Catholic Irish, would have been astonished at any such notion. They were ordinary Americans with a grievance so engrossing that they gave little thought to the consequences. In the larger analysis, the strike was part of the general pattern of industrial unrest that accompanied the dislocations of the postwar period. Nineteen-nineteen was a year of strikes—the great steel strike, the Seattle general strike, railway and transit strikes, a coal strike, longshoremen's strikes, strikes of actors in New York, even a buyers' strike. Their immediate cause was inflation: the failure of wages to keep up with what was then known as the High Cost of Living. The more underlying cause was, however, that sense of restlessness that runs through every society in the anticlimax following the artificial unity of a war.

As for the policemen's grievances, they were real enough. In spite of a small raise, their minimum pay was still only $1,100 a year—less than half of what many a war worker had been earning—out of which they had to buy their uniforms. Beyond the question of pay there was the even larger grievance of the two-platoon system that kept them on twelve-hour shifts. Station houses were old, crowded, and dirty. To the ordinary Boston patrolman a union seemed the answer. The police in thirty-seven other American cities already had unions.

The Boston Police Strike was not unique. That same year over a thousand London policemen struck, and in Liverpool there was a strike almost as large. Many police strikes before and since then have been passed over or forgotten. In Boston, though, there was no one to replace the police when they struck. That the city was left without protection was due directly to Police Commissioner Curtis. Indirectly, Mayor Peters and Governor Coolidge shared the responsibility. Ironically enough, Coolidge, who did the least, received the final credit for doing everything.

Twenty-four years before becoming Police Commissioner, Edwin U. Curtis had been, at the age of thirty-four, the youngest mayor that the city of Boston ever had. He came from an established and wealthy family, and he felt that in taking public office again he was doing his duty to the community and to his country. His position as commissioner was anomalous. A generation before, when he was mayor, the old-line Bostonians still controlled the city they considered theirs by inheritance. But even then they were being pushed by the Irish offspring of the Famine years. When it became obvious that Irish Democrats would take over Boston politically, the Republican State Legislature engineered a law to place the appointment of the Boston police commissioner in the hands of the governor. Thus the Jim Curleys might possess City Hall, but they would not be able to get their fingers on the Police Department.

Curtis, in his middle age, had become an autocratic Puritan with supercilious eyes and a puffy, disdainful face. His attitude toward the police was that of a general toward his troops. They were "his" men, and in the hierarchy of command his orders were to be obeyed cheerfully and without question. At the core of Curtis' unbending self was a sense of insecurity. The Boston in which he had grown up, the class to which he belonged were being superseded. His class had governed Boston since the Revolution. Now it was being steam-rollered by the second-generation Irish. Curtis despised and feared this new emerging group with its alien religion and its eye for political plunder. In his heart he was convinced that Boston would never again be a decent city until the ephemeral Honey Fitzes and Jim Curleys and Dan Coakleys had been replaced by Curtises. That was why, in the period of Boston's decline, he accepted the office of police commissioner from Governor McCall.

During the early summer months of 1919 the policemen began organizing themselves into an unofficial union, the Boston Social Club. Curtis countered with a general order stating that a police officer could not consistently belong to a union and perform his sworn duty. In spite of this warning the Boston Social Club applied for a charter from the American Federation of Labor.

Curtis at once announced the addition to his department rules and regulations of Rule 35: "No members of the force shall join or belong to any organization, club or body outside the department."

On August 11, the American Federation of Labor granted a charter to the Social Club as Boston Police Union, No. 16807. Curtis then charged the eight leaders and officers of the new union with insubordination and ordered them placed on trial. The union countered by warning him that if these men were disciplined the police would strike. The union also maintained that Curtis' regulation was "invalid, unreasonable and contrary to the express law of Massachusetts." Curtis found the men guilty but postponed sentence. On August 29, he found eleven more leaders guilty but again suspended sentence—as he later said—to give the men a chance to withdraw from the Federation. He then announced that he would pass sentence on September 4. This was the impasse at the end of August.

No one was more distressed at the prospect of a police strike than the Mayor of Boston, Andrew J. Peters. By nature, Peters was a more conciliatory type than the Commissioner. In addition, he belonged to the same political party as the policemen. He was that rarity, a Yankee Democrat. Here and there they were to be found in Massachusetts, of Colonial descent, of inherited wealth, Harvard-educated, and yet by some twist of family allegiance standing outside the old Bay State Federalist tradition. President emeritus Charles W. Eliot of Harvard was such a Democrat, as were the Russells of Cambridge, Winslow Warren, the President of the Cincinnati and descendant of the Bunker Hill general; and ex-Governor Eugene Foss.

Peters was an interim mayor between the first and second administrations of the flamboyant James Michael Curley. He had been elected with the help of the Good Government Association—Goo-goos to Jim Curley—while Curley and Congressman James Gallivan were at each other's political throats.

To the more optimistic old Bostonians, Peters had seemed a sign of the city's redemption. The new mayor was in the *Social Register*. He was wealthy enough to be personally honest, he was conciliatory as befitted a Democrat, but his dominant quality was ineffectuality. In Woodrow Wilson's first administration he had served casually as Assistant Secretary of the Treasury. In Boston he was lost. While he sat in the mayor's office, bagmen did business in the anterooms and greenbacks were passed routinely in the corridors. Under the rule of Mayor John F. "Honey Fitz" Fitzgerald contractors had a habit of charging the city for each side of a granite paving block. Under Peters they sold the foundations of City Hall.

Peters resembled an aberrant Scot more than a Yankee. He

had a domed forehead fringed by rufous hair that gave him the spurious look of a thinker, and curiously tufted, almost Mephistophelian eyebrows. He spoke in a high voice with a precise, exaggerated Harvard accent.

Politics was an avocation rather than a vocation with him. He preferred golf and yachting to long hours at his desk. Somehow he was able to shut both his mind and his eyes to the corruption of his administration. He gave the impression of an easy, superficial man, inclined to bore. Yet beneath his brownstone exterior was a perverse personality, unrecognized at the time and only to come to vague light long afterward.*

With dazed impotence Peters watched the August days recede. The threat of the coming strike was too much for him, and like other weak men in a crisis he looked for some way to shift responsibility. The safest and easiest way was, as always, to appoint a committee. So in the last week of the month the Mayor named a Citizens' Committee of Thirty-Four to investigate and advise on the situation in the Police Department. The committee was made up of old Bostonians with a lacing of others that included several wealthy Irish and Jewish merchants. It was headed by James J. Storrow of the ultraconservative firm of Lee, Higginson & Company, that somewhat over a decade later was to go to the wall following Ivar Kreuger's suicide.

At the outset the committee opposed the police affiliation with the American Federation of Labor. Except for this they felt a compromise could be worked out, if Curtis did not force the issue. From August 29 to September 2 they met daily with the president and leaders of the Police Union. But the chief obstacle to any settlement was the Commissioner whose adamant personality stiffened the intransigence of the police.

On Wednesday, September 3, the Commissioner refused Storrow's request for a few days' delay in passing sentence, but,

* For years Peters maintained a Lolita-like relationship with an eleven-year-old playmate of his children. See Morris Markey's "The Mysterious Death of Starr Faithfull" in Isabel Leighton's *The Aspirin Age,* Simon & Shuster, 1949.

when Peters asked formally for a postponement, Curtis finally agreed to put off his decision until the following Monday.

Meanwhile Governor Coolidge sat aloof in his State House office two hundred yards from City Hall. At this point, as Claude Fuess in his definitive life of Coolidge admits, "a single word from him [Coolidge] would probably have led to a compromise, but that word he would not utter."

William Allen White in his *A Puritan in Babylon* tells the story of Calvin Coolidge as a student at Black River Academy. Calvin was in bed one evening in the dormitory while several other boys of a more prankish disposition pitched an old stove downstairs. He remained in bed. When one of the masters asked him next day if he had not heard the noise, he said that he had. When the master asked further why he had not done anything, he replied, "It wa'n't my stove." The looming police strike "wa'n't" his strike: The Commissioner and the Mayor should resolve it as best they could. Since he had not appointed Curtis, he felt no responsibility for him. If a strike should occur it was up to them to safeguard the city. The attempts of the Committee of Thirty-four to get Coolidge to intervene were in vain. As events moved to their climax over that first weekend in September, the Governor left for the western part of the state. No one in Boston knew where he was. He made sure of that.

"Coolidge ran away," my father used to say. "He got scared and cleared out. Just what we expected, but afterward they made a hero of him." At the time my father was in the Massachusetts House of Representatives. Like most of those who came in such close contact with Coolidge, he did not like him. "The laziest man who was ever governor of Massachusetts," my father maintained. "He'd sit in his office mornings with his feet on the desk reading the *Herald* and smoking a cigar. In the afternoon he used to take naps." My mother, meeting Coolidge at the annual reception for legislators and their wives, said that shaking hands with the Governor was like shaking hands with a codfish.

Calvin Coolidge was the product of the Republican escalator system that worked for decades with great smoothness until the depression years destroyed its mechanism. Up the escalator went the more astute and adaptable local politicians under the benevolent surveillance of Boss Murray Crane and the general staff of the Republican State Committee. Coolidge in his typical career went on from mayor of Northampton to become a state representative, state senator, president of the Senate, lieutenant governor, and then governor. Though patricians like Henry Cabot Lodge might be scornful of his bucolicisms, his nasal Vermont accent, and his two-family house on Massasoit Street in Northampton, Coolidge meshed into the machine. After two one-year terms as governor he could look forward to the sinecure reward of a directorship in some life insurance company or the peace of the First National Bank.

Such were the inducements for those who stayed in line. For those who did not, there was arctic isolation. My father, though a regular Republican, had his maverick side. He once ran for the State Senate before the Republican hierarchy gave him the nod. And he was defeated. Though subsequently he was elected to several additional terms as representative, the escalator entrance was henceforth barred to him. He might sit in the House, but he would never again be appointed to so much as a committee on fish hatcheries. His political career was over.

Storrow and the members of the Citizens' Committee spent a baffling weekend trying to locate the Governor. They themselves wanted no open break with the police. Their compromise plan, approved by Mayor Peters, would have allowed an unaffiliated union. If the men would call off their strike there would be no disciplinary action taken against the leaders, and the various other grievances would be submitted to an impartial board. The counsel for the union urged them to accept. If the Governor and the Commissioner had agreed, the plan would undoubtedly have been accepted by the police. Curtis declined to accept any solution "that might be construed as a pardon of the men on trial." On Monday morning he suspended the nineteen police leaders.

Peters, as fluttery and ineffectual as ever, scurried about trying to find some last-minute solution, although by now he was convinced that the strike was unavoidable. As mayor he had the right in an emergency to call out the units of the State Guard stationed within the Boston area. Characteristically, he was not aware of this.

Coolidge returned suddenly to his office on Monday afternoon in a testy mood at about the same time that the police were voting 1134-2 to strike. The strike was set for the following day at five o'clock. Monday evening Coolidge had dinner with Storrow, Peters, and several members of the Citizens' Committee in a private room of the Union Club. Before the dinner, Storrow and Peters begged him to sponsor the compromise plan as the last hope of averting the strike. He refused. Finally they asked him to mobilize three or four thousand troops of the State Guard. He maintained that the situation could be left safely in Curtis' hands. Curtis was still convinced that the majority of the police would remain loyal to him.

Meanwhile, after a series of calls from Peters, the adjutant general, Jesse Stevens, decided that a certain amount of preparation might be wise after all and sent out verbal orders for the first—and only—mounted squadron of the State Guard to assemble at the Commonwealth Armory. Not until several hours after the Union Club dinner did Coolidge learn of this minor mobilization. Knowing by politician's instinct that to call out the militia prematurely is political suicide, he called Curtis and started at once for the armory, his anger glowing through his pinched features.

With a pale and silent Curtis just behind him, Coolidge strode through the armory arch. A hundred or so troopers were standing about on the lower floor with their newly drawn equipment. They stared in surprise as the irate Governor quacked at their commanding officer, Major Dana Gallup: "Who told you people to come here? Go on home!" With that he stalked petulantly up the stairs to the orderly room, followed by Gallup and Curtis.

Then occurred one of the dramatic (and so far unrecorded) minor episodes of the strike. Peters, repulsed and desperate, had set out in pursuit of the evasive Coolidge. Ten minutes after the latter had arrived, the rumpled and excited Mayor burst through the armory door demanding to see the Governor, at the very moment that Coolidge was coming down the stairs.

The two men faced each other, Peters stammering accusations until Coolidge cut him short with a waspish, "You have no business here!" At that, Peters made a rush for him, swinging his arms wildly and somehow landing a punch square on the Governor's left eye. Coolidge did not attempt to strike back nor did he make any move to retreat, but merely leaned against the balustrade with his hand to his face. Troopers at once seized the gesticulating Mayor. It was fortunate for the Governor that he was not called on to make any public appearances that week, for those who saw him could not fail to notice his shiner.

Peters, Curtis, and Coolidge were all at their desks on Tuesday morning. At one o'clock in the afternoon the Mayor called the Commissioner who assured him he had ample means to protect the city. Four hours later the three key figures held a last acid conference. To Peters' renewed plea to call out the State Guard, Coolidge ironically informed him of the mayor's powers within the Boston limits. Curtis insisted he did not need the State Guard. "I am ready for anything," he told the Governor.

Of the 1544 men in the Boston Police Department, 1117 went out on strike. There was no authority on hand to replace them. Although a force of citizen volunteers had been enrolling in the preceding weeks, the Commissioner did not use them. Years later, Coolidge wrote in his autobiography that he felt afterward he should have called out the State Guard as soon as the police left their posts. "The Commissioner," he added as an apologia, "did not feel that this was necessary." Peters, faced with a sudden decision, could not bring himself to call out the local guard. The strike was left to follow its own pattern.

As the police left the station houses, still in uniform but minus their badges, they were cheered by some, and a few furtive adolescents crept up to throw mud against the station doors. At first nothing more happened. Then in the twilight little groups began to start dice games all over Boston Common. Seen from the top of Beacon Hill, they looked like mushrooms springing up on the slope by the Frog Pond as they formed circles to shoot craps under the shadow of the State House. It was harmless enough at first, a naïve gesture against authority. But with the darkness crowds began to gather on the other side of Beacon Hill in the vicinity of Scollay Square with its honky-tonks and flop-houses. For some time they milled about restlessly, as yet uncertain, waiting only for that unifying act of violence that would turn them into a mob. Then it happened. As with all such events no one could be quite sure afterward how it started—a broken store front, an overturned truck, a woman's scream, and the mob was off.

The Boston mob that first night was truculent but aimless. Around Scollay Square plate-glass windows were smashed and stores looted. Pedestrians had their hats knocked off, there were holdups here and there in open view, and later in the evening several women were dragged into doorways and assaulted. Some of the streetcar lines were blocked with mattresses and railroad ties. In the Celtic matrix of South Boston an unfocused rowdyism swaggered and held to such japes as stoning the empty police stations and pulling the trolleys off the wires. But there was a sinister air about the carnival of those streets that made respectable middle-class observers think back uneasily to *A Tale of Two Cities*, read long ago in school. For a few moments the lid was off their stratified social structure, and the glimpse they had of what lay underneath was cold and cruel, something they did not like to think about.

Tuesday night Peters vanished as effectively as had Coolidge over the weekend. Then late Wednesday morning he finally called out the State Guard in Boston, and before the end of the afternoon the guardsmen were patrolling the streets. Peters then issued a statement to the press, remarking plaintively that in this crisis he had "received no co-operation from the Police Commissioner and no help or practical suggestions from the Governor." Now, with the authority he claimed he had found under an old statute, he removed Curtis and began calling up citizen volunteers.

During the day the city remained quiet, but in the evening the mob gathered again, a harder and more menacing mob than the night before, many of its members armed, and reinforced by professional criminals who had been heading toward Boston all the afternoon. Striking policemen moved through the crowd, encouraging the more violent. Behind the closed doors of the banks and the larger stores, blocked off now by barbed wire, employees stood ready with pistols and rifles. In Scollay Square, at the center of the disorders, steel-helmeted guardsmen advancing across the cobbles with fixed bayonets were showered with bricks, stones, and bottles. Not far from the site of the eighteenth-century Boston Massacre, they finally opened fire on their assailants, killing three. Near Cornhill four Harvard undergraduates, acting as volunteer patrolmen, were almost lynched. On the other side of Beacon Hill several guard companies cleared the Common in a flanking movement, rounding up the surly groups still gathered there. Somehow a sailor was killed in the scuffle. Two other men were killed in South Boston. After that the mob melted away.

The Citizens' Committee reported that "by Thursday morning order had generally been restored in the city." The strike was broken. During this interval Coolidge had been consulting with Murray Crane and the Republican elders, all of whom felt it was now time to take a stand. So, nettled by the Mayor's statement and by the removal of the Commissioner, Coolidge belatedly acted. By executive order he called out all the State Guard and assumed full control over the Boston Police Department, instructing Curtis to resume his post at once.

After the rioting the strike overshadowed other news, capturing the headlines and alarming newspaper readers all over the country. By the time it had made its full impact Coolidge had taken over. Out of what seemed to the rest of America a chaotic situation a man had emerged. At once this Yankee governor with the dour expression became a national figure. His pictures papered the land. Even President Wilson sent him a letter of congratulation. And when the Governor replied to President Gompers of the AF of L who had asked for reinstatement of the strikers, he provided a slogan with the copybook phrase: "There is no right to strike against the public safety by anybody, anywhere, any time." Whatever Peters and the members of the committee might think, he became in the words of the Boston *Herald*, "the pilot that weathered the storm."

To those businessmen who as volunteers received badge and revolver from the downtown police stations, the strike was an adventure. For once again, if briefly, the old Bostonians had achieved physical control of their city. As one leafs through the old newspaper files one sees them in faded rotogravure, smiling, self-assured faces, the younger men dressed in trench-coats copied from the war-time British officers. Here and there one finds a sterner note: some Beacon Hill relic of the Civil War days patrolling the financial district with golf cap and night stick. Ex-Harvard athletes-turned-broker are abundant.

My father became a special policeman in Dorchester, but Dorchester Hill where we lived was as placid during the strike as before. Blue Hill Avenue and the Dorchester streets below us were equally calm. It was probably quite a disappointment to my father. His single adventure was in commandeering a private automobile to chase a suspicious character who had been observed boarding a streetcar at Mattapan Square. The character was suspicious because he was foreign-looking and had tried to change a ten-dollar bill at McHugh's drugstore. However, he turned out to be merely an Italian workman, and the bill all that was left of his week's pay.

One of my father's fixed beliefs was that he had a natural talent for things military, a talent under which he now subsumed police work. For several days he directed traffic at the corner of Morton Street and Blue Hill Avenue, the busiest intersection between Franklin Park and Mattapan Square. In those days there were only about a twentieth as many cars on the road as today, but somehow each morning my father managed to create a traffic jam of dimensions previously unknown in Dorchester and not to be seen again until the introduction of traffic lights. He maintained that the tie-up was caused by all the drivers coming in town after the strike, and that no regular policeman could have managed better. Whatever the jam, he enjoyed himself thoroughly. Badge, revolver, whistle, and white gloves were authoritative symbols that made his law office seem tame when he went back to it a week later.

To my father the police strike was a kind of compensation for not having served in two wars. The World War found him in his late thirties with a wife and two children, and he had to content himself with the second-best of serving in the legislature and being on the Mattapan Legal Advisory Board. Twenty years before, as a boy of seventeen, he had stood in line with my Uncle Charlie at the outbreak of the Spanish-American War to join the Roxbury Horse Guards for service in Cuba. However, somebody tipped off my grandfather in his South Boston office and he whipped down in his buggy to pick up the two of them before they reached the recruiting sergeant's desk. My father never did wear a uniform. The Boston Police Strike was the closest he ever came to being on active service. I expect he regretted that he was not in Scollay Square that second night.

Before the strike, the police of Boston still wore dome-shaped helmets like the English police. They also wore high-necked frock coats above which protruded the ends of a wing collar. With their leather outer belts and long wooden night-sticks they resembled the old Keystone cops.

The only policeman I knew by sight was Mr. Fitzgibbons. His daughter Susy was in our fourth-grade room. Susy was a bright, aggressive little girl who wore paper hair-ribbons, could write in Palmer Method without making blots, and got double promotions. As I look back now at our old fourth-grade picture I can see that she was the most attractive one of our group, but I did not think so then. She was the oldest of seven children.

The Fitzgibbonses lived in a square little two-and-a-half story house down the street from the Martha Baker School. They were all neat, well-behaved children, and though they went to St. Angela's, not like those tough shanty Irish who lived on Mulvey Street. Mrs. Fitzgibbons belonged to the Mothers' Club. There were such a lot of Fitzgibbonses that they used to have benches along the dining room table instead of chairs. People like my mother were dubious about so many children, but they thought Mrs. Fitzgibbons was a wonderful manager.

I can remember Mr. Fitzgibbons coming up over the Hill on the way home from the station, a tall, striding figure in his gray helmet and blue coat with the shining badge and buttons. Even the Mulvey Streeters who used to yell "Cheese it, the cop!" when they saw other policemen, were quiet when he went by. No one would have dared to challenge his presence. Mr. Fitzgibbons, that proud and handsome man, walking up the street with the sun shining on his helmet, saluting Miss Sykes, the head teacher, as he passed with courtly reserve, was the Law. But on that Tuesday afternoon he went on strike with the others. "If I hadn't been in my last month, I'd have seen that Mike never walked out," Mrs. Fitzgibbons told my mother afterward.

On Friday the striking policemen, dismayed by the reaction against them, voted almost unanimously to return to work on the same basis as before the strike. They had counted on organized labor to back them up, but the two days' rioting had made public opinion too hostile. Commissioner Curtis would have nothing to do with them. He issued an order that none of the striking policemen would ever be taken back—and none of them ever were. He also fixed the minimum wage at $1400 a year and began recruiting a new force.

Meanwhile, the volunteers were sent home and all Boston police duties were carried on by the State Guard. The Guard was a mixture of overage and underage men who had joined this temporary organization when the Massachusetts National Guard—the Yankee Division—had been called to active service in 1917. The guardsmen's aspect was ludicrously unmilitary. They scarcely knew the manual of arms, and they still wore the laced gaiters and felt campaign hats of the Mexican Border Campaign of 1916, that had been replaced in the AEF by spiral puttees and overseas caps.

To us in the fourth grade, though, they were impressive indeed, soldiers in the flesh, objects of military might. It was like having Memorial Day every day in the week to see so many uniforms. The guardsmen carried rifles with fixed bayonets rather than revolvers, just like the pictures of soldiers in the war. That Halloween I was chased by a guardsman who caught me shinnying up the lamppost to put out the gas light in front of the Sands's. As soon as I saw him I jumped and tried to get away by ducking through the back yards, but he ran after me and the fear went down into my legs. I still recall my side glimpse of that looming khaki figure in his wide-brimmed felt hat, his rifle at port, and the light sparkling on the bayonet as he chased me across lots and under clothes lines. At each step he took I could hear the slap of the leather sling against his rifle butt. I was so frightened I wet myself.

By the end of the year Commissioner Curtis had recruited his new police force, and the brown uniforms of the State Guard disappeared. Governor Coolidge was re-elected in November by a tremendous majority and there were whisperings of him as a dark-horse Presidential candidate. "Jack the Giant Killer," William Allen White called him. The new policemen had different uniforms. The long coats and wing collars had been discarded. Caps replaced the helmets. It was the close of an era: the end of the patrolman in his high helmet walking his beat under the gas lamps past the corner saloon, the beginning of prowl cars and bootleggers.

Even in the fourth grade I could sense the change. I remember one sunny October afternoon passing the Fitzgibbons' house on the way from school. The Fitzgibbonses had a tree in their yard that Susy called an umbrella tree. It had wide leaves almost two feet long and a pink fruit that ripened in the autumn and looked like a magnolia bud. Most of the leaves had fallen and the yard behind the clipped privet hedge was buried under with them. One of the Fitzgibbons children who was too young to go to school yet was gathering the leaves in his express wagon. Another, still younger, sat on the edge of the curb in front of the house playing with an old spoon and a gray policeman's helmet.

The Four Mysteries of President Harding

Several months before the Republican National Convention of 1920, the Ohio political boss Harry Micajah Daugherty made the offhand prophecy that none of the leading candidates could muster enough votes to win the nomination, and that after the delegates had reached a dead end a group of fifteen party elders would then get together in some smoke-filled hotel room. There, bleary-eyed and perspiring profusely—at about 2:11 in the morning—they would pick the party's candidate, the almost inevitable next President of the United States. That man, Daugherty predicted, would turn out to be his friend and protégé, Senator Warren Gamaliel Harding of Ohio.

Daugherty's prediction proved uncannily accurate. There have been a number of versions of the "fifteen men in a smoke-filled room," and the casual phrase has taken its place in American political folklore as a synonym for cynical electoral manipulation. Yet when Daugherty made it, his remark seemed no more than a politician's quick quip. Harding was still the darkest of dark horses, a scarcely conceivable candidate. As a favorite son he lacked even the complete Ohio delegation.

The outstanding Republican contender was Major General Leonard Wood. If the nomination had been by popular vote rather than through the maneuverings of the convention, he would certainly have been the party's choice for that year. The most that could be said against him was that he stood out too far for the comfort of politicians. As the ailing boss of Pennsylvania, Senator Boies Penrose, put it, they wanted a man in the White House "who would listen."

The convention, the tinsel-familiar quadrennial spectacle, opened in the barnlike, reverberating Chicago Coliseum on Tuesday, the eighth of June. As usual, there were the bunting-decked balconies filled with strident supporters ready to yammer, the rows of folding chairs in the pit below marked off by state placards, the brass band beyond the speakers' platform. This year the band, in a gesture to modernity, played snappy foxtrots as the delegates straggled in.

Then the ritual began: the chaplain prayed; the band shook the balconies with "The Star Spangled Banner," and the rafters hummed with the atonal attempts of the crowd to sing it. As the brass notes faded, the Director of Community Singing of the Republican League of Massachusetts sprang forward and shouted:

"Now give three cheers and a tiger for the greatest country on earth—the United States of America!"

Obediently three hoarse cheers welled up from several thousand throats: "Hurrah for the United States! And a long-tailed T-I-G-E-R!"

Senator Henry Cabot Lodge, aloof, assured, gray-bearded, gray-haired, and dressed in a gray cutaway, took the rostrum as permanent chairman of the convention. With precise, bitter words he denounced Wilson, the League of Nations, and the Democrats. Then for the next three days the Committee on Resolutions wrestled with a party platform sufficiently straddling to appeal to all men, while the delegates steamed and fidgeted. Not until Friday was the way clear for the balloting to begin, and only then in the afternoon, following interminable nominating speeches for obscure vanity candidates.

Wood's principal and implacable opponent was Frank O. Lowden of Illinois, who had served five terms in Congress and later as governor of his state. Among the many dark horses were Calvin Coolidge and Herbert Hoover. On the opening ballot Wood received 287½ votes for Lowden's 211½. Harding had 65½. By the fourth ballot, Wood had reached 314½ with Lowden close behind at 289. But to the astute bosses it was clear that neither could muster the 493 votes needed to win, that the General and the Governor had canceled each other out. Abruptly the frosty Senator Lodge adjourned the convention until the following morning.

That evening an inner group of senators met in the Blackstone Hotel suite of the enigmatic George Harvey. A former Democrat, an associate of J. P. Morgan, he was editor of the *North American Review* and had formerly edited *Harper's Weekly,* and liked to claim he had "made" Wilson President. Later he had turned against Wilson and Wilson's creation, the League of Nations. Harvey was a man of pontifical solemnity who fancied himself as a statesman behind-the-scenes, a president-maker. For this night's work he would become ambassador to Great Britain. Among the others present were Senator Lodge, the future Vice-President, Charles W. Curtis, Senator Frank Brandegee of Connecticut, Senator James Wadsworth of New York, and Pennsylvania's Joseph Grundy. The man they picked would have the bloc votes they controlled fed to him ballot by ballot until with the disintegration of the Wood and Lowden supporters he would stampede the convention. Such was their plan. Their problem was whom to choose.

As the heat-heavy hours wore away through the blue skeins of cigar smoke, various candidates were discussed and discarded. Harding, by a process of elimination, remained. He was after all innocuous, even if he did talk more about the time he used to play the trombone in his hometown band than about the tariff. As Senator Wadsworth remarked, Harding in the White House could be trusted to sign the bills the Senate sent him and not to send the Senate bills to pass. And he looked like a President. At close enough to 2:11 A.M. to make Daugherty seem clairvoyant, Harvey sent for Harding.

Harding at first glance was an impressive figure. His tall, solid body, his dark complexion, contrasting with blue eyes and white hair, gave the appearance of mental and physical vigor. There were some who compared him to a Roman senator—more justly than they realized, for in his features there lurked the same imbedded sensuality found in Roman portrait busts. William Allen White remembered him as "a handsome dog, a little above medium height, with a swarthy skin, a scathing eye and . . . the harlot's voice of the old-time political orator."

Behind Harding's senatorial façade fluttered the mind and spirit of a banal smalltown editor. But for his grim-jawed wife —whom he, not wholly in affection, called "Duchess"—and the manipulative Daugherty, he would never have given the Presidency a thought. "I found him," Daugherty remarked afterward, "sunning himself, like a turtle on a log, and I pushed him into the water."

When the late summons came from the Blackstone suite, Harding, disheveled and discouraged, had long since lost faith in Daugherty's brash prophecy. Harvey was waiting for him behind his heavy tortoise-shell glasses. "We think you may be nominated tomorrow," he told the stunned Harding, with the urbanity of an undertaker. "Before acting finally, we think you should tell us, on your conscience and before God, whether there is anything that might be brought up against you that would embarrass the party, any impediment that might disqualify you or make you inexpedient either as candidate or as President." Harding asked for a little time to think it over alone. Ten minutes later he came out of the bedroom to say that there was no impediment.

The following morning was sticky and enervating. The delegates were tired and many of them short of funds. On the fifth ballot Harding received 78 votes to 299 for Wood and 303 for Lowden. On the sixth ballot he had climbed to 89 and on the seventh to 105. William Allen White, who as a delegate would go down voting for Wood to the end, saw the emerging pattern and cried out that to nominate Harding would disgrace the Republican party and bring shame to the country. By the ninth ballot Harding led the list with 374½ votes to 249 for Wood. On the tenth ballot—late in the afternoon of the same day, Saturday, June 12, 1920—it was all over.

Though Harvey had relished his solemn catechising of the night before, he had solid reasons then for playing his portentous role, for there had long been ambiguous rumors adrift concerning Harding. Undoubtedly Harvey had heard them. One concerned something very important in politics, indeed in American life—the color of his skin. The other, no less disturbing, raised a "woman question." To these two mysterious stories, two more mysteries would later be added—the manner of his death, and the fate of his private papers. Over forty years later these four mysteries would still remain.

For campaign purposes the new Republican candidate seemed an embodiment of the American success story. He had started out as a poor boy in Marion, Ohio. At the age of nineteen, with a hundred borrowed dollars, he had managed to take over a moribund newspaper, the Marion *Star*, and over the years had built it up into a prosperous daily. Afterward he had been in turn state senator and lieutenant governor, and in 1914 had been elected to the United States Senate. Now the poor boy was to become President.

But the story bore only a nodding acquaintance with reality. Harding was more a creation of his wife than of himself. Florence Kling De Wolfe Harding, five years older than her husband and as dominating as she was lacking in female charm, had been the driving force behind him. Her aggressive qualities, along with her grimly plain features, she had inherited from her father Amos Kling, a self-made real estate operator and banker who had become one of the richest men in town. At the age of nineteen she had defied her father by marrying the flashy Henry De Wolfe whom she had met at a roller-skating rink. The De Wolfes were almost as wealthy as the Klings, but Henry was the family ne'er-do-well, a small-town sport, aimless, a drinker who would in a few more years die of alcoholism. After two years he abandoned his wife and her year-old child.

Ten years later, Flossie Kling De Wolfe married Warren Gamaliel Harding, to the profane rage of her father who preferred even a wastrel of good family to a printer of none. Harding at the time of his marriage had been running the *Star* for almost seven years and had managed to make the paper modestly solvent. Flossie now made it a success, as chief of its business side. Without her neither the *Star* nor Harding would ever have amounted to much. For Harding, jovial and indolent, Marion, Ohio, was the world. He never wanted to be more than just one of the boys whose relaxations were the Saturday-night poker session, the brass rail, and the occasional stag party. As editor he wallowed in the shallow rhetoric of small-town pride. No word of his ever reached beyond the boundaries of Ohio. As a United States senator he had been a popular nonentity. "A cheese-paring of a man," Nicholas Murray Butler described him.

At the convention Daugherty played up the poor-boy-to-President myth where it would do the most good; but another story was also in circulation, one that Harvey must have been aware of when he put his ponderous question to Harding. This counter-myth was derived from a crudely printed circular addressed to the "Men and Women of America" and distributed surreptitiously to the delegates. Harding's family tree was the subject of the circular, which set out to demonstrate through various affidavits that "Warren Gamaliel Harding is not a white man. . . . He is not a creole, he is not a mulatto, he is a mestizo." *

The man responsible for the circular was William Estabrook Chancellor, a professor of economics and social sciences at Wooster College, not far from Marion, and formerly Superintendent of Schools in Washington, D.C. Chancellor was of sufficient intellectual attainments to have had educational and historical books published by such reputable houses as Hough-

* This one obscure sentence in itself could produce an all-day discussion in many parts of the United States. To most Americans, especially Southerners in Louisiana and along the Gulf Coast, *creole* means a white man of whole or partial French or Spanish ancestry, although it is sometimes used elsewhere to indicate a mixed-blood with various racial admixtures and even to mean a native full-blooded Negro, although in that case the proper expression is *creole Negro*. *Mulatto*, in its first meaning, indicates a person half-Negro and half-white, but also in broader meanings a mixed-blood in general, including, for example, a Negro-Indian. *Mestizo*, more properly a Spanish word, also means a mixed-blood, although not necessarily containing either Negro or white.

ton Mifflin and Macmillan, but—although he had nothing against Harding personally—he was obsessed to frenzy over questions of race. Not only did he believe in strict and complete segregation of whites and Negroes, he advocated the latters' disenfranchisement. Harding's nomination, he maintained, was a plot to achieve Negro domination in the United States. Between the nomination and the election thousands more of his circulars were printed. Two hundred and fifty thousand of them were seized by Post Office officials in San Francisco alone.

The rumors that Chancellor unleashed across the country were no novelty in Ohio. They had been current concerning Harding's parents long before his birth. Harding's father was George Tryon Harding, who had served as a drummer in the Civil War and afterward had come back to Blooming Grove, Ohio, where he married and took up the trade of veterinarian. Then, switching from animals to humans, he spent several years picking up what medical knowledge he could by assisting the local doctor on his rounds. Finally he went a few terms to a Cleveland homeopathic college and returned a "paper" M.D. Later "Doc" Harding moved his family to the shabby outskirts of Marion, twenty-five miles away. The Hardings were always itinerant and they remained poor—the mother more successful as a midwife than the father as a physician. Warren was the eldest of their eight children.

Gossip both in Blooming Grove and Marion held that the Hardings were of mixed blood. In 1938 Samuel Hopkins Adams, visiting Marion in search of background material for his book on the Harding era, found that this belief still persisted among the older residents. A reporter who had worked for Harding and the *Star* in the early 1900s told Adams that "it was generally believed that there was Negro blood in the Harding line, but that W. G. had outgrown it."

Professor Chancellor's circular caused such an uproar in Marion County that the Wooster trustees insisted on his resignation. He continued, however, to live in the town and continued his digging into the Harding genealogy. Harding had been President for just over a year when the results of Chancellor's work appeared in a book with the title page:

Warren Gamaliel Harding
President of the United States.
A Review of Facts
Collected from
Anthropological, Historical, and
Political Researches
by
William Estabrook Chancellor
formerly
Professor of Economics, Politics, and Social Sciences of
Wooster College, Wooster, Ohio.

Although a casual reader might (and was presumably intended to) assume that the professor was the author, the title was carefully worded and punctuated to make no such claim. Chancellor later denied that he had written it, although no other author has ever been suggested. According to the title page the book was "sold and distributed by agents only. The Sentinal Press."

Like the earlier circular, the book was distributed surreptitiously. Most of the copies were sold by door-to-door salesmen throughout the main cities of Ohio. Some copies even reached Washington. In the book Chancellor now maintained that there were several Negro strains in the Harding clan, but his chief claim was that Harding's great-grandmother, Elizabeth Madison Harding, born in 1799, was a Negress. Chancellor in his delvings had spent several weeks in Blooming Grove interviewing the oldest inhabitants, some of whom claimed to have known Elizabeth Madison Harding.

With Harding's inauguration, Harry Daugherty had attained his own goal of becoming Attorney General of the United States. When he learned of the publication of Chancellor's book, he at once sent out agents of the Justice Department and the Post Office to gather up the whole edition. Agents spread out all over Ohio buying, borrowing, or even confiscating every copy they could find. They finally managed to locate the "Sentinal" Press, bought all the unsold copies, burned them, and destroyed the plates. So thorough was the Justice Department in its search that this sub rosa volume has become one of the rarest items in American historical bibliography.

Harding himself was troubled all his days by the shadow across his lineage. His father-in-law remained for years Harding's bitterest enemy. Just before the marriage, Kling, on meeting Harding in the courthouse, elaborated profanely on the young man's mixed blood and threatened to kill him. Kling was responsible for a full-page article that appeared about that time in the rival *Mirror* alleging that the Harding family had always been regarded and treated as Negroes in Blooming Grove. Twelve years later, when Harding was running for lieutenant governor, Kling remarked with open bitterness that he hoped to God he would never live to see a Negro governor of Ohio.

Whatever Harding's frustrations and anger at these mocking accusations, he always followed the manly course of disregarding the rumors about his heredity. He himself did not know whether they were true or not. "How do I know, Jim?" he once told his old friend James Faulkner of the Cincinnatti *Enquirer*. "One of my ancestors may have jumped the fence." Nor, in a day when such matters have come to be of less concern, is there anything more to add to that honest comment.

No President of the United States ever suffered such a loss of reputation in so short a time as did Harding after his death. Aloof insiders like Alice Roosevelt Longworth might sum him up waspishly as "just a slob," but when he died suddenly in San Francisco on August 2, 1923, he was as popular and respected among the mass of people as three years before when he had been elected by the greatest plurality ever yet given a presidential candidate. Three million people from cities, hamlets, and open prairie came to watch his funeral train as it slowly crossed the country; "the most remarkable demonstration in American history of affection, respect, and reverence for the dead," according to *The New York Times.* The day of Harding's funeral was proclaimed a day of public mourning. He would, it seemed, be remembered in history as another Garfield or McKinley.

Yet within months the scandals long simmering beneath the amiable "normalcy"—the President himself had coined the word—of the Harding administration boiled over. Harding had surrounded himself with his friends, and now it turned out that many of his friends were vultures. Ominous questions arose concerning the Teapot Dome oil leases, resulting in Harding's Secretary of the Interior Albert Fall's being sent to prison for bribery. Secretary of the Navy Edwin Denby retired in disgrace. There were revelations of graft and corruption in the office of the Alien Property Custodian and the Veterans' Bureau. There were suicides. Under Daugherty and his bagman Jess Smith the Justice Department became—in Senator Henry Fountain Ashurst's phrase—the Department of Easy Virtue, with pardons and bootleggers' permits for sale over the counter. Only two hung juries kept Daugherty from going to jail when he retired to Ohio.

As an aftermath to all the other scandals a book appeared in 1927, *The President's Daughter,* published by an organization called the Elizabeth Ann Guild, Inc., and written by a former Marion resident, Nan Britton, who claimed that for years she had been Harding's mistress and that her eight-year-old daughter Elizabeth Ann—whose photograph served as a frontispiece—was Harding's child. By this time, as *The President's Daughter* circulated briskly, although for the most part under the counter, the public found it easy to believe almost anything of Harding. Nan's 440-page book was convincing not only through its elaboration of details but by its very naivety. She was a determined young woman, she had determined to become Harding's mistress, and she had achieved that inglorious goal. She had no regrets.

She was, she wrote, the daughter of a Marion physician. As a schoolgirl of fourteen she had become infatuated with the handsome editor of the *Star.* Since the Britton and Harding families were acquainted, she knew him to speak to. Often she used to wait across the street from the *Star* office just to catch a glimpse of him sitting in the chair with his feet on the desk. Or she would telephone the Harding house in the hope that he would answer so that she could hear his voice. When he ran for governor of Ohio, she covered the walls of her room with his campaign photographs. Her infatuation was so open that it became a mild scandal. Harding was aware of it; so was Mrs. Harding. In 1916, when Nan was nineteen and the forty-nine-year-old Harding a United States senator, she moved from Marion to New York, and from there wrote him a letter asking for a job. He replied with eager cordiality, saying that he would see her on his next visit to the city. Their first meeting in the Hotel Manhattan was the beginning of their liaison. Before he left her, she wrote, "he tucked thirty dollars in my brand-new silk stocking and was sorry he had no more that time to give me."

The gesture symbolized their relationship. For Harding, it would seem, Nan Britton was young, attractive, and available—a pleasure for which he was willing to pay. For her he was the sentimentalized passion of her lopsided life. They lived together off and on, according to Nan, from 1916 to 1922, registering as man and wife at hotels or sometimes staying in borrowed apartments. It was at a rendezvous in the Senate Office Building, she said, that their child, Elizabeth Ann was conceived. Once Harding even took Nan on tour as his niece. She saw him secretly at the 1920 nominating convention. Even when he was President they managed to have occasional trysts in a White House cloak-room.

After Elizabeth Ann was born, Harding always sent Nan money—a hundred or a hundred and fifty dollars each week. At the time of his death she was visiting Europe at his expense. As a girl Nan had had Harding's sister Abigail for a high school teacher, and when she returned from Europe with her money gone, she went to Abigail in Marion and told her story. Abigail, believing it, sent her small sums of money from time to time—in all eight hundred and ninety dollars. But Harding's sister Carolyn and his brother George Harding were less sympathetic and more skeptical. Dr. George Harding, in a cold four-hour interview with Nan, demanded specific dates, specific places, above all letters. Nan had no more than a few impersonal notes. Her love letters—some of which she claimed ran to as long as sixty pages—she said she had destroyed at Harding's request. She now asked for a tenth of Harding's half-million dollar estate—an amount which she claimed he had promised to settle on her and Elizabeth Ann.

When Dr. Harding refused any settlement, Nan brought an unsuccessful court action against the Hardings. It was in preparation for this suit, she claimed, that she began to write *The President's Daughter,* intending it at first as merely background material for her lawyer. With its publication she made well over a hundred thousand dollars.

Following Harding's death she married a Swedish sea captain, mostly with the intention of providing for Elizabeth Ann, but the captain was poorer than anticipated, and the marriage lasted only a few weeks. Financially safe at last after her book was published, she founded and busied herself with the Elizabeth Ann Guild, the purpose of which was to provide legal aid for unmarried mothers.

Defenders of Harding—there were still some left in Ohio—attacked the book as a fraud, pointing out that for all its gossip no clinching evidence, such as a surviving love letter, was offered. Yet Nan Britton herself was no fiction. Her family was as well known in Marion as Harding's. Although her schoolgirl infatuation for the *Star* editor had been Main Street gossip, beyond that everyone had thought well of her. When Samuel Hopkins Adams talked with some of her old high-school classmates, all of them spoke highly of her character and reputation.

It would have taken the most exact documentary proof to connect Harding's successor, the taciturn Coolidge, with any "woman" scandal. Ike Hoover, who had observed much in his decades as chief usher at the White House, noted tartly in his memoirs that whereas Taft was a ladies' man, Harding was "a sporting ladies' man." When such a man is married to a shrill, nagging, older woman, a certain amount of dalliance may be expected. Even in Marion, there was much that the Duchess had to overlook. Editor Harding had once had an affair with the wife of one of the town's leading merchants. Years later when President-elect Harding returned to a Marion decked with flags and bunting, there was one large store front that remained uncompromisingly blank among the red, white, and blue decorations.

There were other such primrose detours from Main Street in Harding's life. And although his affair with Nan Britton could not be documented to the satisfaction of Dr. George Harding, nevertheless the gushing, redundant pages of her book ring true. Such an enthusiastic artlessness could hardly be counterfeited. Subsequently the Secret Service chief, Colonel Edward Starling, who was then in charge of White House security, confirmed in his memoirs that one of the Secret Service detail had, as Nan alleged, carried letters between the President and "a certain young lady, unnamed, in New York," and once brought her to the White House. "This, I suppose," he wrote, "was Nan Britton."

For several years Nan's book gave flourishing support to the Elizabeth Ann Guild. At one point it employed eight staff members to deal with the flood of letters pouring in from unwed mothers from over the country. Boni & Liveright undertook to publish a second edition of *The President's Daughter.* The book was for a time Gertrude Stein's favorite reading.

Nan wrote various articles, gave interviews, and compiled comparative photographs of Harding and Elizabeth Ann. In a 1928 piece for the *Haldeman-Julius Monthly,* she explained:

> I based my decision to give my book to the world on a platform of faith built on the eternal rock of love, a higher love than mother-love when mother-love is narrow, fearful and absorbing. Never for a moment have I had the slightest doubt of the rightness of my decision in its relationship to my darling child and Warren Harding's.

In October, 1930, a film company was planning to make what Nan called a "picturization" of her book, until film czar Will Hays—who had been Harding's Postmaster-General—

squelched it. In 1932, Nan published her second book, *Honesty or Politics,* more interesting for its assorted pictures of herself, Elizabeth Ann, and Harding than for the 374 rambling pages in which she wrote about her difficulties with the surviving Hardings and with getting *The President's Daughter* into print.

No bills were tucked into stocking tops in *Honesty or Politics.* Lacking the scandal value of its predecessor, the book had only a modest sale. After its publication, Nan and her daughter and the Elizabeth Ann Guild disappeared into anonymity. If Nan is still alive in 1965—the centenary of Harding's birth—she will be sixty-nine years old and Elizabeth Ann forty-six.

It was Harding's good fortune to die when he did, for the scandals of his administration—as he probably knew—could not have remained hidden much longer. He had meant well. With naive sincerity he had hoped to be America's "best loved" President. He had not consciously sullied his office; indeed his cabinet contained men of unquestioned honor and ability, like Herbert Hoover and Charles Evans Hughes. But his closest friend and associate was still Harry Daugherty; his convivial companions, the Ohio politicians who had trailed him to Washington. With Harding in the White House, with Daugherty attached by a private line, the Ohio gang was all there. Alice Longworth described the presidential poker parties that were an evening feature in the early months of the Harding administration:

> No rumor could have exceeded the reality; the study was filled with cronies . . . the air heavy with tobacco smoke, trays containing every imaginable brand of whiskey stood about, cards and poker chips ready at hand—a general atmosphere of waist-coat unbuttoned, feet on desk, and spittoons alongside.

If Harding had lived, it is at least possible that he might have been impeached. By the middle of his term the vultures were beginning to come home to roost. Early in 1923 he discovered that one of his closest poker cronies, Charles R. Forbes, whom he had enthusiastically made director of the Veterans'

Bureau, had rigged his department and had robbed the government and the veterans of an estimated 200 million dollars. It was Harding's first experience of treachery. A visitor to the White House, misdirected to the second floor, was appalled as he passed the Red Room to find the President shaking the cowering Forbes by the neck and shouting: "You yellow rat! You double-crossing bastard!" Shielded as the President was both by his office and his incapacity, the last to learn what had long been Washington gossip, he became by 1923 vaguely but increasingly aware of the other leeches about him. There was Daugherty's loose-lipped Jess Smith, master of the revels at the Little Green House on K Street where, it was whispered, appointments and pardons were sold, liquor permits farmed out, and political deals arranged amidst a profusion of poker chips, bootleg liquor, and accommodating women. There was William J. Burns who, as head of the Federal Bureau of Investigation, was using his bureau as a private detective agency to harass the critics of Daugherty and the Ohio gang. There was Secretary of the Interior Fall, suddenly affluent after his leasing of government oil properties to the Sinclair interests, and now resigned from the Cabinet. There were so many others. Harding, the friendly man, was learning tardily to see his friends in their true light. But even as he learned, disaster was rushing toward him.

So timely was Harding's end in the light of the approaching nemesis, that those in the know soon began to whisper that he had committed suicide. Such rumors were stiffened by certain anomalies of his death. There were contradictory reports of his symptoms. It was uncertain, all now said, just who had been with him when he died. Mrs. Harding had refused to allow an autopsy, had refused even to allow a death mask to be made. Even darker rumors followed, hinting that Harding's death had really been a mercy killing and that the iron-willed Duchess had poisoned him to save his reputation. Fifteen years later Samuel Hopkins Adams found a number of people in Ohio—some of them friends of the Hardings—still convinced that Harding had been murdered by his wife. Many Washington insiders accepted that at the time, although the story did not gain nationwide circulation until the publication in 1930 of *The Strange Death of President Harding* by Gaston B. Means.

Means, a perjurer and trickster whose devious career included a trial for murder, was officially an operative in the Bureau of Investigation but his real function was to operate undercover for Burns and Jess Smith. He lived sumptuously in Washington, renting a house at $1,000 a month and owning a $5,000 car driven by a liveried chauffeur—all on a salary of $88.33 a week. Though his word was always dubious, he maintained in his book that he had also been employed by Mrs. Harding to investigate Nan Britton. Means was to spend two post-Harding terms in a Federal penitentiary, the last (during which he died) for swindling Evelyn Walsh McLean of $100,000 by concocting false clues in connection with the Lindbergh kidnaping. Without saying it in so many words, Means implied that Mrs. Harding had poisoned her husband. Following Nan Britton's revelations, Means's book tore up the last shred of Harding's reputation.

It seemed reasonable enough, after all the other scandals, to believe that Harding had met an unnatural end. Yet the skilled diagnostician Dr. Emmanuel Libman, observing him at a dinner party in the autumn of 1922, had predicted to friends that the President would be dead of a coronary ailment within six months. The year 1923 found Harding oppressed both mentally and physically. He had always played golf with the same compulsive zest that he played cards. Now he tended to become tired after nine holes and often quit at the twelfth or thirteenth. He was unable to sleep except when propped up with pillows. His face aged and grew slack. To his essentially indolent nature the demands of the Presidency had become a relentless burden. With morbid uneasiness he began to doubt himself and to sense the menace to his administration and to his name of the friends he had trusted. Although he still attended the Calvary Baptist Church, he would not go on Communion Sunday, saying that he felt unworthy. He foreswore liquor and gave up his poker parties. For some time he had been thinking of a trip across the continent and to Alaska—"a voyage of understanding," he called it—in which he imagined himself escaping from the isolation of the White House and renewing himself by seeing again the ordinary men and women of America who had elected him.

Originally he had planned the trip as a junket to be made with cronies like Daugherty, Jess Smith, and the court-jester husband of Evelyn Walsh, Ned McLean. The shift to the voyage of understanding developed with the darkening mood of 1923. It was as if Harding were trying to break out of the web of his old associates. Instead of Daugherty, Harding now invited sober-minded men like Speaker of the House Frederick Gillett, Secretary of Agriculture Henry Wallace (father of ex-Vice President Henry Wallace), and Dr. Hubert Work, the former physician who was now Secretary of the Interior. Secretary of Commerce Hoover, then on the West Coast, was asked to join the party there. Dr. Charles Sawyer, the President's personal physician, accompanied him as did a young Navy doctor, Commander Joel T. Boone. Sawyer was a Marion friend, a diminutive country doctor of about the standing of the elder Harding, whom the President had brought to Washington and made a brigadier general. Sawyer cut an absurd figure in his uniform, but he was an honest man. Mrs. Harding of course made the trip, one of her maxims being: Never let a husband travel alone.

The special train with the presidential car *Superb* left Washington on June 20. But before then Harding had had two ominous shocks. In March Charles F. Cramer, Forbes's closest associate in the Veterans' Bureau, had committed suicide. Two months later Jess Smith's improprieties had become so flagrant that they finally reached the President's insensitive ear. Summoned by the White House, Smith confessed, blubbering out the catalogue of iniquities of the Ohio Gang. Harding, aghast, dismissed him with the warning that he would be arrested next day. A few hours later Smith shot himself dead in Daugherty's hotel room.

To the correspondents and those aboard the *Superb* the voyage of understanding seemed more a voyage of doom.

Harding in his restlessness insisted on playing bridge steadily, interrupting his game only to make a speech at each town and whistle stop. He prided himself as an orator, but this time his phrases—always resounding platitudes—had lost their resonance. When he spoke in Kansas City, William Allen White noticed that his lips were swollen and blue and his eyes puffed.

Slowly the *Superb* moved across the continent in the rending summer heat. At St. Louis Harding delivered a ghost-written speech on the World Court. Later the wife of former Secretary Fall, obviously much troubled, visited him incognito at his hotel. The veiled elderly woman spent over an hour talking with him, and when she left Harding appeared profoundly disturbed. Afterward on the train, as if he were thinking aloud, Harding remarked that it was not his enemies but his friends who were keeping him awake nights.

On July 3, Secretary Hoover and his wife joined Harding at Tacoma, just before the party embarked for Alaska. Aboard ship the Secretary was forced to play bridge with the President each day beginning immediately after breakfast and continuing until after midnight. So surfeited of cards did Hoover become that he never played bridge again. One evening Harding sent for him and in the privacy of his cabin asked him what he would do if he knew of a great scandal in the administration. Would he for the good of the party expose it or bury it? Hoover replied that the only thing to do would be to publish it and at least get credit for integrity. Harding gave no further details. But Hoover noticed that as the trip continued the President grew increasingly nervous. In Alaska a long coded message came to Harding by plane from Washington. After reading it he almost collapsed, and for the rest of the day seemed half-stunned. He did not recover on the voyage back. His speeches were listless, their banalities no longer covered by his personal magnetism. In Seattle, on a searing afternoon, he faltered and was barely able to finish reading his manuscript.

That night Harding suddenly suffered such pain that Dr. Sawyer was hastily sent for. The doctor announced that the

President was suffering from acute indigestion after having eaten crab meat—although later it turned out there had been no crab on the menu. Dr. Boone, noting symptoms of high blood pressure and an enlarged heart that had been passed over by the homeopathic general, insisted over Sawyer's objections that it was much more serious and that Harding had had a cardiac attack.

As the *Superb* moved south all speaking dates were canceled. Boone and Dr. Work arranged to have two specialists meet the train at San Francisco: Dr. Ray Lyman Wilbur, president of Stanford University and afterward president of the American Medical Association; and a well-known heart specialist, Dr. Charles Miner Cooper. Harding arrived in San Francisco on Sunday, July 29, walking unaided from the train to the street, although reporters noted that he looked "gray and worn." He was taken to the Palace Hotel where Dr. Wilbur and Dr. Cooper examined him and at once diagnosed his condition as a coronary attack aggravated by bronchial pneumonia.

Under treatment the President seemed to improve. On Wednesday Dr. Sawyer announced that the crisis was past. The President's lungs cleared up and on Thursday his improvement continued. He was able to sit up. Then, without warning, at 7:35 in the evening, he suddenly died of what his death certificate described as cerebral apoplexy.

According to the newspaper accounts by reporters at the hotel, his wife had been sitting beside him reading an article about him by Samuel G. Blythe in *The Saturday Evening Post.* It was called "A Calm View of a Calm Man," and it pleased Harding, for he remarked, "That's good! Go on, read some more." And in that instant a change passed over his face, he shuddered and collapsed. Mrs. Harding ran shrieking into the corridor. A few seconds later Dr. Boone and Dr. Sawyer arrived to find him dead. Doctors Wilbur and Cooper were sent for. They, with the other two doctors and Secretary Work, signed the death certificate.

"Nothing could be more absurd than the poison theory," Dr. Wilbur wrote long afterward. And as Samuel Hopkins

Adams pointed out, to accept it is to assume that five doctors—four of whom at least were distinguished members of their profession—would violate their ethics to cover up a capital crime. Even if they had done so, there would still be the problem of how either Harding or his wife could have obtained possession of a killing drug without the knowledge of others. As for the suicide hypothesis, Harding for all his faults was not the suicidal type.

After Harding's funeral, Florence Kling Harding wasted no time in unprofitable grief. The Coolidges did not press her, and she spent the first few weeks of her widowhood in the White House gathering up and destroying every bit of her husband's correspondence, official and unofficial, that she could lay hands on. Once back in Marion she performed a similar operation on the files of the *Star*. She employed a corps of secretaries to trace Harding correspondents, to whom she appealed on sentimental grounds for any surviving letters. Her last year of life—she died on November 21, 1924—was a busy one, but her motives were incendiary rather than sentimental. When the publishing house of Doubleday, Page asked if it might publish a volume of Harding letters, she refused to consider it. She admitted to Frank N. Doubleday, the head of the firm, that she had burned her husband's correspondence, saying that she feared some of it might be misconstrued and harm his memory.

What the destroyed letters contained remains as mysterious as the Lincoln correspondence destroyed by his son Robert in the 1920s. Yet there were a number of Harding letters that somehow eluded her.

These letters and papers still exist in possession of the Harding Memorial Association where they are kept in the basement of the old Harding house in Marion. They are at present in the custody of Dr. Carl Sawyer, the president of the association and son of the former White House physician, who has been engaged in sorting and arranging—but not destroying—them. Nothing, however, is open to the public or even to scholars or biographers. Dr. Sawyer maintains that Harding was unjustly treated and that the truth about him will show him to have been "a fine, a wonderful man." But it does not seem to be a truth that anyone in Marion is particularly anxious to hasten before the public. Long ago the association decided not to make the Harding papers public until fifty years after his death, in 1973. Dr. Sawyer is not sure that they will be ready even then. "There's something America doesn't know," he told an interviewer enigmatically in the spring of 1962, "and may not for a hundred years." *

Shortly after Harding's death his friends in Marion formed the memorial association and began to raise money for a tomb splendid enough for their President's body to lie in state forever. Businessmen, workers, schoolchildren, Ohioans from every walk of life—and many outside the state—contributed. At first the money gushed in with fanfares of publicity, but as the Harding scandals darkened the sky over Marion, money and publicity began to run thin. To the press, as to the politicians, the proposed memorial became an embarrassing subject. Eventually, however, the dogged committee of the memorial association succeeded in getting together three quarters of a million dollars.

The cornerstone was laid in 1926 and the dedication set for July 4, 1927. On high ground, in the cemetery on Delaware Avenue south of Marion, the white marble monument loomed up—a beautifully proportioned circle of Tuscan columns joined by an equally austere entablature. Harding's remains and those of his wife were moved there early in 1927 to await the official eulogy. This, according to the etiquette of such things, could be spoken by no one less than the President of the United States. President Coolidge was in any case the honorary president of the memorial association.

* After calling a meeting of the association's Executive Committee on September 30, 1963, Dr. Sawyer finally announced that the Harding papers—including some 300,000 letters and copies of letters—would be released to the Ohio Historical Society. On October 10 the steel boxes containing the papers were removed from the basement of the Harding Home and Museum in Marion and transported in a moving van to the Historical Society building in Columbus. At Dr. Sawyer's insistence the van was accompanied by an armed patrol of state police to protect "against any ambush from the Teapot Dome crowd."

Cautious Cal, however, had no intention of getting himself tarred with the Harding brush. At any mention of dedicating the Harding Memorial, Coolidge—according to Herbert Hoover—"expressed a furious distaste."

July 4, 1927, came and went unmarked by any ceremony in the Marion cemetery. So did three more July Fourths. Hoover, succeeding as President, was no more pleased at the prospect of this dubious task than was Coolidge, but he was more the man and less the politician. An article that appeared in the September, 1930, issue of *Plain Talk* called "Harding's Haunted Tomb" stirred Ohio and bestirred Washington. Hoover finally agreed to take his sour medicine and preside over the dedication.

The Marion memorial was dedicated on June 16, 1931. Chief Justice Charles Evans Hughes spoke first, revealing to his surprised audience that if Harding had lived he would have been a hopeless invalid and that he knew it. Ex-President Coolidge then cannily accepted the memorial on behalf of the American people, measuring out his words by the teaspoonful. Finally President Hoover stepped before the battery of microphones. Directly behind him, as a member of the committee, sat the gimlet-eyed Daugherty. Hoover might have dodged the issue that was probably alive in the minds of everyone present, glossing it over with meaningless words. But his Quaker conscience faced it squarely. His words were intended to cut home, and they did:

> Here was a man [he said, as if he were addressing the man behind him] whose soul was seared by a great disillusionment. We saw him gradually weaken, not only from physical exhaustion but also from mental anxiety. Warren Harding had a dim realization that he had been betrayed by a few of the men whom he had trusted, by men whom he had believed were his devoted friends. It was later proved in the courts of the land that these men had betrayed not only the friendship and trust of their staunch and loyal friend but they had betrayed their country. That was the tragedy of the life of Warren Harding.

The Witch of Beacon Hill

Never in the ambiguous history of spiritualism in the United States has there been a medium who achieved such a reputation for psychic phenomena and caused such extended controversy as the woman known as Margery, who suddenly manifested her abilities in Boston in the spring of 1923. Margery, it was claimed, performed under the spirit control of her dead brother Walter. His voice first spoke through her, though later independently of her vocal cords. During a series of Margery's séances extraordinary occurrences took place. Flowers and other objects materialized from nowhere. Ghostly bugle calls sounded. At times ectoplasmic rods sprouted from the medium's body that were capable of touching persons in the dark, moving objects, producing lights, and making wax impressions of themselves. J. Malcolm Bird, associate editor of *Scientific American,* who later wrote a book on Margery, became her partisan, as did Hereward Carrington, Sir Arthur Conan Doyle, and others. Houdini the magician, after attending five of the séances, denounced her almost hysterically. In the next few years hundreds of newspaper and magazine articles appeared about her. A committee from *Scientific American* and one from Harvard investigated her. Their findings were varied. Concerning Margery herself there has never been a final conclusion.

What made Margery's case unique beyond the spiritualist phenomena themselves was the quality of the people involved. Doctors, professional men, and members of the Harvard faculty were among the regular sitters at her séances. No financial considerations ever entered into the mediumship; in fact the expenses of many of the investigators were paid by Margery's husband.

Margery was the Canadian-born wife of Le Roi Goddard Crandon, a well-known Boston doctor and surgeon-in-chief of a local hospital. Dr. Crandon, a Harvard graduate of the class of 1894, had been for some years a lecturer in surgery at the Harvard Medical School. The Crandons lived in a four-story Federalist town house at 10 Lime Street, just at the foot of Beacon Hill. It is a small street of dissimilar houses harmonized by the passage of time, and its antique intimacy makes it seem rather fitting for psychic adventures.

The name Margery was a pseudonym invented for Mrs. Crandon at the outset of her mediumship to protect her from publicity. In her ordinary daily life she was matter-of-fact about her psychic powers and would sometimes jokingly refer to herself—a personable woman in her thirties—as a witch, adding that if she had lived 250 years earlier she would probably have been hanged.

Margery the medium had her origins in Dr. Crandon's library. Early in 1923, more or less by chance, he happened to occupy himself with books on spiritualism, at first in a desultory way and later with more concentrated interest. Although his wife did not take spiritualism seriously, they talked about it together, and one day as a joke she went with a friend to a Boston clairvoyant. She did not identify herself, and she was astonished when the medium, in a trance, told her that a spirit by the name of Walter was present. The messages that he then transmitted from Walter consisted of small personal incidents from her girlhood.

A short time after this the Crandons, with four of their friends, made a private attempt at spirit communication, gathering around a table in the Lime Street living room under a red light. Before long the table began to rotate and then tilt. One by one the sitters were sent from the room. Only in Mrs. Crandon's absence did the table remain dead. A code of responses was soon established by which the table-tipping intelligence, who maintained he was Walter, could reply to questions. Subsequently Walter began to communicate by a series of raps, and then after some time his voice asserted itself through Margery. About this time Dr. Crandon constructed a cabinet for his wife, and her séances were conducted with the sitters joining hands in a circle.

Walter's presence was usually announced by a sharp whistle. His voice now became a standard feature of all Margery's séances, and the table tipping and the raps were discarded. Over the months her mediumship seemed to follow its own curious progress. At one point all the clocks in the house were stopped at a time predetermined by Walter. At another séance Walter announced he would play taps, and shortly afterward the notes were faintly heard in the lower part of the house. Sometimes the furniture in the living room would move. Once, after he called attention to the possibility, a live pigeon was found in the next room.

Finally Dr. Crandon claimed that he had observed "faint aurora-like emanations" projecting from the region of Margery's fingers. This was the beginning of the ectoplasmic materializations that were to produce organs and hands of various kinds. A wax cast was made of one of these hands. Others were photographed. Walter registered his thumb-print in wax. The ectoplasmic limbs rang bells. Accompanying these materializations were psychic lights that floated about the room glowing and fading.

In 1922, *Scientific American* offered to pay $2,500 for any objective demonstration of psychic phenomena and appointed an investigating committee of five prominent persons interested in this subject. The members were Dr. Daniel Comstock, formerly professor of physics at the Massachusetts Institute of Technology; Dr. William McDougall, professor of psychology at Harvard and president of the American Society for Psychical Research; Dr. Walter Franklin Prince, former clergyman and research officer of the society; Dr. Hereward Carrington, the author and psychic experimenter who had tested the European medium Palladino; and Harry Houdini, the magician and escape artist. J. Malcolm Bird, who had first brought Margery into contact with the committee, served as its secretary. During 1924, in the course of the committee's investigations, three articles by Mr. Bird, essentially favorable to Margery, appeared in *Scientific American.* These spread the interest in her mediumship quickly and widely.

The report of the committee a few months later was, however, unfavorable. Mr. Bird accepted the Lime Street séance phenomena as genuine, as did Dr. Carrington. Houdini, with a showman's eye for publicity, published a lurid pamphlet denouncing Margery. Dr. Prince was not convinced. Yet it must be said that his and Houdini's attendance at the sittings was scanty. Dr. Comstock was present more often than any of the others. He found difficulty in making up his mind, and concluded merely that "rigid proof has not yet been furnished." Dr. McDougall also seemed hesitant during the séances, but in his report he wrote: "As long ago as November . . . I was inclined to regard all the phenomena I had observed as produced by normal means. . . . Since that date . . . the inclination has grown steadily stronger in the main, in spite of some minor fluctuations, and has now become well-nigh irresistible." The report and the committee were sharply attacked by the growing number of Margery's defenders.

In the summer of 1925, another briefer investigation was conducted by a group of younger members of the Harvard faculty, this time in a room of Emerson Hall in the Harvard Yard. Walter made the transition from Lime Street easily, but the principal Emerson phenomenon was Margery's trance production "after the manner of a birth" of an ectoplasmic hand. For these séances she wore luminous bands on her legs as controls, but during one sitting it was discovered that she had slipped a foot out of the band and was free to manipulate it. Afterward a committee member, by a similar free use of his foot, managed to duplicate all the phenomena except the production of ectoplasm. The ectoplasmic hand impressed itself on a lump of plasticine, which on later examination showed skin markings and lint microscopically identical with that in the medium's slipper. At another Emerson séance two observers noted that the medium had worked both hands free, and one of them detected her conveying objects from her lap and afterward returning them.

At a subsequent series of séances with an English representative of the Society for Psychical Research, Margery produced varieties of ectoplasm including a much more embryonic hand than the earlier one, spongy and feeling like blancmange. This hand was photographed under red light. When these photographs were examined by Dr. W. B. Cannon, professor of physiology, and Dr. H. W. Rand, professor of zoology, both of Harvard, they reported that the so-called ectoplasm was composed of the lung tissue of some animal.

There were rumors that the Harvard group had disagreed about Margery. To correct this the members issued a statement that they were "in absolute agreement; that the only conclusion possible is that trickery accounted for all the phenomena; and that the only possible difference of opinion is to what extent the trickery is unconscious."

Perhaps the most directly damaging evidence against Margery was the discovery in 1932 that the wax impressions shown for six years as Walter's psychic thumbprints were really those of a Boston dentist. The dentist, still alive and practicing, admitted that he had once made several such impressions in dental wax at Mrs. Crandon's request. To this charge the Crandons never replied.

My later friend, the writer Robert Hillyer, who was at that time an English instructor at Harvard, became a regular attender at the Lime Street sittings along with another young Harvard writer, S. Foster Damon. With Damon, Margery developed an almost maternal relationship, and he came to her for advice on all his personal problems. Subsequently, he wrote a glowing book about her. Robert had just published his fourth book of poems, *The Hills Give Promise*. What he experienced in the séance room at first convinced him, and he gave Margery a copy of his new book in which he had written: "I have seen, and I have believed." In the course of further sittings, however, he came to change his opinion and in the end very much regretted that he had given Margery the inscribed book.

"At one séance," he told me, "Margery produced an ectoplasmic hand and we were asked to feel it. As soon as I touched it I knew it was the hand of a dead person. It was small, either a child's or a woman's, but dead. I understood then. Dr. Crandon was a surgeon, and he could sneak such things out of the hospital."

"But," I asked him, "if it was a fraud, why did they do it?"

"It was a weird business," he said. "Crandon was much older than his wife, and he was an educated man of some standing. She had neither education nor background. There may have been some sort of psychological conflict in that, each trying to prove something to the other. Of course he faked, but perhaps he felt that in spite of the trickery there was something real behind it all. He may have believed in Walter. I don't know. After that night I never went near Lime Street again."

It was in 1940, in the second autumn of the war, that I happened to be asked to 10 Lime Street. I was surprised to learn that Margery still lived there. In the ominous quiet of an America preparing its first peacetime draft, the controversy she had caused a decade and a half earlier seemed remote and irrelevant. Yet though the fashions of publicity had passed her by, Margery still continued her sittings with her followers. Dr. Crandon had died the winter before.

A Dr. Richardson introduced me. He had been a friend of the Crandons from the beginning of Margery's mediumship. Just after World War I he lost his two sons in a polio epidemic and this had turned him toward spiritualism. To his satisfaction at least, he had found his boys again in all the brightness of their youth at Margery's séances. On our way to Lime Street he showed me a spirit photograph of Margery in a trance with a cloud like a double exposure above her head on which were the blurred outlines of two faces. These faces, he told me, were his sons beyond doubt.

We arrived at eight o'clock of a rainy, line-storm evening. Margery herself opened the street-level door for us, shook hands, and led the way to an upstairs drawing room. She was an overdressed, dumpy little woman, amiable, yet with a faint elusive coarseness about her that one sensed as soon as she spoke. Dr. Richardson said that in recent séances they had been trying to reach Dr. Crandon and that tonight they hoped to get a wax imprint of his fingers. The room was a homely one with chintz curtains, leather and fabric armchairs, imitation upright Chippendales, a tapestry brick fireplace with a sofa in front of it at one end and lengths of bookcases at the other. On a side shelf was a silver-framed, autographed photograph of A. Conan Doyle, and another of Sir Oliver Lodge. Near the window stood an old-fashioned Victrola. There were eight or ten people standing about.

"Everybody ready?" Margery asked us. We arranged our chairs in a circle. Margery sat in the center in a straight-backed chair. "Let's have a little music," she said as we settled down.

Someone turned on the Victrola. She squatted there with her eyes half-closed, and there was no sound but the rasp of the needle and then the notes of "Ah, Sweet Mystery of Life" scratched out of the wax grooves.

The song ended, and as the mechanism shut itself off, Dr. Richardson turned out the lights. For several minutes there was no sound at all. The tension hung suspended, like that empty moment before the bull comes into the arena. Then I noticed Margery's breathing. At first it sounded no more than a repeated sigh, but with each breath she took it deepened until it became a stertorous moan. Only once before had I heard such sounds—when I passed a hospital room where a man was dying.

Then, breaking in suddenly over this animal noise that stopped abruptly, came a rush of air and an ear-cracking whistle, and after this a man's voice talking very fast. The sound seemed to come from a spot several feet above Margery's head.

"Almost thought I couldn't make it," said the voice nasally. "Lot of interrupters, lots of trouble, plenty of them."

Dr. Richardson spoke back. "Walter," he said, "we have a new sitter with us I'd like you to meet. This is Mr. Russell."

"How do you do," I said awkwardly, in what I thought was his general direction, realizing as I said it that my voice sounded strained and somewhat artificial.

"How do *you* do," said Walter mimicking me. "I don't think you do very well. Is that a Harvard accent you have?"

"You mustn't mind Walter," said Dr. Richardson. "He's often rude, but he doesn't really mean a thing by it."

"That's what the doc thinks," said Walter.

A woman in the darkness opposite asked if Dr. Crandon could give them any message.

"Roi's busy," Walter answered her. "He said to say he was OK, but he's still tied up. He can't come through yet."

"When do you think he can?" Mrs. Richardson asked.

"Not for a while yet, not for a while yet. Keep your shirt on." Walter's voice was edged. "Leave him alone, give him time. He's got his troubles, too."

There was more talk, and then Dr. Richardson asked Walter about the fingerprints.

"Not tonight, Doc," said Walter. "Next time, maybe."

Then there was silence, as if a radio station had gone off the air, and a few seconds later Margery's voice broke in casually. "Will you turn on the lights?" Although pitched in another key, the tone bore a certain resemblance to Walter's.

The lights went on and we stood up blinking, while Margery smiled at us in an indolent, good-natured way, stretching her plump arms and yawning. As we left she shook hands with each of us at the top of the landing. "You must all come to tea next Sunday," she said. "I have a feeling it's going to be important. All of you, next Sunday—but not before five o'clock. I have to see about Roi's grave earlier." She giggled. "The landscape gardeners have made an awful mess of it, planted hydrangeas. Roi hates hydrangeas. Now don't forget—next Sunday at five."

It was the only time I ever saw Margery. At that séance there had been no wandering lights or ghostly music, no bells ringing, no psychic touch I could feel, no ectoplasm or even fingerprints. In a committee sense there had not been enough phenomena for anyone to pass judgment; yet Walter's voice was real, and he was the core of the matter, the leading spirit—if one could excuse the play on words. Those earlier productions of ectoplasm had been a contrivance, part of the paraphernalia that Dr. Crandon had assembled. A less gullible medical man than Dr. Richardson was afterward to describe the psychic rods sprouting from Margery's body as some sort of animal intestines stuffed with cotton. The lights and the bells and the rest Houdini could have managed as well.

That left Walter, a spirit with a taste for Victor Herbert, brash and crude of speech, a kind of poolroom johnny from the other world. As an audible actuality he was capable of three interpretations. Either he was a disembodied entity that had once been Margery's brother; or he was a subconscious element of Margery developed in a trance; or he was merely Margery's normal self play-acting.

If one were to believe the first interpretation, as did Dr. Richardson, that glimpsed other world must be a shabby, static place. For Walter, since parting from his body, showed no development in mind or personality or tastes.

In regard to the latter two interpretations, the first seems the more likely. For Margery to contrive such a conscious Walter-fiction during hundreds of sittings over a period of years would be too demanding a feat. Walter was a complete individual. He never hesitated, never lacked for words, never stepped out of character. Rather than to assume that Margery was merely a clever actress, it seems a more likely assumption that her trances at least were genuine and that Walter was a second personality developed in them.

Several years after that Lime Street séance, when I had been sent overseas to an infantry reinforcement unit in England, I happened to pick up a pink paperbound copy of *Whitaker's Almanack* in the mess anteroom. While I waited for dinner, I thumbed through it—the events of the year before, tides, eclipses, weights and measures, and finally a list of noted people who had died during the year. There, under November's obituaries, I suddenly noticed: "Mrs. L. R. G. Crandon, the medium Margery, at Boston, Massachusetts, U.S.A."

It was not quite, however, my last contact with Margery. One heat-struck August afternoon just after the war, I happened to be walking along Cornhill behind Boston's City Hall. As a relief to that empty, sun-bleached street I stopped under the shadow of the awning in front of Colesworthy's secondhand bookstore. On the sidewalk was the usual tray of twenty-five-cent books. As I glanced over them I saw one with a faded brown cover that looked familiar. I could scarcely decipher the lettering of the title, *The Hills Give Promise.* I picked it up and opened it. There on the flyleaf, just as I had somehow expected, was Robert's neat, almost prim inscription: "I have seen, and I have believed."

The Hill, the Hollow, and the Jews

Dorchester Hill was the fixed point of my childhood. I cannot recall a time when I was not aware of Boston, the smoke-blurred seaport lying beyond the welter of three-decker tenements between the Hill and Dorchester Bay. From the Hill's summit, under the shadow of a line of pignut trees, one faced the sweep of vast windy horizons. To the north, enveloped in a pastel haze, sprawled the tentacular city, dominated by the granite obelisk of the Custom House tower, and on bright days reflecting the glitter of the gilt State House dome (of solid gold we supposed those arched blocks to be, where one need only climb with a cold chisel on a dark night to hack out one's fortune). To the south was the low saddleback range of the Blue Hills, as thickly wooded as when the Puritans named it three centuries before, and broken far to the left by the spars and masts of the Quincy granite quarries. On the other side of Canterbury Ridge and the Bellevue water tower lay the whole continental expanse of North America, stretching away unimagined miles to Mexico, the Pacific, Alaska, and the straits of Asia. Eastward, the sea curved into infinity, beyond the massed three-deckers of Jewville and the Codman Square Meeting House and the yellow brick bulk of the Dorchester High School. Within that curve were the green harbor islands with their deserted beaches and their eighteenth-century forts, the ledges and warning beacons of the Brewsters, and the final unbroken gulf of water touching the sky's rim. To live on such a hill was like living on the roof of the world.

Originally the Hill had been owned by the Holbrooks, a land-hungry Puritan family that in its decline sold its possessions and its land piecemeal, thereby retarding but not avoiding the inevitable. At the turn of the twentieth century this final remnant of the Holbrook holdings was developed by a syndicate of builders in partnership with Wellington Holbrook, the last of the family. They cut through streets, leveled gradients, and built a series of small wooden boxlike houses, gambrel-roofed, in a style known as Dutch Colonial, and each varying slightly in cut and color from the next. The houses were built cheaply and in a hurry, either one-family houses of seven very small rooms or two-family houses containing two suites of six rooms each. The lots were narrow. There was a small strip of grass before each house and a scattering of forsythia and other ornamental shrubs. Quick-growing Norway maples were planted along the edge of the street that from the vanity of the last Holbrook was named after him.

It was a fairly typical American-Protestant lower-middle-class settlement of clerks and shopkeepers, salesmen, petty officials, minor professional men, and occasionally a teacher. Those who lived on the Hill conformed unconsciously to an accepted pattern, convinced that they thought things out for themselves, and almost unaware of possible dissent. They believed firmly in the American success myth of beginning at the bottom and working to the top, although in their cases they were only a jealously-held rung or two above working-class status and sometimes in such precarious financial condition that they had a third mortgage on their homes. The more prosperous bought one-family houses; the two-family houses cost more to begin with, but the rent of the second flat was expected to pay for the interest on the mortgage plus the upkeep.

As a community it was homogeneous, its racial origins scarcely remembered but predominantly Yankee-English with a certain admixture of Scots, Scandinavian, and Pennsylvania Dutch. Its religion was, of course, Protestant, the more fashionable going to the Episcopal Church of the Holy Spirit at Mattapan Square a mile away, the rest being either Presbyterian or

Methodist. Politically it voted straight Republican, partly for the myth's sake, partly because of the Irish-Democrats, who, as in other seaboard cities, controlled the municipal political machine.

The Hollow was another matter altogether. River Street, running between it and the Hill from Dorchester Avenue to the Boston Elevated Railway terminal at Forest Hills, was the dividing line. This bowl-like depression, also originally part of the Holbrook estates, but considered of no value, had been let go for a settlement of its back taxes to John Mulvey, a relative of the building commissioner under Mayor "Honey Fitz" Fitzgerald. There was no need for Mulvey to worry about the vagaries of the building laws. He cut a road running from River Street down to the swamp edge of the Hollow and, without bothering to pave it, lined it with closely-set three-deckers. He called the street Mulvey Street—more in his case from lack of imagination than out of vanity.

Three-deckers, three-storied rectangular wooden houses with a triple porch and bay window at the front, take their name from their characteristic flat roof. Each story contains a flat of five rooms. Being of flimsy construction, they are cheap to build. In the past they brought a quicker return on one's investment than any other form of real estate.

The three-deckers of Mulvey Street were scarcely finished when they filled up with the overflow from the Irish matrix of South Boston. Such jerry-built houses, with several families in each flat, deteriorated rapidly. Almost before it was inhabited, the section became a depressed area, solidly Irish, solidly Catholic. Below the railroad bridge a mile away on the road to Milton, a Roman Catholic church, St. Angela's, was built, at first merely a low red-brick utility basement. It would be some years before the money was raised for its near-romanesque upper structure.

The Hollow was a casual phenomenon. All the large seaboard cities of the northeastern United States where the immigrants arrived en masse contained these scattered islands of racial groups. Coming to a strange land and as the lowest stratum of the population, the immigrant quite naturally held to his own both for protection and company. In Boston the Famine exodus made solid Irish settlements of Charlestown and South Boston; later, the Italians from Naples and Sicily swarmed into the North End; the Jews filled Chelsea until the fire of 1908, then migrated to Dorchester; the Negroes occupied the South End and parts of Roxbury; a German colony went farther out and settled Germantown near Dedham. There were dozens of smaller areas: Chinese, Russian, Armenian, Scots, French-Canadian, almost everything except English. Occasionally there was a certain spilling over, a drift from the older centers of settlement, a spreading out into the suburbs to such little racial islands. At the time of Mulvey's building activities the Jews were just beginning to come into Dorchester, a few miles north of the Hill.

Such minor folk movements followed a fixed pattern. The Irish would drive out the old Yankees, as they did from the handsome swell-fronted town houses of Charlestown. The Poles, although religiously akin, nevertheless replaced the Irish rather than mingled with them. The Jews displaced the Irish with harsh words, and sometimes more took place than words on both sides. The Negroes infiltrated and the Jews moved out, but with little friction, as the Jew does not tend to emphasize the color line. Long after the Negroes, came the bulldozers of urban redevelopment.

Mulvey Street was one of those spillovers, a small Irish plantation in the Hollow above which was the small Protestant Ascendancy of the Hill, both of which were to be swept away in the next generation by the overwhelming pressure of the Jewish population of Dorchester. In my childhood nobody gave a thought to that new influx a few miles north, although even by then the section near Franklin Field had begun to be called Jewville. The Hollow had its own thoughts about the Hill; to the Hill the Hollow was both an eyesore and a stronghold of belligerent superstition.

Among the adults of the two communities there was no real contact. They took the same Egleston Square street cars each morning to go to the city, but even those at different hours, the Hollow going to work at 7:30, the Hill at 8:15. The young

Hill and the young Hollow met in the neutral territory of the Martha Baker School, but although the children sat in the same classrooms, outside the school they kept apart.

I can still remember that contingent from Mulvey Street in the first-grade room. They were tough, unkempt, dirty, and pugnacious, foul-mouthed almost from infancy. Someone has described the progress of literacy as the graffiti on walls becoming lower and lower. If so, the Killian boys were unusually precocious. This prolific family was the toughest of the tribe. The oldest Killian was the leader of the Mulvey Gang, made up of boys ranging from ten to fifteen, who would periodically attack the Hill Gang—really more a self-protective association than a gang. A stone fight would ensue in and about the Dutch Colonial houses and small gardens, and once up to the very hill crest by the pignut trees.

Old Mulvey was the symbol of his street. As he prospered and grew older he became grossly fat, and long after autos had become common he still drove about in a buggy, holding a frayed whip in his dimpled fat hand, his obese belly wedged behind the dashboard where he sat like a toad, blue-jowled, with overhanging eyebrows that met in the middle above his pinkish eyes. His connection with the commissioner always gave him advance knowledge of any impending building developments, so that whenever the City of Boston came to buy land in Dorchester for a school or fire station, it was usually found that John Mulvey had an option on the property and that the City had to pay his price for it. New Calvary Cemetery, west of the Hollow, was another venture of his, perhaps his most profitable, on waste land unfit even for jerry-building. Haphazard, unkempt, with long rows of weedy neglected graves, it was, nevertheless, a consecrated cemetery and received the bones of the faithful to the profit of the Mulvey Cemetery Corporation. Farther down Walk Hill Street was the Protestant Cemetery of Mount Hope. Here the landscape was trim, the lawns clipped, the borders green, chestnut trees sheltered the macadam walks, and instead of makeshift wooden markers or sorry little iron crosses that soon rusted away, there were great lumps of polished granite that shone like mirrors and indicated by their relative size the social and financial position of the deceased. The Hill felt that the differences between the cemeteries were symbolic of the two communities—in Mount Hope order, quietness, dignity; in New Calvary, from the rotting, mansard-roofed chapel to the dump beyond where the faded wreaths were thrown to disintegrate in full view, a blot on the landscape.

In the Hill's opinion, Catholicism was the next thing to paganism. It is true that not one Hill person in five had ever been in a Catholic church, but they were convinced nevertheless, that it was a form of idolatry, a gross superstition, and only a literal fear of Hell fire crowded St. Angela's basement on a Sunday morning. Confession consisted of telling your sins to a priest and then going off and acting as badly as you pleased.

From its outside the low basement of St. Angela's was a desolate-looking building. The brisk trade that the noisy newsboys did selling Sunday papers on the steps after High Mass would never have been tolerated in front of the Church of the Holy Spirit by the Reverend Allen MacLane Taylor.

There was one Catholic, however, living on the Hill, Robert Emmet Egan, who had come from an obscure mid-western college to attend the Harvard Graduate School, where he had received his master's degree, and then became headmaster of an elementary school near Codman Square. Not only was he a Harvard man who in spite of his name identified himself in no way with the Irish of the Hollow, he had even written an autobiographical novel of his boyhood called *Little People of the Dust* that he had published at his own expense. That such an intelligent man as Mr. Egan could still be a Catholic and go to a church like St. Angela's was a great mystery to the Hill. Most people blamed his childhood training that persisted in spite of all his education and just went to prove how hard it was for a man to shake off his early superstitions.

To my child's mind Catholicism, the Irish, and Mulvey Street were synonymous. It always gave me a sense of uneasiness and bewilderment at the Sunday Morning Prayer and Sermon at the Holy Spirit when we repeated the Apostles' Creed together: "I believe in the Holy Ghost; The Holy Catholic Church. . . ."

What was the Catholic Church but that red-brick basement and the crowd of Mulvey Streeters coming out after mass and crowding on the steps while the paper-boys howled their wares? The uneasy feeling never left me until we sat down again and Mr. Taylor stood in the pulpit, tossed back his silvery hair with a rather theatrical gesture, and began his sermon. In spite of that dubious passage in the Prayer Book, Mr. Taylor did not mince words. There were no two ways about what he thought of the Catholic Church.

The Hill's political allegiance to the Republican Party never wavered. Although the Irish Democrats controlled City Hall, the Republican State Legislature so gerrymandered the outlying districts that the Irish vote in the State House was nullified. By linking the Hill (Ward 21) with Hyde Park (Ward 24), a similar but much larger Protestant community, the Irish of the Hollow and of the Lower Mills were kept in a minority. Tom Buckley was our perpetual Democratic candidate for the legislature, but it was a joke really, for he never had a ghost of a mathematical possibility of winning with the Hyde Park votes against him. The politics of Boston was a different affair, as sinister as the outline of the gray city itself from the Hill on a louring afternoon. To the Hill the city's personification of evil was its feared and hated mayor, James Michael Curley. I remember the turbulence of his second election, when he was opposed by a reform candidate who carried the suburbs, Dorchester, West Roxbury, and Hyde Park, but failed ignominiously with the massed voters of Boston proper. The evening of Curley's victory was one of chagrin and frustration for the Hill. Several groups of grownups stood with us children near the pignut trees watching Curley's triumphant torchlight parade as it swung down Walk Hill Street below us, a cavalcade of autos with the tops down that wound along toward Forest Hills under the arching elms like a grossly iridescent and enveloping snake.

Molded into me with my acquisition of language was the consciousness that there were two groups of people in the world, ourselves on the Hill and the Irish below us. The Irish were tangible. A third group, the Jews, intruding later into my awareness, was much more elusive. Where we played our games in the meadow beyond the pignut trees we looked out toward Dorchester High School and the harbor. I suppose it was there playing with the older children that I first heard the word Jew. Somewhere in that nebulous past I have the vaguest recollection of myself asking, "What are Jews?" But the answer, if answer there was, is lost, and all I know is that between the age of four and five I had the feeling of Jews as people who were different and somehow threatening, who lived mysteriously in those gray three-deckers between the Hill and the city among that maze of twisting streets I had never visited.

Mass emigration of the Jews from Polish Russia to the United States began with the anti-Jewish riots in Kiev and other Russian cities during 1881, followed by the "May Laws" of 1882 which expelled great numbers from the smaller Polish towns and villages. Before 1880 there were fewer than 500 Russian Jews in Massachusetts out of a foreign-born population of 350,000. Between 1900 and 1914 they formed the largest racial bloc coming into the state.

This large-scale migration was accelerated by the Kishinev pogroms of 1903 and by the great Russian massacres of 1905. Of the 100,000 immigrants arriving in Massachusetts in 1913, 21,000 were Jews from the Polish Pale.

The greater part of them settled in Chelsea, a sordid industrial-slum adjunct of Boston, along the dumps and pot-hole wharves of the Mystic River. Unfamiliar with the language of the country, unassimilable, in earning a living they followed the customary pattern of newly arrived immigrant groups. Only the lowest and most menial tasks were open to them, those scorned or abandoned by the previous wave of immigrants. The Jews took to peddling and junk-dealing, a haggling existence to which they were adapted by their harsh and limited life in the Pale, and which was considered beneath the dignity of previously arrived groups.

Chelsea, with its dreary massed tenement blocks, its narrow, purulent streets and swarming waterfront, became a ghetto, nonetheless real for lacking the sanction of legality. As yet, except against Orientals, there were no restrictive immigration laws in the United States, but the Jews of Chelsea, like the Italians of Boston's North End, made many a native New Englander wonder if any process could make such alien people Americans. A Jewish sociologist, Oscar Janowsky, wrote of this period:

> Between 1880 and 1914 almost two million Jews came to the United States from Eastern Europe. [The number was nearer three million.] They made one of the most difficult transitions ever recorded of a migratory group. Leaping across several centuries in time as well as thousands of miles in space, they left a seventeenth-century, pre-industrial, Torah-regulated society for the twentieth-century machine culture of America. The wonder is not that there was some friction but that there was so little. By settling for the most part in the congested quarters of the larger cities, they increased the visibility of the Jew. Non-Jews saw Yiddish signs, *Kosher* markets, bearded and gabardined Jews; and all these externals served to sharpen the difference between the Jewish and Gentile communities.

The ghetto of Chelsea was suddenly destroyed in a fire that began on Palm Sunday, 1908. Perhaps set deliberately in some junk yard—for Chelsea had the highest arson rate in Massachusetts—it came on a day of spring winds that made it impossible to check the flames as they swept through those matchbox tenements. Only by dynamiting whole streets did the firemen at last gain control. Most of the Jewish population of Chelsea were left homeless.

Then began one of those folk migrations in miniature that make the history of American racial groups so absorbing a study. Like some ancient tribe driven out by war or in search of new pastures, the Jews of Chelsea migrated south some ten miles, across the Mystic River, the other side of Boston to Dorchester.

Dorchester was originally a rural township that forty years before had been annexed by Boston, becoming gradually a solid, respectable, if not fashionable suburb. The Jews first took over the more congested sections near Roxbury, already built up with three-deckers. Because of their poverty, three or four families moved in where one had lived before. Speculative builders ran up more three-deckers to meet the demand: dark, shabbily constructed houses, with only that fourteen feet between that the law required—and paying a safe annual twenty per cent. Still, Dorchester was an improvement on Chelsea, and those who prospered spread out and moved to better homes in other parts of the town.

In a few more years Jewish shops with their foreign wares and *Kosher* signs began to appear along Blue Hill Avenue, starting at Franklin Park, and each year creeping closer to Dorchester Hill. Side street after side street, district after district, became solidly Jewish. The pattern was set. So soon as a few Jews bought into a street, the native families became restive, *For Sale* signs would appear in their windows, and in a few seasons they would have moved away. The whole appearance of the area changed. Dorchester was becoming the most thickly populated district in greater Boston.

The Jews of Chelsea dressed as they had in the ghettos of the Pale, the older men wearing boots and *kaftans* and *payoth* —the traditional earlocks. But in Dorchester even the elders began to make some concessions to their environment. They still wore their long coats and beards, still sat on the front porches on summer evenings with black skullcaps on their heads, but one no longer saw the boots or the *payoth.* Some of the older women wore a *shaitel*—the wig that distinguished married women—under their closely knotted shawls. The common speech was Yiddish. Yet Dorchester was not a ghetto as Chelsea had been. It was, rather, a *kahal,* an expanding Jewish community with its institutions of synagogue and Hebrew school and council, its inbred social life without the former boundaries.

In Dorchester, too, the second generation was making itself felt; young people, American-educated, wearing American clothes, looked about them as they emerged from the long tunnel of the past. They spoke colloquial American-English with the undertones of Yiddish running through their speech and breaking out in particular expressions. The memory of the

Pale was still with them, but not the haunting fear. They were self-assertive in consequence, eager to get ahead in the many ways that America had to offer, resentful of the disability of their birthright. Such resentment would later attract some of the intellectuals to the raceless promise of communism, and with others of the blunter extrovert type produce the relentless go-getters described in the novels of Jerome Weidman.

As I grew older I came to know Jewville at first hand, but to walk along Blue Hill Avenue always seemed to me like paying a brief visit to a foreign country. There were such swarming masses of alien people littering the pavement, surrounding the pushcarts. Outlandish they were to me, the bearded men, the twisted old women in their shawls, their gray hair peeping out from under the dark *shaitel.* The air was thick with Yiddish.

In November the Park Department flooded Franklin Field for ice skating, and often on winter days after school a group of us from the Hill would go there and skate long into the twilight. I liked skating after sundown, under the crude blue-white glare of the arc lamps. Our hollow-ground blades gave a hissing echo with each stroke that rebounded from the long-shadowed stone wall by the old cemetery where the lights of the Avenue glittered. Later, my fingers numb from unlacing my boots, I would walk the mile back to the Hill, past the little shops with their *Kosher* signs and strange wares—pumpernickel bread, rolmops, poppy-seed cakes, bagels, odd-looking fish, and tripes and wrinkled sausages hanging on long skewers in the butchershop windows.

In summer, the Avenue held a mixed savory aroma of pickles and spices that I could never quite decide whether I liked or not. But I came to enjoy knocking about aimlessly and alone through that crowded district so far removed from my own folkways. Once the owner of a hardware shop where I bought a bicycle pedal gave me a pomegranate, laughed when I tried to eat it as I would an apple, and showed me the way to split it in two. On soft June afternoons the murmur of pupils' voices through the open windows as I passed the Hebrew School Hashahar was like the hum of bees in a hive. It was a languorous sound under the fragrant lime trees that had just begun to blossom. Beyond Franklin Park a few thunderheads were piling up in the cobalt sky, and crickets chirped antiphonally in the waste of gold-pointed tansy by the Donnelly Advertising Company's billboard. I used to be sorry for those pupils on such a summer day sitting at their desks reciting a dead priestly language in unison. But I no longer thought of the Jews as a threat. They were merely people living in a separate world, apart from us. Beyond that I did not think much about them. I knew nothing of their history, where they had come from, or why.

The *kahal* of Dorchester increased yearly like a spreading ripple. With the group loyalty and desperate altruism of the immigrant, those who had arrived earlier used their savings to bring over their cousins and their cousins' cousins in turn. After the war the new immigration laws stopped the mass flow, but those who could manage it either through the quota or their own acquired citizenship still brought in their relatives. They were a prolific community. The balance of the population was still with the older foreign-born members, but it was shifting.

At that time elections were held annually for the upper and lower houses of the Massachusetts Legislature. Three representatives were chosen from wards 21 and 24. Each year the names of four or five candidates for representative would appear on the primary ballot for the Republican nomination—itself equivalent to election. There was no great public interest. After one or two terms, a representative—usually some local lawyer—would either drop out of politics or go on to the Senate, being replaced by one of the unsuccessful candidates of the previous year. Through the good offices of the Republican State Committee there was a gentleman's agreement about succession.

The year after the war the Hyde Park Republican Committee had as usual arranged its primary slate, with three representatives up for re-election and two redundant candidates who were being given a trial run for the following year. Then at the very last minute, as a complete surprise to the committee, nomination papers were filed for Samuel P. Garfinkle as the sixth Republican candidate from wards 21 and 24.

The older-generation Jews who read *Forworts* and thought in terms of the class struggle were by conviction Socialists. After they had become citizens, as most of them tried to do when their five-year residential period was over, they voted in the presidential elections and in the municipal elections for mayor of Boston, but they were unfamiliar with and did not concern themselves about state politics. The Jewish vote as a whole, however, was considered Republican, not from any tendency toward conservatism, but because the Irish, who held traces of anti-Semitism, were hereditary Democrats.

Samuel P. Garfinkle, who had been brought over from Poland at the age of six, was a self-made lawyer, a graduate of the Harvard Law School, past president of the Mattapan-Dorchester Zionist District, and a man of integrity far above the average run of state politicians. He was the unanimous choice of the Dorchester *kahal.* In running its first candidate, the Jewish community had united on one of its ablest members. This was in the historic pattern of each minority racial group as it emerged from its European background. To achieve office they would put forward their best. Only when it became clear to the rank and file how easy it was to win, how thin the apparently solid Yankee veneer, did the mercenary second-raters take over.

At first the Republican Committee in Hyde Park did not consider Garfinkle seriously. Nobody had thought much about the Jews and their vote. A Jewish candidate was a novelty, a source of dialect jokes. Only on the afternoon of the primaries did those in the know realize what was happening. Each voter could vote for three candidates on the ballot sheet. A vote for only one, leaving the other two blank, was known as a "bullet" and felt to be undemocratic, not to say unsporting. But by the middle of the afternoon the checkers in the Franklin Field precincts had reported back to Hyde Park that "Jewville's all voting bullets!" Things looked bad for someone. No one, however, was quite sure of the size of the Jewish vote.

It turned out to be enormous. Eighty percent of Jewish Dorchester had voted for Garfinkle, as opposed to the customary thirty percent that turned out in the rest of the two wards. Garfinkle was nominated by three votes to one over the second name on the list. And the fourth name, a young Ashmont lawyer who was counting on some day taking the next step up on the Republican escalator, found himself next morning abandoned on the lower level.

The following year Garfinkle, now the Honorable Samuel P. Garfinkle, ran for state senator. This was considered highly unethical in the Gentile parts of Dorchester and Hyde Park. According to unwritten law, a representative served two terms in the House, then consulted the local Republican Committee, which advised him whether he should run for the Senate. He disregarded the advice at his peril, for even if he were elected he would find himself snubbed at the State House and barred from all committees and any chance of advancement. Old Senator Seth Clarke of Dorchester Lower Mills had been in the Massachusetts Senate for five years. He was chairman of the Committee on Banks and Banking and a friend of Calvin Coolidge, for whom he had occasionally acted when the latter was President of the Senate. This was to be his last term. Even so, with all the aroused votes of upper Dorchester and Hyde Park against him, Garfinkle beat Senator Clarke by almost two to one and became the first foreign-born Jew to enter the Senate of the Commonwealth of Massachusetts. He served for only one term, and then—as if he had proved his point—went back to his law practice.

Professional politicians now recognized the Jewish vote as a power. The Legislature, in one of its periodic gerrymandering redivisions, separated Hyde Park and Dorchester. From then on Dorchester produced nothing but Jewish candidates. None of them was of the caliber of Senator Garfinkle, and they became progressively worse, following a kind of Gresham's political law that the bad politician drives out the good.

Garfinkle's first election was the handwriting on the wall, although no one on the Hill at first understood it. Blue Hill Avenue still remained the dividing line. The Hill was an outpost, a redoubt of Protestant middleclass America. The only Jews with whom the Hill had any contact were the dreary-looking pedlars who drove their hired carts and hacks along the street once a week, calling out "Rags'n butl" in a mournful singsong.

There was a mild autumnal calm to that last season of the Hill as a community. The war for democracy had been won, the troubled years were over. Where Norfolk Street joined the Avenue near the Tileston Grammar School, they named the junction Anslow Square (after Freddy Anslow, killed in the Argonne attack), and his five maiden sisters sat on the platform on Memorial Day while Senator Clarke made the dedicatory speech. The Price boy, who had been gassed overseas with the Yankee Division, now ran the fishmarket, although he still had a hacking cough. There was talk of organizing a post of the American Legion.

Just before the war the Boston Park Department had planted a double row of Norway maples along Wellington Street over the crest of the Hill, and these had grown so high with the years that they met in a spreading arch from pavement to pavement. There were more members than ever in the tennis club, and in spite of the high labor costs, the committee had managed to build a second clay court. On Christmas Eve every house on the Hill had lighted candles in the windows. If it had not been for the High Cost of Living, everything would have been well on the way to the old pattern. Prices kept rising, but everyone felt they were bound to drop again, particularly if one sat tight with his Liberty Bonds.

Then came the catastrophe. Suddenly, and in secret, the Robinsons sold their two-family house to Jews. They had paid $3,500 for it in 1915, and after the war Wellington Holbrook had brought them a customer who offered $5,000. They were considering it and had almost signed an agreement, when a fur dealer by the name of Isidore White offered, first $5,200, which they refused, and then a thousand dollars more. They took it.

The news soon leaked out. Everyone on the Hill was appalled. At the tennis club they talked of nothing but the perfidy of the Robinsons, who, during their remaining month on the Hill, stayed in semi-retirement with the shades drawn. Oscar Dodds, their neighbor across the street, was all for a boycott of the new owner. Wellington Holbrook, who now spent his days sitting pompously in a little green shack the other side of the tennis courts labeled REAL ESTATE AND INSURANCE, selected a committee of ten to meet at his house. The only thing to do, he maintained, was to buy the Robinsons' place back again. If twenty people would give fifty dollars apiece, that would be enough to buy off this Isidore White.

They agreed. Fifty dollars apiece, even if they lost it, would be cheap enough for saving the Hill. They were protecting their homes. Yet even the committee members knew in their hearts that they were whistling down the wind.

The neighborhood "changed." That was the expression currently used when one racial element in a community displaced another. After the Robinsons had gone, the balance shifted with astonishing quickness. A year later half the old families on the Hill had moved away.

The physical aspect changed as rapidly as its population. A builder named Feldman bought up most of the remaining house lots and built three-deckers that took up all the open space that had been a meadow, and made the street look mean and narrow. The Tileston School, to which I had now advanced, began to fill up with precocious Jewish children, all of whom seemed to be taking either piano or violin lessons. Finally, the Rabbi Sheshevsky bought a two-family house on the side street running behind the Dodds'. For the remnants of the old community this was the end.

The Rabbi looked a medieval character direct from the Krakow ghetto. He was a solid little man with a full beard and wary eyes. Winter and summer he wore a long kaftan-like broadcloth overcoat and a wide-brimmed black hat with a flat crown. Invariably he carried a heavy walking stick. He was, we discovered, terrified of dogs. Bob Egan had a smooth-haired fox terrier, named Peter, who always started barking when he saw the stocky black figure of the Rabbi coming down the street. Peter would rush at him playfully as he often did with us, but as soon as the dog came near, the Rabbi would stop in his tracks and brandish his stick. Of course this sent Peter off into a spasm of barking and he would circle, yapping and pretending to nip, while the old man kept turning, always facing him, shaking his stick and calling out hoarsely in guttural broken English. Bob thought it funny, and instead of checking Peter would quietly sic him on. Peter with his little teeth could not have hurt anyone. If the Rabbi had held out his hand, he would have come to him wagging his tail. But the old man was afraid. Not until long afterward did I realize that his fear came from having had dogs set on him in Poland.

Although looking like a grandfather in his white beard, the Rabbi had two sons, Abraham and Solomon, both of whom now went with the rest of us to the Tileston School. There was war between us. Solomon would whimper and take any blow, but Abraham was different. He would spit and strike back, and he had an uncomfortable accuracy in throwing stones. Several afternoons a week Bob and Georgie Hunter and the older boys used to lay for Abraham as soon as he came out the school door. He used to leg it back to the Hill, stopping when he could to shy a stone at his pursuers. Luckily for him he was a good runner, but sometimes they would catch him just the same and hold him down screaming while they took turns pummeling him. Once while they were doing this he seemed to go mad, and bit and frothed at the mouth. When they let him up, instead of running away sobbing as he usually did, he threw stones at close range, cutting Georgie on the forehead. After that they fell on him again.

The Rabbi came to school next day with Abraham. Anyone could see how angry he was by the way he thrust with his walking stick. He spent a long time in the headmaster's office with Old Man Beveridge. After he had gone, Old Man Beveridge called the older boys in and warned them that if they bothered the Sheshevskys again the Rabbi would take them into the juvenile court. From then on the boys left Abraham and Solomon alone. They came and went each day with their books, unspoken to, pariahs among us.

The Hill was rapidly becoming an adjunct of Jewville, with

the difference that there were less of the Rabbi's generation than on the Avenue. Most of those moving in had been born in Poland, but they had come to America as young men, had learned a Yiddish-inflected English, and though they were not far removed from the ghetto, considered themselves Americans. We considered them Jews. Across the street from where I lived a man named Magazine moved in with a sickly son and pretty red-haired daughter. Bronstein bought the house next to him, a man whose father had started as a pedlar not so many years ago. Now they both had a large wastepaper business. Bronstein owned a bright yellow Kisselkar.

Wellington Holbrook, in his little green shack, adapted himself soonest to the new situation. Having in one way or another cheated most of the people who had bought houses on the Hill, he was nevertheless dishonest within the ethic of the community. Never misses a trick, they said of him half-admiringly. But the Jews were different. They did not operate within the rules.

Feldman was often seen in Holbrook's office now. The latter had a new set of contracts printed, not in general terms as before, but covering every contingency, each last detail. "My Jew contracts," he used to call them.

I left the Tileston School at the year's end. For the next four years I went to the Roxbury Latin School, a small private day school in Roxbury. It was an old-fashioned informal sort of place, with six classes, eight masters, and only about a hundred pupils. Everyone knew everyone else and the atmosphere, although it had overtones of the school's Puritan foundation was a friendly one. When I was fifteen I had to change from Roxbury to the free Boston Latin.

Someone once remarked that a person has to be either very poor or very rich to live in Boston. The middle classes who work in the city live for the most part in the surrounding dormitory suburbs that are themselves independent townships with their own school systems. But in Boston people of even small means send their children to private schools. The result is that the secondary schools, the ordinary high schools, are of low academic standing.

Boston Latin School is the exception, the one Boston school that makes a specialty of college preparation. Its six-year course is a rigid, unimaginative grind, its one goal to push its students over the annual hurdles of the College Entrance Examination Board. For years its graduates have entered Harvard as the largest single group from any school in the country, and with the highest scholastic average.

In my day, the majority of the Boston Latin students were Jewish. To the Jews, the "people of the book," all means were acceptable to get into a university. Every Jewish junk-dealer from Chelsea, every shopkeeper or delicatessen proprietor in Dorchester, every tailor or fur-worker in Mattapan, wanted above all else for his son to become a professional man. And because Harvard was America's oldest and most illustrious university, he wanted him to go there and to no lesser place. For this, any and every sacrifice was worthwhile, for this, the first-generation Jew would grub away his working hours. Life in America was hard, but this was its opportunity.

As a result, second-generation Jewry produced an excess of professional men, particularly in law and medicine. Outstanding Jewish lawyers had made their mark in America. There was the great and splendid tradition of Justices Brandeis and Cardoza, and of Professor Frankfurter of the Harvard Law School. But if a Jewish lawyer or doctor was merely average or a little above it, although he might have two Harvard degrees, nevertheless he was forced to practice within the *kahal*. There were too many Jewish doctors and too many lawyers for their community to furnish them an adequate living.

For me, Boston Latin was a formidable brick building with its long tiled corridors, coldly antiseptic classrooms, and steel stairways. It had the regulated aspect of a jail rather than a school. Everything ran by bells. At the end of each hour a fire-alarm rang and we had three minutes to change classes—a great rushing about in those bare corridors, with an extra period to stay after school if we loitered. There were no pictures in the building, nothing but glazed brown tiles, brown painted woodwork, and set rows of desks. The discipline was rigid and unvarying, the conversation during six years for the most part about College Entrance Examinations and getting into Harvard.

My home room—as they called it—from which I set out at nine in the morning and ended up at two in the afternoon, was 208. There were always thirty-six pupils to a room, and I remember Room 208 beyond all forgetting because of our curiously symmetrical division into twenty-four Jews and twelve non-Jews.

I hated the Boston Latin School as an impersonal prison of the mind, and on my first intimate contact I disliked Jews. No longer were they people of a foreign world whom I could observe with detachment on leisurely summer afternoons. Now they were boys of my own age, in the same room with me.

In theory, the democracy of the public school system mixes all classes and groups of a community together, and by the demonstration of the worth of each human being as an individual, breaks down artificial barriers and teaches a mutual understanding and respect. The theory did not work very well in Room 208. Everyone was aware of an invisible dividing line, and the very closeness of our association emphasized that line. In the school the non-Jews were a minority, but in the world outside they were dominant—a fact neither group ever forgot.

At the Roxbury Latin School we had been an unself-conscious community with our unwritten laws and customs. The boys lived in a state of war with the masters but it was a genteel eighteenth-century type of warfare with its etiquette and truces and established rules for both sides. The members of each class formed a united front against their particular master. They pooled the results of their homework, they covered for each other. If anyone was unprepared it was the duty of the rest to help him out, to draw the master off the track of a difficult translation, to spar against time by asking long pointless questions. Some of us of course did better than others, and for the cleverest there were prizes at the end of the year, but it was considered bad form to work hard at one's lessons, and those who did kept the fact modestly concealed. Roxbury Latin did not admit Jews. Of course the shadow of the College Entrance Examination Board hung over Roxbury as over all preparatory schools, but it was a joint enterprise for us all, we were not competitively minded, and if we could have swindled each other over those formidable barriers we should have done so.

Taken from my friends at Roxbury, suddenly thrust into a crowd of pushing little Jews, I was aware only of their unpleasantness, knowing nothing of the relentless, grinding processes that had made them so different from the boys I had known. I had always taken it for granted that I should go to Harvard because my father in his time had gone there and I never doubted the possibility of this any more than I stopped to consider whether I really wanted to or not. That Harvard could be the goal of anyone's ambitions never occurred to me.

To be imprisoned in the brick intellectual sweatshop of Boston Latin gave me the feeling of being abandoned. At first I was appalled by the Jews of 208. The early awareness of their racial handicap had given them two things: an apparent thickness of skin, and a frenetic, driving ambition. They knew—as I did not—that what I had taken for granted was for them an elusive hope. Freed from ghetto and government quotas and the fear of pogroms and the yellow benches, they were determined to get ahead. They worked far into each night. Their lessons next morning were letter perfect. They took obvious pride in their academic success and talked about it. At the end of each year there were room prizes given for excellence in each subject, and the Jews were openly after them. There was none of the Roxbury solidarity of pupils versus master. If anyone reciting made a mistake that the master overlooked, twenty hands shot into the air to bring it to his attention. They competed one against the other, and no one ever helped anyone else as at Roxbury, where we used to sit round the hot-air furnace in the basement each morning before school and construe Virgil. It was a fierce and grueling competition. To stay in it at all one had to work at least four hours each evening. Some of us in the gentile rump were fair students, most of us lazy and mediocre ones, and by our very position at the foot of the class we despised the industry of the Jews.

They looked different, they were different. The undertones of their speech still bore a Yiddish intonation, and many of their expressions were Yiddish—the familiar *goy*, and *shiksa* for a non-Jewish girl. "An' so what ahv it?" An' so what ahv it?"—that expression seemed to dominate the room, that room down which we twelve with the uncomprehending cruelty of the young drew our invisible line.

There had been no assignment of seats in 208, so that we twelve managed to occupy the lefthand rear corner. From there we could either look out the window or over at our Jewish classmates. Aaronson sat in the forward opposite corner, a chubby oratorical boy with thick tortoise-shell glasses. His name began the recitation list, and among the aggressive group he was the leader. Then there was Lipshitz, who was swarthy and looked more Sicilian than Jewish. His most engaging quality was a certain reckless insolence and the fact that he was, by 208 standards, lazy. Lee had been Levi the year before. His voice was shrill. Stanley Epstein was quiet in a hesitant olive-skinned way, and he had a premature growth of down on his upper lip. His mother was continually visiting the headmaster to complain about her son's grades, the favoritism of the teachers, and other grievances. The pallid Meier Hirschfield sat in the righthand corner, and always won the Latin prize. Kabatznick, the smallest boy in the room, was three years younger than the rest of us. He was a kind of infant prodigy, and later entered Harvard at thirteen. Then there were the others: Applebaum, Fish, Klein, Sydney Kotzen—who had the profile of an Assyrian bas-relief—Seymour Weiss and Milton Belsky, Berliner, and Herman Pill, who had brown eyes and fine-cut features and was, I think, Sephardic, whereas the rest were Polish. There was also Harry Isaacs, gentle and lacking the aggressive qualities of the others. His father was a tailor in Mattapan, and in time he became my friend. Through him I received my first lesson, not in tolerance—for tolerance is an unpleasantly touted word—but in the understanding that in their common bewilderment all human beings are essentially the same.

It was a slow lesson. We hated the Jews because they worked so hard, because they were so relentlessly competitive, because their one thought was to force themselves ahead, to win the prizes at the year's end, to get top College Board marks and admission to Harvard. They hated us in return with the accumulated resentment of the past, and because they knew the way was easier for us. I disliked them in addition because they had come in and broken up the community where I had lived all my life.

Our homeroom master was a bald little Yankee named Dole. For some reason no one knew, he had been nicknamed the Gunner. The Gunner had been teaching at Boston Latin since that dim past when the City of Boston and the Boston school system were still run by people of his stock. He had gone to Bowdoin as a young man and was very proud of being of the college of President Pierce, Longfellow, and Hawthorne. Over his desk hung a sepia photograph of the Bowdoin campus, with the twin-towered college chapel in the background—the sole decoration that I remember in that prison. He had a low-slung jaw that snapped like a rat trap, small, roving, pig eyes, and his characteristic remark was: "Read the notes. You've not read the notes! If you don't study the notes how do you expect to pass?" Probably he was anti-Semitic at heart, but, Puritan-like, he never showed it except by keeping completely aloof from all his pupils, giving currency to the tale that his wife and child had been killed in a subway accident and that he had become crabbed and silent afterward. Actually, he was a bachelor.

The Latin School curriculum was unalterable. It prescribed certain courses and books to read. There was no choice. In English we first read Burke's "Speech on Conciliation with the Colonies," then "The Deserted Village," of which the Gunner would say with his Yankee twang, "This is a good pome, but bad political eeconomy." And his jaw would snap to.

Half the term we spent reading *The Merchant of Venice.* We read it scene by scene, we dissected it, we mapped out the plot and subplots, the exposition, the climax, the suspended climax, the resolution. We memorized "The Quality of Mercy" and a dozen other passages, we drew semimathematical outlines of the characters in the order of their appearances. By the year's end we had come to loathe the play and to withdraw suspiciously at Shakespeare's name.

Yet to those of us left in the rear corner of Room 208 *The Merchant of Venice* gave a kind of poetic revenge. Richardson beside me would read in his already sonorous voice,

> . . . You may as well do anything most hard
> As seek to soften that—than which what's harder?—
> His Jewish heart. . . .

and imperceptibly glance over in Epstein's direction to see how he was taking it. He had bent Epstein's glasses pushing through the door one day, and Epstein's mother had come to the school to complain. As a result he had to pay to have them repaired. Now he was getting his own back. The Jewish boys seemed impervious, however, just as they did to the not-too-veiled slurs coming from any of us twelve. Even the passage:

> . . . the dog Jew did utter in the streets:
> "My daughter! O my ducats! O my daughter!
> Fled with a Christian! O my Christian ducats!
> Justice! the law! my ducats and my daughter! . . . .

did not faze them, as Lee recited it. The Gunner called on us in strict rotation. When Lee finished, Gavin, sitting in front of me, snickered.

"What are you making that noise for?" the Gunner snapped.

"Nothing, sir."

"Well, I'm giving you *something.*" And he gave him a Misdemeanor mark.

The florid Aaronson's ambition was to win the Declamation Medal at the end of the year. His delivery was baroque. One day his turn came to read Shylock's apologia.

"I am a Jew," he began throatily. "Hath not a Jew eyes?" He seemed absurdly plump in his plus-fours, gesticulating, his tortoise-shell glasses sliding down his nose while he mouthed the Elizabethan words. "hath not a Jew hands, organs, dimensions, affections, passions? fed with the same food, hurt with the same weapons, subject to the same diseases, healed by the same means, warmed and cooled by the same winter and summer, as a Christian is? If you prick us, do we not bleed? if you tickle us, do we not laugh? if you poison us, do we not die?"

Suddenly, to my embarrassed amazement, I realized that his voice was trembling.

At the end of the year we moved away from the Hill, one of the last of the old families to go. In the spring of 1948 I returned for the first visit since my school days, drove down Blue Hill Avenue and up the steep side of Dorchester Hill under the now towering arch of maples just beginning to bud. Except for the trees everything looked smaller and meaner than I had remembered. Even the hill slope seemed less steep. It was solidly built up now, with new streets cut through, the houses closely wedged together, and not a vacant lot left.

Dorchester is still a *kahal,* the most thickly populated area of the city, but it has changed much in the years. The Hill has changed too, not as obviously as when the first street was laid out on that green drumlin by Wellington Holbrook, not as dramatically as when the Robinsons sold their house, but even at a casual glance I could see the new patterns beneath the surface. A few shops along the Avenue had *Kosher* signs in the windows, but most had discontinued them. There were Jewish chain delicatessens now, large and sanitary. Posters in Hebrew script had been discarded. No more old men sat on the porches, *yarmolkas* covering their bald heads, nodding and talking in the May sunshine. The gnarled old women with their shawls and wigs had vanished too. So had the pushcarts and the pedlars. The one increase was in the number of doctors' and lawyers' shingles.

A decade after we left Dorchester, some of the more prosperous second-generation Jews began to move away to the garden suburbs of Brookline and Newton. Much of their Torah tradition was left behind in the *kahal.* Dorchester still has the orthodox synagogue and Hebrew school. In Brookline or Newton there are reformed temples, externally often resembling New England meetinghouses, and with Sunday services that do not differ much from those of Unitarians. There are no Newton Hebrew schools, nor young people who could be coerced into going to them. These third-generation Jews are not like the frantic hard-pressed students I knew at Boston Latin. They are casually American, and though they often preserve a slight burr in their speech and a certain cast to their features, they seem much less a type than the boys of Room 208. Gifted through the ancient ghetto processes of natural selection with a more than average intellectual acuteness, they work within more moderate limits, content with the suburban *status quo* and at peace with themselves.

For all that its cohesive quality lessens, the Jewish community persists. As sociologist Nathan Glazier, an editor of *Commentary*, wrote in 1950: "Despite their prosperity, Jews show very little tendency to assimilate: they intermarry less than any other ethnic group. They do *acculturate*—that is, they drop traditional habits and speech, and become culturally indistinguishable from other Americans; yet the line that divides them from the others remains sharper than that separating any other white group of immigrants."

I climbed the road behind our old house and saw in the yard below me the peach tree which my father had planted years before. A massive three-storied structure with the name Solomon Lewenberg School carved on the pediment stood where the tennis courts had been. The road curved over the hill crest where once there was a stone wall near the straggling line of pignut trees, and now nothing but the boxlike wooden houses. Through a slit between adjoining roof-tops I could just make out the yellow outline of the Dorchester High School and a few harbor islands beyond it, although the sea's rim blurred on the smoke-heavy horizon. To the north, the Custom House tower still dominated the uneven Boston skyline, while to the south and much nearer I could see the familiar rounded shape of Great Blue Hill and the acres of scrub oak and speckled alder in Canterbury Hollow. These had not changed with the years; they at least had remained as fixed and firm as in my boyhood memories. There was still something of the past I could catch hold of in the soft May weather.

Sheiks and Shebas, Dance No More: The World of John Held, Jr.

It is always the autumn of 1926, the last Saturday in September or the first in October, the ivy leaves on the stadium wall crisping to scarlet, the sun still warm, the lucent air all blue and gold. It is a midwestern university, *the* midwestern university—mock-gothic library and chapel, mock-classic classrooms, the lush tapestry-brick veneer of fraternity row. With the big game only hours away the saxophones of the college band are giving anticipatory brays between the chapel and the gymnasium. At some remote date a few years back the flappers here wore their skirts a foot longer and their overshoes unbuckled. The cake-eaters favored plus-four knickers. Now the fringed skirts sway above the knees to Charleston rhythms, and the plus-fours have swelled to plus-sixes or even plus-eights. The vague transition figures of the cake-eater and the flapper were still part of the postwar revolt. They have left the Greek-lettered houses to their successors, the sheik and the sheba, who are too all-sufficiently themselves to need to revolt from anything.

Over that pied and milling campus the sunshine is almost tangible. The sheiks wear Fair Isle sweaters of gaudy intricacy, checked plus-eights with tasseled socks, or gray flannels so bell-bottomed that they completely cover the saddle-strap shoes. Most of the sheiks are hatless and their hair, parted in the middle, is lacquered with Slikum or Staycomb to a mirror-like stiffness. The shebas have close-cropped shingled hair. Beneath their sweaters or sheath dresses there is only the vaguest convexity of breasts. Their knobby knees are topped by frilled garters.

A Theta Delt (one can tell by the ΘΔΧ on his cap) is strumming "Bye Bye Blackbird" on his ukulele for a covey of shebas sitting on the library steps. They sit with legs apart, displaying the V-shaped pattern of their lace panties with provocative unconcern. Couples are chinning, charlestoning, cheering, all in the syncopated good humor that has become college humor. A freshman, still marked with the grotesque innocence of Central High School (he will shed it before spring), passes timidly by the insouciant sophs and juniors, a beany cap on his head branded with the numerals 1930. The date is, of course, part of his absurdity. For every sheik and sheba knows that 1930 will never come, that there will never be anything but here and now, this timeless moment throbbing to the beat of "The Varsity Drag."

Why should a sheik
Learn how to speak
Latin or Greek
Badly?
Give him a neat
Motto complete:
Say it with feet,
Gladly!

It is warm, mindless, immediate. It is the Plastic Age of Percy Marks's forgotten novel, of the quintessence of a thousand campus paper cut-ups (*Bowdoin Bearskin, Dartmouth Jack O'Lantern, Notre Dame Juggler,* and the rest), of *College Humor* with its: "College bred—a four-year loaf!" It is the world of John Held, Jr.

That nature imitates art is one of those paradoxes Oscar Wilde confected to startle the dinner tables in the nineties. Since then it has been repeated so often that it has become a truism. Yet a truism for all its acquired banality may be nonetheless true, and art does in fact have a way of nudging nature. In any age there is first the amorphous urge toward a pattern, a malaise seeking an outlet. And always the artist appears to embody the age or the time-spirit, whether it is Mr. Pope in his grotto at Twickenham or Mr. Eliot listening to the melancholy notes of St. Mary Woolnoth.

A generation before Held, Charles Dana Gibson sat at his drawing board, and at the command of his pen, Gibson girls appeared like daisies on the American scene—haughty yet chastely alluring, an aureole of hair beneath their flowered pancake hats, and with floor-length skirts and leg o' mutton sleeves. Lady Astor in her American youth was one of the first Gibson girls. And there was a Gibson man as well, an earlier eternal undergraduate, who wore his varsity sweater inside out so that only the Y stitching showed, smoked a pipe, and was accompanied by a bulldog on a leash. He returned the Gibson girl's glance, ardently from afar—and he came to actuality in the person of Richard Harding Davis.

Gibson outlived his creation, even as Held was to outlive his. In the era when the sheiks and the shebas charlestoned and black-bottomed their way through the pages of the old *Life*, Gibson continued to produce his fine-drawn society sketches for the same magazine. But his genteel figures, though the women shortened their skirts and bobbed their hair, appeared pathetic revenants in the dazzle of the Heldian campus world.

Curiously enough, Held was about fifteen years older than his abounding collegians. Nor did he himself ever attend college. He was born into the Mormon community of Salt Lake City in 1889. His father, an engraver, had been discovered in Switzerland by Brigham Young—on one of his periodic European journeys in search of people of talent—and brought back to Utah as his adopted son. When young Held was nine years old, he sold his first woodcut. At fifteen, under the influence of Mahonri Young who designed Salt Lake's Gull Monument, he decided to be a sculptor, but had to earn his more immediate living as an apprentice cartoonist on the Salt Lake City *Tribune*.

In 1910 he came to New York with a young wife on his arm and four dollars in his pocket. Almost at once he found a job drawing car-cards for Colliers Street Railway Company. Restless as he was creative, he spent his spare time working on cartoons and woodcuts, and soon was selling them regularly. "I was looking for success. I found it," he wrote later when he was making several thousand dollars a week as the tone-giving cartoonist for *Life, Judge,* and *College Humor.*

After the United States entered World War I he left his drawing board to join Naval Intelligence, serving in such unwarlike areas as Guatemala, Honduras and Nicaragua. When he was discharged, in 1919, he went back to his cartoons but not to his wife. His first post-war job was with *Life.* The old humorous weekly had grown stuffy, but now Robert Sherwood as editor and Robert Benchley as dramatic critic set out to revivify it. The new-life infusion was not at once apparent. At first, more than anything else, the pages reflected the uneasiness of the period. They looked back nostalgically to 1914, welcomed the newly elected Harding as a symbol of "normalcy," resented the strikes and the High Cost of Living, feared the agitator, the Bolshevik, and the anarchist. Even the humor was uncertain of itself, much of it being a play on anachronisms, applying the situations of the mechanized world to the Stone Age or the Middle Ages. The captions beneath the cartoons tended to the old he-she variety, as with two young people in evening dress at a concert:

She: Tell me, are you fond of Brahms?
He: Oh, very! But I think I like shredded wheat biscuits even better.

Charles Dana Gibson still continued his double-page spreads. The cover was often by Maxfield Parrish or one of his imitators.

During the transition period between the Armistice and the Coolidge prosperity, John Held, Jr. remained one of the obscurer signatures in *Life.* Woodcuts were at first his favored medium, as if he sensed that the moment was not yet his. He made a number of such cuts to illustrate Sherwood's rhymed series, "The Cinema Primer." Meanwhile the small fillers fell to him, such as the sketches at the top of Benchley's moving-picture page. It was in these tentative drawings that he began to feel himself into his final style.

His moment came with the season of Coolidge prosperity, a season so warmly sunlit that few noticed the slanting rays were autumnal. The conflicts of the postwar adjustment period were over, 1914 with its fashions and its foibles had sunk below the horizon, the "now" was here. Intellectuals sitting in self-conscious exile at the Dôme drinking their cognacs might consider themselves the lost generation, but the new generation in America was the one that, just about halfway through the decade, John Held found.

His round-headed button-nosed shieks with enameled hair and hip flask, his shingled shebas with long chin, pert nose, and tapering cigarette holders are models rather than caricatures, hey-hey sayers to life that reaches its thundering climax in the cheering sections at the Saturday big game. For that game the campus casuals of the morning have donned their uniforms. The sheiks wear derbies and racoon coats of enormous bulk that hang within a foot of the ground. Only an occasional nonconformist sports a felt fedora with a striped hat-band, the brim turned down all round. The shebas wear helmetlike hats, and their shaggy coonskin coats do not quite reach their garter frills. There is not a vacant seat in the fur-lined stadium. The saxophones of the band are muted. It is that hushed moment before the two teams surge onto the empty field and the rival captains walk toward each other for the toss-up. Any hushed moment, however, is apt to be shattered by the crash of a hip flask inadvertently dropped on the concrete.

After the game there are the ritual dances along fraternity row. Over the fieldstone mantel of the fraternity house living room stand the cabalistic letters ΨΥ or ΚΔΣ or ΛΝ. The sheiks have changed to tuxes and white waistcoats, the shebas' evening dresses—with large bows in the back—are even shorter than their campus skirts. In the corner the saxophones wail and a bulb flashes on and off in the interior of the bass drum to light up a windmill or a waterfall or a sailboat by moonlight painted on the drumhead. A few couples are dancing, a few more are in the kitchen mixing drinks, but most are twined in each others' arms within the convenient alcoves or up and down the wide staircase as they neck with concentrated unconcern.

After the dance there is the ride home. Some of the dough-heavy sheiks may drive a Jordan Playboy with port and starboard lights, but most settle for the modified Model T, the tin-lizzy touring with the top and windshield removed and its sides daubed with legends: FOUR WHEELS—NO BRAKES; STOP ME IF YOU'VE HEARD THIS; ENTER BY REAR. Under the trees the last sheik parks with the last sheba for the last drink and the last neck. Yet for all this hip-flasked groping in the moonlight, it is all somehow innocent, or almost so, and with the poignancy of everything that is brief.

The lengthening of women's skirts was the curtain ringing down on John Held's campus world, and it was the skirts rather than the stock market that marked the end. Sheiks and shebas danced no more. Held himself turned back to his earlier woodcut style and forward to *The New Yorker,* where with mock-primitive sophistication he illustrated the Frankie and Johnnie songs of the nineties. With his first surge of success he had bought a stock farm in Westport, Connecticut, and lived there until the thirties as a dapper country gentleman. Tall, dark, and still exuberant (heavily tattooed with eagles, girls, anchors, and roses) he often amused himself by tap-dancing in public. He married again, this time an older woman, and they adopted three children.

Money was never anything that concerned him, and he left his investments to be handled with maladroit conservatism by a proper Boston banker who capped his other judgments by investing heavily in Kreuger & Toll just before the Swedish match king's empire burnt out. Held had very little left but his farm and his insurance. These he left to his children and his now-estranged wife and went to New York alone.

Once more he arrived in the city of his younger days to start a new life. From drawing, he turned to his first love, sculpture, and to writing. He modeled a series of small animals. In several volumes of short stories that he now wrote—*Grim Youth, The Flesh is Weak*—he attempted, unsuccessfully, to recapture the coon-coated past. His third wife, a runner-up for Miss America, he met while judging a beauty contest. This marriage lasted scarcely longer than the birth of their daughter.

He lived on in sad isolation, with his infant daughter, in a single room over his favorite eating place, Barbeta's, while continuing with his drawing, writing, and sculpturing. For awhile, to support himself, he ran Friday evening collegiate talent broadcasts, each week from a different college. Just before World War II he became an artist-in-residence at Harvard and later at Georgia.

In 1942, in spite of his age and an old head injury, he managed to join the Army Signal Corps. In that same year he married his fourth wife, Margaret, and bought the old Schuyler Farm in Belmar, New Jersey. The remaining fifteen years were the most serene of his life. There, in Belmar, with Margaret and his mother he raised turkeys, ducks, chickens, dogs, sheep, cows and pigs, and grew strawberries and tomatoes of enormous size. The farm was a great success and became almost self-supporting. Dirt farming and sculpture, he told his friends, were the only things he was interested in any more. Most of his sculpturing was of animals, and he held several successful exhibitions. To help finance the farm he still made occasional linoleum prints.

When, in the fifties, another generation began to look back with a certain sentimental wistfulness at the twenties, Held was often approached to revive the bright and brittle dream of his lost midwestern campus. Always he refused. Even before the end of the twenties he had come to detest his sheiks and shebas. Like Finley Peter Dunne with Mr. Dooley, his spirit finally revolted against his prime creation. He died of cancer in 1957.

When the twenties began I was ten years old, just a few years too late to be really part of that coruscant era. But during Coolidge's first term, as I sat up in my room evenings grubbing through my twenty-four lines of the Third Oration Against Cataline or puzzling over the problems set in Hawkes, Libby and Touton's *Revised Algebra,* I could hear Jack White cranking his flivver in the drive below. Jack was a nonacademic sheik. He owned a banjo ukulele on which he could strum "If

You Knew Susie," and he would change the line "Back to Yonkers, she's the one that hadda walk" to "Back to Roslindale" or "Mattapan" or wherever his sheba of the moment lived.

"Collegiate" was the song of the day: "Yes we are c'llegiate." Jack preferred the term *colleege.* Though he had left Mechanic Arts High School after his first year, he was just that—*colleege.* How I at my desk with my Cicero trot and my algebra used to envy him on such nights, chugging away in the flivver with the oval rear window to places of mystery and delight like the Roseland Ballroom, where beautiful shebas waited for their sheiks and the saxophones wailed "Where's My Sweetie Hiding?"

The syncopation of the twenties echoed only dimly through the paint-flecked walls of the old Roxbury Latin School set in its Roxbury slum. That pre-Civil War battleship-gray building repelled the present. We fourteen- and fifteen-year-olds in the Fourth Class could not hope to be *colleege,* like Jack White, but within our Victorian bastion we imitated art as best we could. The art was that of John Held. Old Man Farnham, the sixth class master, used to bring in *Life* every week and keep it in the drawer of the side cabinet. During the lunch hour we could go upstairs and look at it while we ate our sandwiches. Held's cartoons were our dream of the future, the sunny campus with its bustling sheiks and shebas in wistful contrast to the musty un-coeducational corridors of Roxbury Latin.

Those cartoons were our models. We doused our hair with Slikum and parted it in the middle. Slikum was a mystery fluid the color of benedictine. If applied when the hair was wet it gave the effect of spar varnish. A tornado could not have ruffled a hair. When we could, we changed our gold-rimmed glasses for mock tortoise-shell. We wore plus-four knickers and patterned golf socks and elastic bow ties called William Tells (pull back the bow and hit the apple!). Bell-bottom flannels were not yet for us, though there were some in the upper school.

No one at Roxbury Latin, however, had that *ne plus ultra* of the Heldian hero, a coonskin coat. Mills, the cheerleader at our few small private-day-school-league football games, was the closest Roxbury approximation to the Held type. In winter he left his overshoes unbuckled and never wore garters. Between the halves of the Brown and Nichols game he shocked Dr. Thompson, the headmaster, by playing "Saxophobia" on his saxophone. He had a sheba in Jamaica Plain. For most of us, for me certainly, shebas were as yet far over the horizon.

From present-day musical comedies and television skits on the twenties one would gather that the striped blazer, like those worn in club colors in England, was then the dominant form of jacket. Possibly it was in the nineties, but in the twenties such striping was unknown. Because of a certain confusion in the minds of costumers and scenarists about such things I should like to set down here what I wore to my first dance.

It was in the summer of 1926 at the Manomet Grange Hall near Plymouth, Massachusetts. Because of a shortage of boys at our little beach resort, the girls there taught me to dance on condition that I take two of them to the Grange Hall on Saturday night. After the somber segregation of Roxbury Latin I was glad enough at the chance—my first encounter with girls.

Penelope and Isabelle were my two—the fair and the dark. I walked from the beach with them on that lingering summer evening, scared stiff at the prospect of appearing on a live dance floor, and yet at the same time delighted. My slikummed hair was parted in the geometric middle and I had a new pair of tortoise-shells that had a tendency to slip down my nose. My necktie was yellow with purple stripes, nothing so bright as those handpainted things that came out just after World War II, but bright enough. I had a blue serge jacket. My plus-fours were of white linen checked with black lines. I was particularly proud of the plus-fours, wheedled from a reluctant father by a more indulgent mother. Below them I displayed a pair of purple and white argyle socks. My shoes were white with black toes. In my piebald shoes and purple diamond socks and dishcloth knickers I felt very smooth, or in the lingo of the day, I thought I looked "the snake's hips."

Penelope and Isabelle had shingled hair, and Isabelle had disconcerting blue eyes. I have forgotten what they wore. Gradually overcoming my petrifying fear, I edged out onto a corner of the dance floor, first with Penelope, then with Isabelle. The orchestra consisted of a piano, a violin, a saxophone, and a snare drum with a hole in it. "Bye Bye Blackbird" and "The Girl Friend" were the hits of the summer. They played them both intermittently. Also they played "I'm Gonna Charleston Back to Charleston." Some of the older couples could Charleston, but all I could do was to stand with my two girls and watch the flashing knees. Still, perhaps next winter. . . .

Isabelle took my arm in the darkness going home and said she particularly liked my socks. I felt then that I was on my way to becoming a Held hero—a real sheik.

The Last Anarchist

On the evening of January 11, 1943, a tall middle-aged man in a wide-brimmed hat locked the door of his small third-floor office in the building at the corner of New York's 15th Street and Fifth Avenue, then—a little stiffly because of his bulk—walked down the narrow darkened stairs. A scar running down his left cheek showed up even in the shadows, in spite of the pointed gray beard meant to conceal it. From his appearance he might have been Scandinavian. He was accompanied by a smaller, darker man, obviously Italian.

The building had two entrances, one on 15th Street and one on Fifth Avenue. The men walked out of the 15th Street entrance into the dank dimmed-out street and headed eastward for Fifth Avenue. The time was 9:30 P.M. At the corner they stood under a dimmed street lamp, waiting for the traffic light to change. As they stood there, a man stepped up behind them, raised a pistol and fired four shots. The bearded man dropped to the pavement, one bullet in his back, a second in his brain. Before the smaller man could grasp what had happened, the gunman sprang into a dark sedan that disappeared at once down 15th Street. The bearded man died almost instantly. He was Carlo Tresca, the last leader of the American anarchists.

When the police arrived and searched the vicinity, they found a loaded .38 caliber revolver in an ashcan at the Fifth Avenue entrance to the building. Since the bullets found in Tresca's body were from a .32 caliber automatic, they reasoned that there must have been a gunman waiting at each entrance. After the first gunman had fired, the second had thrown away his pistol and slipped off.

Two passers-by managed to catch a glimpse of the murderer. He seemed to them to be between thirty-five and forty, about five feet five inches tall. Several hours later the police found a Ford sedan abandoned about five blocks northwest of the murder spot. All four doors of the sedan were open and a bunch of keys hung from the ignition lock. Tresca's friend Tony Ribavich recognized the car from its unusual side mirror. The driver of such a car had tried to run Tresca down two days before as he and Ribavich were walking past the New School for Social Research on West 12th Street.

The abandoned car had been licensed in the name of a nonexistent man at a nonexistent Queen's County address. The Con-Field Automobile Company at 1902 Broadway had sold it to "Charles Pappas" on the twenty-second of December. Two days after the killing the police arrested a thirty-two-year old paroled convict, Carmine Galante, who had been seen to enter the car only an hour and a half before Tresca was shot.

On that evening Galante had made his routine weekly report to the Parole Office at 80 Centre Street. He left the building at 8:10 P.M. Because the supervisor of parole inspectors had learned that Galante was again associating with criminals, he assigned two officers to follow him. During this period of gasoline rationing the officers expected Galante to enter the subway. Instead, about a block from the parole office, he stepped into a Ford sedan that had apparently been waiting for him. The officers, on foot, could not follow him further, but they managed to get the number of the car. It was the number later found on the plates of the abandoned Ford.

On his arrest Galante denied that he had been in any car that night. Although the police were convinced that he had killed Tresca, they could get nothing out of him. He was held in the Tombs for eight months. "Prison wise and a tough witness to crack," the district attorney described him. Galante had never known Tresca or anything about him, and he would have had no reason to kill him (so the police reasoned) unless he had been hired for the job. From the Tombs, Galante was returned to Sing Sing for violation of his parole.

Eight months after Tresca's murder a second suspect was arrested—Frank Nuccio, a small-time racketeer who lived less than a block from where the police had picked up Galante. Nuccio ran an eight-car garage where the escape car had been kept until the night of the killing. The police had traced the garage through keys found in the ignition lock of the Ford. A locksmith who made one of the keys said that he had changed the lock on Nuccio's garage a few hours before Tresca was shot—presumably to prevent the sedan being returned there afterward. Nuccio—as uninformative as Galante—was held for two months, then released.

There the investigation ended. On various unrevealed grounds neither the district attorney's office, the mayor, nor the United States attorney general seemed to be much interested in solving the mystery of Tresca's death. "Is there some political reason?" Tresca's old Boston friend Aldino Felicani asked in an open letter to Mayor La Guardia, published in his miniscule anarchist monthly *Controcorrente* (*Counter-current*). "Would it complicate our international relations . . . if the forces which inspired that murder were revealed at this time?"

In his earlier years Tresca had been a doctrinaire anarchist, a believer in—if not a practicer of—the propaganda of the deed. But as he grew older—in spite of his broad-brimmed anarchist hat and black butterfly tie—he became less concerned with anarchist theory and more and more concerned with the rights and freedom of individuals. Fascists and Communists—those who talked of breaking eggs to make omelettes, and who would suppress the individual for the sake of the cause—came to hate him. Others, whatever their politics or religion, could not resist his abounding personality. Even the police who arrested him became his friends—and he was arrested some thirty-six times on charges varying from blasphemy, libel, disorderly conduct, incitement to riot and criminal obscenity to conspiracy, sedition and murder. Even the district attorney who denounced him as an enemy of society would eat and drink at his table. Tresca relished the mere fact of being alive, and he loved to the full the smaller personal things life had to offer him—women and wine, talk, food and song. "Big, bearded, boastful, life-loving," his friend Eugene Lyons saw him, "and as unlike the embittered anarchist of popular tradition as possible. Priest-baiting and spaghetti were among his chief passions, and his hairbreadth escapes from enemy bullets everywhere from Abruzzi to the copper empire of Montana were ample proof of his charmed life." Suzanne La Follette, who served with him on the Dewey Commission, remembered him as "tall, very heavy, with gray hair and beard and the kindest blue eyes twinkling through glasses (if my memory is correct he wore a pince-nez with a black cord). He always wore a black hat with rather low crown and wide brim. Altogether a most impressive looking man—warmly affectionate toward his friends, wise and humorous, without a touch of the fanatic about him."

Tresca's funeral was held in the old Manhattan Opera House on 34th Street, and even that building was too small.

> It was packed [Suzanne La Follette wrote] and as one looked and listened one knew that these people were no mere sensation-seekers; they were mourners—mourners of all sorts and conditions, sharing a common grief and a common awareness that with Carlo a vital warmth had gone out of their lives that could never be rekindled.

Carlo Tresca was born in 1879 in Sulmonia, an ancient hill town of the Apennines. Like Galleani, Malatesta, and many of the anarchist leaders, he came from an upperclass family, his father being the wealthiest landowner in the vicinity. He became a Socialist before he had left school, and at the age of twenty he organized a local branch of the Socialist party and mustered and marched his father's peasants behind the red flag. Oddly enough, his radical views caused no family conflict, and eventually he was even able to convert his father to a Socialist point of view. At twenty-two the buoyant and irrepressible Carlo had become secretary of the Italian Railroad Workers' Union and made his mark as one of the most popular undesirable citizens in southern Italy. The tone of his revolutionary paper *Il Germe* (The Seed) was scarcely scholastic. He soon found himself indicted for libeling his father's friend, the political boss of Sulmonia. To defend their bright young man, the Socialists sent on two of their deftest lawyers. Tresca was so certain he would go free that while the jury was out he went across the square to a café to celebrate with his friends. While they were drinking a toast to Garibaldi and the new war for freedom, the bailiff appeared on the courthouse steps shouting "Carlo! Carlo!" Tresca dashed over to the courthouse with a bottle of wine in one hand and a piece of cheese in the other—only to hear himself sentenced to a year and a half in prison. His lawyers entered an appeal, he was released—and he then *forgot* to file his appeal.

With jail closing in on him, Tresca left for Switzerland. For a time he joined a group of Italian radicals in Geneva. Among those noisy café exiles, one of the noisiest was a comrade by the name of Benito Mussolini. He and Tresca did not take to each other. Mussolini thought that Tresca was not enough of a radical. Tresca thought that Mussolini talked too much.

In 1904 Tresca sailed for the United States. He still considered himself a Socialist, although in those days the distinctions between Socialists, Communists, and anarchists were much vaguer than they were later to be. For several years in the coal mining region near Pittsburgh he edited *La Plebe* (The People), the paper of the Italian Socialist Federation. Whatever remaining energy he had—and he had much—he spent in organizing and leading his Italian compatriots, the workers who had now replaced the Irish as a source of exploitable labor. The America that he knew in those years was scarcely more than an extension of Italy. He learned only a few words of English, and he would never really master the language. After a few months editing *La Plebe* he found himself in jail for libeling the local priest. On his release he was warned to leave town. Shortly afterward, as he was leaving his office, someone seized him from behind and slashed his face with a razor from the left nostril down to his collar. Instinctively he raised his shoulder and managed to protect his jugular vein. Spurting blood, he staggered into a drugstore. A policeman—

one of three who had seen the attack—followed to arrest him. Tresca was still able to muster enough strength to bellow at him: "Why don't you take a dead body to the morgue?" Instead he was carried to the hospital where it took twenty-six stitches to bring his face together. The man who slashed him was caught and tried, but even though the three policemen testified that they had seen him lunge at Tresca with the razor, he was acquitted.

In June, 1905, the one-eyed giant Big Bill Haywood, Daniel DeLeon, "Mother" Jones, and other militants founded the Industrial Workers of the World, soon to be known as the Wobblies. In the decade of their strength the Wobblies organized among the unskilled and migratory workers and led strikes in New England textile mills, Minnesota iron mines, and Pennsylvania steel works, that were as much social rebellions as economic conflicts. The Wobblies were syndicalists whose goal was not the Socialist one of having the state own all the means of production but to have the mines owned and run by the miners' union, the land by a union of agricultural workers, the factories by textile workers, all in a vast non-capitalistic non-nationalist co-operative society. Tresca was attracted to the I.W.W. at once. At this period he considered himself an anarcho-syndicalist.

It was the strike in the textile mills of Lawrence, Massachusetts, beginning on January 12, 1912, that stamped the letters I.W.W. in burning red on the American imagination. The year before, the Massachusetts Legislature—with the best of liberal intentions—had passed a law reducing the working hours of women and of children under eighteen from fifty-six to fifty-four hours. When the law went into effect, the mill owners countered by reducing wages correspondingly. Since many of the juvenile mill workers received five dollars a week or less, the reduction amounted to only about twenty-five cents, but its calculated meanness caused 23,000 workers to strike in aimless anger. They were a polyglot mixture of Italians, Germans, French-Canadians, Poles, Lithuanians, Belgians, and Syrians, with a scattering of Russians, Jews, and Greeks. After a number of riots, the governor called out the militia.

It was then that Joe Ettor of the I.W.W. executive board came on from New York with the radical poet Arturo Giovannitti to give the strike force and direction. The winter was unusually bitter and the workers suffered much from cold and hunger. Sympathy for them grew as the wretchedness of their condition became known. "Their demands were justified," William Allen White wrote in distant Kansas, "and there was no excuse for the violence by police and military."

Clashes between the strikers and the militia became more and more frequent, the Wobblies flaunting red banners reading NO GOD! NO MASTER!, the soldiers replying with bayonets. Finally one afternoon, shots rang out and a girl striker, Annie Lopizza, fell dead. No one ever heard who shot her, but the police welcomed the chance to arrest the "troublemakers" Ettor and Giovannitti.

With the two leaders in jail, the Wobbly hero, Big Bill Haywood, came on from the West to take charge. He arrived in Lawrence at about the same time as did the slim, dark-haired, blue-eyed "East Side Joan of Arc," Elizabeth Gurley Flynn. Decades later, in an antithesis unanticipated by Marx, her almost spherical figure was to be seen waddling in militant complacency across the platform of Communist conventions.*

By March the textile owners capitulated, granting the strikers pay increases of from five to twenty per cent. Ettor and Giovannitti still remained in jail waiting trial. Tresca, who had long been a friend of Giovannitti, hurried to Lawrence to help in organizing mass agitation for his and Ettor's release. Everything that Tresca did had a way of turning into an adventure, and in Lawrence he was a marked man. Early one morning a militia squad came to pick him up at the tenement where he was staying, and he escaped out a rear window, dashing through a network of alleys stark naked. At another time when he was leading a parade to lay wreaths on Annie Lopizza's grave the police cornered him, but a group of workers formed a flying wedge to snatch him away. Two policemen were injured, and after that the police preferred to look the other way when they saw Tresca coming.

* In 1961 she became General Secretary of the Communist Party of the United States.

The Lawrence strike made the I.W.W. famous, and for a while it seemed to the Wobblies and their sympathizers a harbinger of social revolution in the United States. Soon, however, the flame of indignation died down, the textile workers shed their militancy, and Lawrence relapsed into its grubby obscurity.

Lawrence had a more lasting effect on Tresca, for in a May Day parade there he met Elizabeth Gurley Flynn. Her combination of beauty and radicalism he found irresistible. He had married in Italy, but had left his wife with relief. "I no like married life," he once explained to his friend Max Eastman in his not quite basic English. "I like one woman an' then time pass an' I like another. I make many good frien' ship with women because I always say ver' frank: 'Don' trus' me. My character ver' emotional. I have gran' an' real passion now, but when dat gone, I gone too!" His grand passion for Gurley—as she was called—outlasted all his others. They lived together until 1923.

After Lawrence, Tresca moved to New York and started to publish and edit another anarchist paper, *L'Avvenire* (The Future). He and Gurley were soon involved in a strike of the hotel and restaurant workers, whose degrading working conditions had turned them from the gradualism of the American Federation of Labor to the militancy of the I.W.W. A meeting of the strikers in Bryant Hall on Sixth Avenue, with a squad of hostile police standing by, turned into a riot, and Tresca, as the most conspicious person present, was at once arrested. When a group of strikers tried to rescue him, a policeman pointed his revolver at Tresca's head and stopped the rescuers in their tracks by threatening to shoot him. Somewhere between the hall and the patrol wagon, Tresca lost a copy of Elizabeth Barrett Browning's *Sonnets from the Portuguese* that Gurley had given him with an affectionate inscription and with many of the love passages underlined. Accounts of the "hidden I.W.W. romance" appeared in next day's papers.

After the hotel strike came the silk strike in Paterson, New Jersey. Paterson was known both as the silkweaving center of the United States and as the Red City. Most of the workers were Italians, and the Red City had a long and turbulent anarchist tradition. Luigi Galleani had thundered revolution there in his *Cronaca Sovversiva.* The international anarchist leader Errico Malatesta had been shot at while on a visit. Gaetano Bresci, the editor of an earlier anarchist paper, had left Paterson in 1900 and sailed for Italy to assassinate King Humbert. The city was a dreary, smoke-encrusted industrial hinterland, seared by poverty, belligerently class-conscious.

The strike broke out in February, 1913, when the mill owners attempted to increase the number of looms each weaver had to tend. Before the strike ended, all the leaders and a thousand strikers had been arrested. Two workers were shot dead in clashes with the police. Tresca and Gurley arrived within days of the walk-out. They were picked up by the police at their first platform appearance. Big Bill Haywood came to Paterson, as did the fledgling revolutionary John Reed, lately hatched from Harvard. Reed was soon arrested and spent a dynamic interlude teaching the imprisoned strikers songs of the French Revolution and writing such realistic accounts for the New York papers of imaginary filth and vermin in the jail that the furious sheriff finally had "that writing son of a bitch" ejected to freedom.

In and out of jail, Reed, Tresca, Gurley, and Big Bill kept right on speaking. In addition, Reed, with the help of his friends in the New York theatrical world, organized the Paterson Strike Pageant and staged it in the old Madison Square Garden. New York had never seen anything like this massive spectacle with its cast of 1,029 actual strikers. It was both a pageant and a morality play, and it thrilled its nonproletarian audience in the boxes with the feeling that a new proletarian art form had been born.

On the night of June 7, the letters *I.W.W.* shone out from the top of the Garden's tower under Diana's statue. To middle-class Manhattanites, those glaring red letters seemed the modern abbreviations for Mene, Tekel, Upharsin.

Unfortunately for Reed, the expenses were heavy, and when after a single performance the Pageant closed, it had added much more to the notoriety of the strike than it had to the strike fund. Some of the disgruntled Paterson workers accused the New York committee of profiting at their expense. The closing of the Pageant was followed shortly afterward by the collapse of the strike.

To enthusiasts like Haywood and Tresca and Gurley and Reed, each new strike in its moment of incandescence seemed a dynamic thrust forward toward a new dawn. The pattern, however, became static—an initial spontaneous walkout; agitation and organization; violence, with more often than not a striker or policeman killed. Sometimes, as in Lawrence, the strikers won; sometimes, as in Paterson, they lost; but in any case the life of the gray industrial communities soon moved much as before, a little better or a little worse, but with no beguiling prospect of revolution just round the corner.

In 1916, Haywood asked Tresca to help organize a strike of iron miners in the Mesabi Range of Minnesota. Haywood's Western Federation of Miners—the genesis of the I.W.W.—had long conducted what was almost a civil war with the feudalistic mine owners of the great western ranges. After the miners struck for an eight-hour day, the companies replied by importing strike-breakers. In that bleak countryside of scarred red earth where even the landscape seemed violent, the law was an irrelevant abstraction. Both sides were willing to fight. No sooner had Tresca arrived with a group of speakers and organizers than he was hustled off to jail.

While he was locked up, four deputies forced their way into a Montenegrin worker's house and, when the man's wife objected, they beat her up. Three boarders jumped to the woman's defence, there was a scuffle, shots were fired, and an instant later a deputy lay dead on the floor. The boarders and the woman were held for murder. Tresca and three other organizers were charged with being accessories.

In spite of Tresca's predicament, Haywood did not come to the Mesabi Range. The old direct-action agitator was beginning to show signs of turning into a bureaucrat. At this point he was preoccupied with setting up central offices for the I.W.W. in Chicago. To Gurley and the others in Minnesota, Haywood's interest in the strike appeared unhappily remote. They, on the spot, made what they considered the best deal they could with the state's attorney. Since he wanted to avoid a long, spectacular, and expensive murder trial, he was willing to allow the three boarders to plead guilty to manslaughter. After serving one year of a three-year sentence, the attorney agreed, informally, that they would be released. The Montenegrin wife, Tresca, and the other organizers would be freed. When the boarders appeared before the judge next day, they—to the shock of Gurley and Tresca—received sentences of five to twenty years. From Chicago, with no knowledge of the details, Haywood furiously denounced the outcome. Actually the prisoners were released after three years, but Haywood's arbitrary long-distance reaction to the episode was enough for Tresca who scornfully severed his connection with the I.W.W.

Tresca returned to New York's Little Italy and to editing *L'Avvenire,* his interest in unions now limited to those of predominantly Italian membership. From this time on, according to Elizabeth Gurley Flynn, "he wrote and spoke only in Italian and made little or no effort to learn English or to participate in American affairs."

Like all anarchists, Tresca opposed the First World War and America's entry into it. When he wrote flaming editorials in *L'Avvenire* denouncing conscription he found his paper banned from the mails. After President Wilson's declaration of war, the United States government moved against the I.W.W.—Tresca, Gurley, Ettor, Giovannitti, Big Bill Haywood, and 164 others were indicted in Chicago under the 1917 espionage and sedition laws. Ninety-three were sentenced to prison terms. Tresca and Gurley were among those released, since they had broken with the I.W.W. before the new laws became effective.

Undaunted by his narrow escape, Tresca traveled through the Italian enclaves of the East, denouncing Wilson's imperialist war and proclaiming that the real war for freedom was being fought by Lenin and Trotsky in Russia. Because he proclaimed in Italian to Italians, he managed to escape the more assiduous attentions of the monolingual police, although in

Canton, Ohio, he came as close as he ever had to dying. As he arrived, the police were waiting for him at the station platform, but he, wise in their ways, managed to drop off the train just outside the station. He made a detour through back alleys to the hall where he had been billed to speak, only to discover that it, too, had been taken over by the police. An anarchist comrade spotted him on the street and took him home. There, among his Italian friends, he was relaxing over a meal in the kitchen when the police burst in, led by the chief with a drawn revolver who fired almost point-blank at Tresca. The men shouted, a woman screamed, but Tresca seemed bulletproof.

"Arrest me," he told the chief, "but stop shooting at my friends!" He did not notice at first that one old friend sitting beside him had slumped forward, mortally wounded. Years before he and that friend had marched behind the red flag in Sulmonia. The young radical had followed Tresca across the ocean to become in middle age, a conservative businessman. Now he was dead because he had merely dropped in with a bottle of wine to chat reminiscently with the friend of his youth.

Such wild and ironic happenings were the very substance of Tresca's life. When Mussolini, after his march on Rome, began to organize the overseas Italians, Tresca organized his own direct-action groups to drive the New York *fascisti* from the streets of Little Italy. It was his boast that from 1925 on he had made it impossible for the fascists to hold meetings in New York. Stung by such obduracy, the Duce arranged to have a New York gunman eliminate his former comrade. But Tresca's apparently bullet-proof figure was so formidable, and his popularity in Little Italy so massive that the gunman hesitated. His hesitation became panic when the Mafia, for inscrutable reasons of its own, "suggested" that Tresca was not to be harmed. Finally, the would-be assassin came to Tresca, confessed his hired intentions and begged forgiveness.

Unlike many of his comrades, Tresca had never felt the need of protecting himself with a weapon. Now, during his struggle with the New York *fascisti,* when for the first time he found himself compelled to move with a bodyguard, he decided to buy himself a revolver. On the very day he bought it he accidentally pulled the trigger and shot himself in the foot, an accident that he considered even more comic than did his friends.

Ever since the Haymarket Massacre of 1886 when six policemen had been killed by a bomb thrown at a Chicago anarchist meeting, the name "anarchist" in America conjured up the cartoonist's image of the bearded foreigner, bomb in hand. Anarchism's own vision was of a golden age when all governments would be done away with and each individual would accept his innate responsibilities in a world of voluntary cooperation. The means to this goal—in Malatesta's portentous words—would be revolutionary destruction; the immediate instrument terrorism, the politics of the deed. By spectacular acts of political assassination, anarchists would stamp their image on the world. One bomb, the anarchist high priest Kropotkin insisted, made more propaganda than a thousand pamphlets, and to demonstrate this the direct-action anarchists had struck down presidents and kings. Denjiro Kotoku had tried to kill the Mikado, Mateo Morral made an attempt on the King of Spain, Luigi Luccheni assassinated the Empress of Austria, Santa Ceserio killed President Carnot of France and Leo Czolgosz had shot President McKinley. Although after the First World War the anarchists lost much of their mass support to the Communists, their individual acts of violence continued. At the Peace Conference in 1919 the anarchist Emile Cottin shot and wounded Clemenceau. Most anarchists—as Emma Goldman in her later days—rejected the politics of the deed, but they were not prepared to reject their comrades who did not. Nor did native Americans, who generally attributed spectacular events like the 1920 Wall Street explosion to anarchists, make any distinction between theorists and bombers.

The year following the war seemed to bring more problems to the United States, or at least more disillusioning problems, than the war itself—nationwide strikes, inflation, a crime wave, jobless ex-servicemen. In their wake came distrust of foreigners and the search for a scapegoat. The scapegoat itself accommodatingly turned belligerent. Radicals, anarchists, socialists, and the two nascent American Communist parties saw a great light in the East, and hailed the Bolshevik Revolution as the harbinger of the second American Revolution. John Reed expected such an overturn almost momentarily. Even the mild Eugene Debs announced that he was a Bolshevik "from the crown of my head to the tips of my toes."

The Attorney General of the United States, A. Mitchell Palmer, shared with John Reed his belief in the imminence of revolution, which he predicted for May Day, 1920. Under Palmer's direction large numbers of the foreign-born, whether naturalized or not, were illegally and often brutally rounded up and herded into detention centers. Those aliens among them who could be identified as Communists and anarchists were deported.

To this blunt harassment the direct-action anarchists replied even more bluntly with dynamite. Bombs were found in the packages mailed to the Attorney General, the Postmaster General, the Secretary of Labor, the Commissioner of Immigration, J. P. Morgan, John D. Rockefeller, and others. In May, 1919, when the leader of the American anarchists, the leonine Luigi Galleani was deported there were reprisal bombings in eight cities. The chief target was Attorney General Palmer in Washington. Just as he was going to bed, a bomb blew in the whole front of his house. Palmer was not injured. Apparently the bomb had gone off prematurely and killed its carrier, for fragments of a body were found up and down the street.

In time the Department of Justice concluded that the dead bomber was Carlo Valdinoce, a former associate of Galleani's. One of the few who knew this for a certainty was Tresca, who had replaced Galleani as informal leader of the anarchists in the United States. Without any intention, merely by the force of his personality, the now-gray and bearded leader assumed the role of a father figure for comrades and associates who, at least in theory, did not believe in father figures and leaders. In the sea of troubles that the anarchists found themselves in, theorists and direct-actionists turned to Tresca almost automatically. He knew their thoughts and their deeds, he shared their innermost secrets. He gave them his skilled and unstinted help. They in turn gave him their admiring trust.

Flyers calling for the proletariat to smash the tyranny of capitalism, signed by "The Anarchist Fighters," had been found scattered in the neighborhood of Attorney General Palmer's shattered house. Government agents traced them to two anarchist printers in Brooklyn, Roberto Elia and Andrea Salsedo, who had once worked for Galleani. Elia and Salsedo were taken to the Manhattan offices of the Department of Justice and detained for some weeks. Tresca and a committee he had formed to aid the Palmer raid victims tried without success to help the two men. Elia was eventually deported, while Salsedo—who gave evidence and then regretted it—committed suicide by jumping out the fourteenth-floor window. While the printers were still confined by the Department of Justice, an inconspicuous Massachusetts anarchist came to see Tresca. He, Bartolomeo Vanzetti, had been sent by his Boston comrades to inquire about the two prisoners. Nine days before Vanzetti's arrival in New York there had been a hold-up murder in South Braintree, Massachusetts. Eight days after Vanzetti returned home, he and a comrade, Nicola Sacco, were—by sheerest chance—plucked off a street car a dozen miles from South Braintree and held on suspicion of this murder.

As soon as Sacco and Vanzetti were arrested, the Boston anarchists hired local lawyers to defend them. Vanzetti was identified by several witnesses as having participated in an earlier robbery attempt at Bridgewater, Massachusetts, where, although there had been much shooting, no one was killed. Vanzetti was tried first on this lesser charge, found guilty of attempted armed robbery, and sentenced to twelve to fifteen years in prison.

Tresca was furious at what he considered the bungling of the Boston anarchists and their local lawyers. He now engaged Fred Moore, a bohemian radical and a former general counsel of the I.W.W., to take over the defense.

If it had been left to Massachusetts lawyers to defend Sacco and Vanzetti, the two obscure Italians, whether convicted or acquitted, would never have shed their obscurity. It was Moore, with his flair for propaganda and his contacts with so many radical labor groups all over the country and even abroad, who took the fate of the two immigrants and made it into a blazing international issue.

Tresca's continuing attacks on the Duce and the Italian monarchy were duly noted by the Italian Embassy in Washington. When in 1923 he printed a small advertisement in his paper *Il Martello* (The Hammer) for a book on birth control, the Embassy complained to the postal authorities and Tresca was prosecuted for sending obscene matter through the mails. He was convicted and sentenced to a year and a day in the Federal Penitentiary in Atlanta. In protest, H. L. Mencken reprinted the advertisement in his *American Mercury* and vainly challenged the government to prosecute him.

Congressman Fiorello La Guardia managed to persuade President Coolidge to pardon Tresca after the impenitent anarchist had spent three months in Atlanta. As soon as it was learned that he was a friend of Eugene Debs, he passed the time like a star boarder. Debs had served his time in Atlanta earlier, and his genial nature and simple goodness had made an unforgettable impression on both guards and prisoners.

On his way North from Atlanta, Tresca stopped off in Washington like any tourist to see the sights. A group of children happened to be standing before the main gate of the White House, and Tresca, as he passed, stopped to talk to them. He was fond of children and, like a benign uncle, soon found himself in the middle of a chattering circle. Then a White House attendant appeared and beckoned to the group to come inside. The children insisted on taking Tresca along on what turned out to be a tour of the White House that ended with everyone shaking hands with President Coolidge. It must have been an incongruous sight when the ebullient Italian grasped the flabby hand of the taciturn Yankee. Reporters thought so when they spotted Tresca on the way out. Next day the headlines announced: CRIMINAL ANARCHIST RELEASED FROM ATLANTA MAKES PEACE WITH PRESIDENT. Tresca's embarrassment was voluble. Coolidge's was not, but the attendant who brought in the anarchist with the children lost his job.

In the twenties, anarchism was an obviously dwindling cause, its more violent adherents absorbed by the Communist wave, the others turning to socialism. In America the emerging second-generation Italians for the most part forsook the radical politics of their fathers to become Democrats and Republicans. Tresca changed too, in emphasis if not in theory. In his middle years, he turned more and more from the heady dream of an international working class to the defense of the individual against oppression.

Just as in the circle of political thought the discipline of fascism and the compulsion of communism come to coincide, so do anarchism and conservatism approach one another with their emphasis on the responsibility of the individual. Tresca, the last great anarchist leader, ended in the conservative belief that the ultimate discipline is self-discipline and that the just society must be built on loving-kindness.

In 1919, as Emma Goldman was deported on the *Buford* she thumbed her nose at receding America. To her Russia was the northern Promised Land. The promise, however, lasted only the few months it took her to find out that the Russian anarchists were being liquidated in the cellars of the Lubyanka. In 1921, after Trotsky's merciless suppression of the anarchist revolt of the Kronstadt sailors, she left Russia. For the rest of her life she remained convinced that the brutalities of the Soviet Union far exceeded anything known in the capitalist world.

Tresca, now chiefly concerned in fighting the imported *fascisti,* did not react as did Emma Goldman. He continued to cooperate with the Communists even when the Boston Sacco-Vanzetti Defense Committee, in the later stages of the case, was bitterly and publicly denouncing them. In 1925 when James Cannon, on orders from Moscow, organized the International Labor Defense Tresca allowed his name to be included among the non-Communist decoy minority on the executive committee. Not until 1934 when the Communists maneuvered to disrupt a strike of New York hotel workers did he break with them, and two years later he was still willing to cooperate with the Popular Front to support the Spanish Republic in the civil war. But word soon came to him of the ruthless Communist control of the International Brigade volunteers and of the Communist liquidation of the anarchist militia. His old friend Camillo Berneri, an Italian anarchist intellectual, was assassinated by OGPU agents in the streets of Barcelona. Communists seized and executed another acquaintance of his, the old Trotskyite Andrés Nin, who had been for a time minister of justice in the Catalan Government.

But whatever the vagaries of politics and policy, Tresca never let them interfere with his emotions. The end of his relationship with Gurley Flynn came not through any political differences but when a man presented her with a package of love letters that Tresca had written to the man's wife. After Tresca had left Gurley he took up with a Communist sculptress, and lived for a while in a *ménage à trois* under her roof, with the roof expenses provided by her husband. OGPU agents often dropped in at the studio, and in that period before the Spanish Civil War Tresca remained on friendly terms with many of them. Subsequently he had a more lasting affair with another Communist, Juliet Stuart Poyntz. She, with a hard veneer of physical attraction, a Daughter of the American Revolution, aristocratic in appearance and revolutionary in ambition, was until 1934 a member of the Communist District Executive Committee. Then she officially dropped out of the party to become a spy for the OGPU. Following the assassination of Stalin's associate, Sergei Kirov in Leningrad in that same year, she was called to Moscow and took part in some of the OGPU interrogations there. The horror of what she saw was too much for her. When she returned to New York, broken in nerve and belief, she refused to take on any new OGPU assignments. Orders to eliminate her came from Yagoda the OGPU chief in Moscow. It was her murder, as the culmination of similar murders in the Spanish Civil War, that set Tresca irrevocably against the Communists.

Juliet Poyntz disappeared in the autumn of 1937, the same year that the Communists drove the anarchists to the wall in

Barcelona. She left her room in the American Women's Hotel, an unfinished letter on her desk and none of her friends ever saw her again. Tresca would not let her disappearance rest, although it took him several years to fit together enough bits and pieces of elusive fact to discover what had happened.

She had been enticed from the hotel by a telephone call from one of her former lovers, Shachno Epstein, an editor of the New York *Freiheit*. He, fearful to the point of collapse, had been forced by the OGPU to act as her decoy. The two met at Central Park. Epstein led her along an isolated path close to a large parked car. Then he stopped. Two OGPU agents sprang out of the car, seized her, forced her inside, and drove away, leaving Epstein shaking and alone. With the woman muffled in back, they drove through Westchester and into Dutchess County. Not far from the Roosevelt estate, at Hyde Park in a remote wooded area, they garroted her and buried her body.

Tresca, when he felt that he had gathered enough clues, went to the district attorney's office and demanded an investigation. Communist publications at once began to refer to him as a police spy, and party members hinted that he would be next on the OGPU list. He, through his Italian followers, let it be known that if anything happened to him, the Communist Party Secretary, Earl Browder, would be killed in retaliation.

For the Communists, Tresca committed the ultimate sin when he agreed to serve on John Dewey's commission to sift the treason charges made against Trotsky during the Moscow Trials. After sittings held in New York, Washington and Mexico City, the commission found Trotsky innocent. Tresca was singled out for attack by the *Daily Worker,* and the Italian Communist leader Pietro Allegra published a pamphlet calling attention to Tresca's "moral suicide" and demanding the "elimination from society of beings who are hateful to themselves and to society."

It was of singular and long-standing annoyance to the Communists that Tresca was able to keep them out of the Garibaldi Society, the leading organization of Italian anti-fascists.

Even in the hothouse period of Russian-American friendship during World War II, he continued to bar the way to their infiltration. In 1942, the Office of War Information organized the Italian-American Victory Council to arrange overseas broadcasts and prepare for political changes in Italy after the war. So great was Tresca's influence that he was able to exclude Communists as well as ex-fascists from the new organization. For the fellow travelers of the Italian section of the OWI Tresca was as awkward an obstacle as he was to the Communists.

When the awkward obstacle was eliminated that January evening in 1943, it seemed both simple and convenient to let the blame fall on the elusive ex-fascists. Washington was willing to let it go at that. So was New York's Mayor La Guardia, tipped off by his friend Congressman Vito Marcantonio. So was the district attorney. The man who arranged Tresca's murder remained officially unknown.

He had not been unknown to Tresca, however. His name was Vittorio Vidali, alias Carlos Contreras, alias Enea Sormenti, and he had come from Mexico on a special mission to get rid of Tresca. "Where he is, I smell death," Tresca told a friend a few days before he was shot down, when he learned that Vidali had been seen in the city.

Tresca had known him in New York in the twenties. In 1928, Vidali had been deported to Mexico. There he developed his talent for political assassination by arranging the murder of Antonio Mella, a Cuban ex-Communist who had turned against the party and was living in exile.

With the outbreak of the Spanish Civil War, Vidali went to Spain and under the *nom de guerre* of Colonel Carlos Contreras became the political commissar of the Fifth Brigade, which conducted the bloodiest of the Communist-directed purges. It was by his arrangement, and in spite of the protests of the Spanish Republican Prime Minister Juan Négrin, that Andrés Nin was executed. At the war's end Vidali escaped to Mexico where he managed the first attempt on the life of the exiled Trotsky. In May, 1942, Tresca denounced him on the front page of *Il Martello* as a "commandant of spies, thieves and assassins." Within months Vidali took his revenge. He was the type who liked to take his revenge personally. Possibly he was the gunman waiting near the Fifth Avenue entrance to Tresca's office building. Almost certainly he was in the getaway car.*

Carlo Tresca's death marked the end of the great anarchist leaders. Kropotkin, Merlino, Malatesta, Galleani, all were gone. Three years before Tresca was killed, Emma Goldman died. "A mountain of integrity," Rebecca West called her. The same was true of all the anarchist leaders. They were what they said they were, they believed what they said they believed, and no cause or end was for them worthy of a lie.

When Tresca sent Moore on to Boston to represent two unknown anarchists in a local murder trial, he created the Sacco-Vanzetti case. It developed into one of those world-encompassing issues that occur perhaps once in a generation and that polarize a society. Conservative New Englanders defiantly insisted that the two men were guilty. But in the liberal intellectual world that prevailed outside New England it became a dogmatic conviction that Sacco and Vanzetti were two innocent radicals willfully done to death for their political beliefs by a reactionary and corrupt social order. According to this dogma their innocence was self-evident, the trial a frameup, the jury composed of Yankee bigots, the district attorney a scoundrel, and the judge a senile and profanely biased old man. Massachusetts itself became the arch-criminal when the governor and a special committee appointed by him refused to revoke the death sentences.

Most of the books, pamphlets, plays, articles, and poems about the Sacco-Vanzetti case have all taken the dogma of the men's martyrdom for granted. The dogma long ago became a fixed liberal canon, closed to debate. Yet, ironically, the man who shaped the canon was the man who shattered it.

If there was one man who possessed the ultimate inner knowledge of the Sacco-Vanzetti case, that man was Carlo Tresca. Just as Tresca had known that it was Valdinoce who

* Vidali is at present the leader of the Communists in Trieste.

had blown himself up on the steps of Attorney General Palmer's town house, so he knew the whole hierarchy of direct actionists and their secrets. A few weeks before he died he was talking with Max Eastman, who, whatever his own shifts in politics, had remained his close friend over the years. Some time before, Eastman had written a Tresca "Profile" that appeared in *The New Yorker.* Eastman was perplexed by recent rumors he had heard of Moore's later doubts about the innocence of Sacco and Vanzetti.

"Carlo," he asked his friend suddenly, "would you feel free to tell me the truth about Sacco and Vanzetti?"

Tresca could have answered in many ways. He could have simply said no. He could have said that he did not know the truth. He could have said that the men were innocent. Instead, and without hesitation, he told Eastman: "Sacco was guilty, but Vanzetti was not."

And with the unqualified honesty of his reply, in those seven bare words, he rent the most cherished American liberal myth of the century.

Coolidge's Vermont: Plymouth Notch in an Off-season

The afterglow of the sunset was sallow against the hills as I drove up from Ludlow. I could see some planet—Jupiter or Venus, I did not know which—lucid in the fading metallic sky, and then the cloud-rack blotted it out and the wind buffetted my car halfway across the empty road and the rain pelted down. There were a few farmhouse lights, but the solitary filling station I passed was closed, and when I saw the sign ROUTE 103—RUTLAND wet and gleaming under my headlights I knew I had lost the road. I turned back.

Mid-May seemed to bring no spring to this Vermont hill country. Driving north had been like driving back in time—for in suburban Boston the elms arched over the road in all their light-feathered greenness and the lilacs were almost in flower. Here the elms tossed nakedly in the wind, and the maples and the hickories were a mass of interlacing bare branches. A dead landscape it seemed. Yet here and there the headlights picked out a solitary shadbush in blossom like a bridal dress of translucent shimmering whiteness. The roadside ditch held occasional clumps of marsh marigolds, and as I drove through a hollow and the wind died down temporarily, I could hear the iterant treble of the spring peepers, a sound I had not heard for three weeks past in Massachusetts.

What with the weather, I decided to stay the night in Ludlow. Tomorrow would be time enough to take the back road to Plymouth. As I came down the hill at the end of Route 103 the Ludlow streets were rain-sodden and deserted. I spent the night in a bathless creaky room in Ye Olde Touriste Home.

It was ten years ago at least that I had first thought of Plymouth. Plymouth was one of those places—cities or towns; in this case a remote New England village—that I had stored up carefully in my mind, locked away, with a promise to myself of some day going there. I wanted to see it because of that atavistic Yankee, John C. Coolidge, Jr., who was born there in 1872 and who as Calvin Coolidge became the thirtieth President of the United States. Curiously enough it was here again, fifty-one years later, in the Coolidge family homestead that he learned of the death of President Harding and at 2:47 of an August morning took the Presidential oath of office from his father, a local justice of the peace. That simple inaugural in the front parlor lit by a kerosene lamp on the table next to the family Bible, with the grizzled taciturn farmer facing the sharp-faced rufous little man he was then to make President was one of the dramatic incidental scenes of American history. In the jazz-hot twenties it seemed a harking back to a lost rural past, to the vanished decencies of a simpler way of life. Vermont—the only state in the Union never to have voted Democratic—was, as William Allen White said, a waxworks museum of nineteenth-century America, and here was a living tableau out of that period.

The tremendous impact of the Roosevelt era has dwarfed the Coolidge interlude, making most people forget that there was ever such a thing as a Coolidge myth. Coolidge has receded into a minor Presidential figure, commemorated with the others on a postage stamp, a man of limited understanding if with no blemish on his personal integrity. His nasal twang is forgotten—he is supposed to have pronounced "cow" as a three-syllable word. His occasional acid remarks are no longer quoted. No one reads the adulatory books like *Coolidge Wit and Wisdom* or even the amusingly scurrilous *Rise of Saint Calvin,* subtitled *Merry Sidelights on the Career of Mr. Coolidge.*

In the normal course of events Coolidge might have ended up as a state senator, a lieutenant governor at most, but by a set of curious chances, by disaster and death, that inbred Yankee who was so aptly named Calvin, who always kept the copybook maxims of his school days in his mind and the Vermont hill country in his heart, became President of the United States in a period as opposite to his nature as Plymouth was to Chicago. It was this contrast between the small man and his large destiny that appealed to me, that made me attempt an awkward verse play called *Calvin Coolidge* when I was a Harvard undergraduate, that sent me now on this detour of a day to Plymouth. Whatever his destiny, Coolidge never moved inwardly beyond the hill country of his birth. Only Vermont could break down his almost surly taciturnity. In 1928, toward the end of his Presidency, he made an impromptu speech from the train at Bennington, typically brief, in the somewhat archaic language pattern of his boyhood, that for once came close to poetry. "Vermont is a state I love," he said, touched by the immediacy of his leaving it. "I could not look upon the peaks of Ascutney, Killington, Mansfield, and Equinox, without being moved in a way no other scene could move me. It was here that I first saw the light of day; here I received my bride; here my dead lie, pillowed on the loving breast of our everlasting hills."

Next morning was warm with the softness of spring, as if the season had relented; and the sun slanted lazily along the Ludlow pavements by the time I left the angular town and started again along the Rutland road. In the clearness of the morning I could see where I had made the wrong turn, for Route 103 and Route 100 parted company in a wooded hollow, and the latter—a dirt road—veered right to Plymouth Union. The road funneled into the hills. There was ground mist in the valley as I jolted along a track glistening with puddles and still humped and broken by the winter's frost. In every swamp I could hear the red-winged blackbirds chattering with a sound like a rusty gate, and sometimes they would flutter upward, their orange-and-red wing bands startling in the subdued morning colors. Bluebirds had come back too, and the sun caught the azure of their flight. The road wound ambiguously in and out, following the course of the Black River that connected Rescue Lake, Echo Lake, and Lake Amherst like a thread. There seemed to be no far shore to these lakes. The hills plunged down to the water that spread out glaucous and reflective with streamers of mist wisping along the surface. Occasionally a fish would break and leap, and the hills would echo back even that brief sound, and the concentric ripples spread and spread like a silver tide until they dissolved against the shore. I saw two painted turtles on a log, just out of hibernation. The air held the scent of spruce and balsam in such crystal transparency that it was as if I could see each budding leaf and samara across the water. Always the road continued along the shore, past screens of speckled alder and aspen with the long catkins drooping from the lead-gray branches, past summer cottages and a wooden jimcrack-ornamented hotel now all boarded up, and several abandoned farms with disintegrating stone boundary walls and empty cellar holes and lilac bushes grown dense to mark the old threshold.

The landscape turned from wild to derelict as I left the finger lakes behind under the shadow of Salt Ash Mountain. Abandoned farms clung to the edges of overgrown fields, and there were other farms apparently on the point of being abandoned, banked with sawdust against the winter cold, their doors and windows sagging, the yards littered with rusty cans. As I approached Plymouth Union I came to a settlement of tar-paper shanties, where the rural jetsam holed up, workless, kept alive by the parsimonious assistance of town welfare. Here along the road the decay of Yankeedom was inscribed in rotting farmhouse and squatter shack. The young and enterprising had gone away long ago. These harsh upland acres, scored by the Northern winter, with the granite so close below the level of the soil, had nothing to hold the newer generation. There was no economy to sustain them—unless one counted the monstrous hooked rug industry; the land was too poor even to be sold for taxes. Here lay the sweepings of an old tradition.

A man guiding a horse harnessed to a small sledge heaped with boulders moved the minimum distance in inches to let me pass without looking up at me, and some children playing in the dismantled tonneau of a Model-T Ford before their front door stopped to stare. In front of one unpainted house I saw a sign: FRESH EGGS—FRESH COW.

One hundred years earlier Plymouth Township had held 1400 inhabitants. When Calvin Coolidge died in 1933 there were about 400. Now there are under 300. Yet, when one penetrates the seedy outskirts to the old settlements of Plymouth Union and Plymouth Notch, the ancient structure is still intact, reminiscent, like an aged soldier sitting in the sun.

I had no interest in stopping at Plymouth Union. The center of the village, composed of square white buildings with corrugated roofs—the usual meetinghouse, store, town hall, and frame dwellings of the more substantial—though in the New England tradition, was of no great charm. I drove past what had once been a small factory and then sharply uphill toward Plymouth Notch.

The road grew even more rutted as the gradient steepened; trees encroached on the verges; then I came to a final crest and slipped down through masking trees, until at one last bend I could see the few buildings of Plymouth Notch ahead of me set in their bowl of hills. From my vantage point they had an air of coziness about them with nothing really identifiable in their grouping except the spire of the meetinghouse.

Plymouth Notch was a straggling collection of houses near the crossroad: what would usually be called a "corner" in rural New England. At the large white general store, with an empty obsolete Socony pump in front of it, the road turned left and up under a pale blur of elm buds into the background of the hills. Crows were cawing above the meadow hollow to the right. There were no other sounds in the morning quiet but the crows and the trickle of running water in the gulleys beside the road; no sign of any living being until a small boy in a checked lumber jacket appeared, trotted up the long steps of the store, and came out with a loaf of bread wrapped in wax paper. That was no doubt Miss Cilley's store, the one that once belonged to John Coolidge. In its back room Calvin Coolidge had been born. It was there too that the famous Moxie episode occurred the night he was sworn in as President. For on that sweltering evening, just before he took the oath of office, he had walked over to the store with Congressman Dale and a local newspaper man. "A hot night," he remarked laconically, and ordered himself a nickel glass of Moxie, a pre-cola New England tonic. The other two did the same. When the three glasses appeared the President-to-be downed his with quiet deliberateness, then took out an old-fashioned purse with a snap clasp, laid a single five-cent piece on the counter, and walked out.

The Coolidge homestead lies along and parallel to the hill road about 150 yards beyond the general store. Originally it was a one-story colonial type building, a narrower adaptation of the Cape Cod cottage, with a later el of smaller size added to connect it with the barn. The el has a triangular gable in the roof and a porch running the length of the recessed front. Some time in the eighties, probably at the same time that the old-fashioned window squares had been taken out and the glazing bars removed, a two-story bay was added that bulges out ludicrously, destroying the earlier symmetrical pattern. The large blank rectangles of window glass give the house an empty, almost desolate appearance. A barrack-like two-story annex on the far side was added when Coolidge was President. The homestead looked squat, framed by billowing sugar maples that would nearly hide it under their summer foliage in another month, a nondescript place that no tourist would have glanced at twice if it hadn't been for Coolidge and that dramatic night in August, 1923.

First I took a snapshot from across the road. Then I walked up to the porch and knocked on the side door that led to the main house. After a few seconds I heard shuffling, deliberate footsteps and finally a bent old woman opened the door and looked me up and down without speaking. She had on a kind of tam-o'-shanter and her leathery desiccated face with its thin set of mouth suggested the Indian blood that was part of many a rural Yankee inheritance. I asked if I could see the room where Calvin Coolidge was sworn in as President. She said it was pretty early, but she guessed I could come in. Her cracked voice had the overtones of the New England past that still suggested psalm-singing dissenters. Coolidge had that same kind of voice. Over thirty-five years ago he had become President. In another thirty-five years there would be no solitary survivor, not even in wax-works Vermont, who would have kept that nasal twang.

"Right here's where Pres'dent Coolidge took his oath of office," she said with a snap to her jaw. "Look about."

The door opened directly into the room. It was small and mean. There was a rocking chair in the window bay and empty cast-iron flowerpot holders fastened to either side of the molding. The wallpaper was a faded imitation brocade, and the gray floor paint had worn off in patches, especially around the black Glenwood parlor stove with its nickel trimmings. In an alcove near the window stood a cumbersome Victorian walnut secretary-desk. The old woman went over to it. In the light I could see the cords of her neck standing out like clotheslines and the bobble of her Adam's apple under the serrated skin as she began to speak.

"There's the table he took the oath on," she said pointing to the middle of the room. It was a splay-footed center table with a maple base and a cherrywood top. On it were postcards showing pictures of the homestead, and the meetinghouse down the road "where several generations of the Coolidge family have worshipped" and a blurred likeness of Coolidge in a cutaway. There were also little red-and-green felt banners price-tagged 25c, with PLYMOUTH, VT. stamped on them, for tourists to tie on their cars. Against the wall was set a horsehair sofa on which were displayed other souvenirs, pottery dishes, dolls, amateurish water colors, and similar bric-a-brac. Several yellowed newspaper photos hung on the wall in makeshift frames—one of Coolidge with his family when he was Lieutenant Governor of Massachusetts, one of his first day as President, another showing his father welcoming him back for a visit. There was also a rather stilted letter of Calvin Jr.'s, the young boy who died in the White House.

I took two postcards, while the old woman watched me in silence, tapping her forefinger on the flat of the secretary. "Do many tourists—er, people—come here now?" I finally asked her.

The commonplace question seemed to thaw her out a little. She nodded and cleared her throat cords and seemed for the moment almost friendly.

"Not so many as used to," she said, rasping the words. "In the summer we get more visitors, of course. I guess it all fades into the past. They forget. But hist'ry was made in this room. An' some people say they wisht we had Coolidge President naow."

I waited for her to go on, but she was through.

"How much are the cards?" I asked.

"Ten cents," she said. "The money goes to help keep the place up. I hear down to Roosevelt's place they're chargin' folk to see it, makin' 'em pay just to get in—as if he hadn't cost the country enough as 'tis!"

"Did you know President Coolidge?"

"Lots of people ask me did I know him, but I say no one knew him. No one ever did. I was a hired girl when I came here. After he died they made me caretaker."

She broke off abruptly, shuffled out of the room and came back with a nickel in change for the quarter I had given her.

"What's the name of the mountain behind the crossroad?" I asked her finally.

"I don't know as it has a name," she said. "It's just a hill."

I turned away from the hill and the brown strip of road that receded into the distance, turned back and went down again to the Notch, past the one-room schoolhouse with its woodpile and the meetinghouse and the general store behind the red Socony pump, still farther down the slope and across the ridge to the old burying ground. There were more dead there under the knotted grasses than would ever live again in Plymouth Township. As I walked along the spongy neglected paths even the names on the slate and granite tombstones seemed remote shadows. No one would be likely to walk this earth again named Ichabod or Zeb, to say nothing of Lemuel, Ira, Achsa, Eli, or Jabez. Calvin Coolidge's uncle had been named Julius Caesar Coolidge; and his grandfather, Galusha Coolidge, known locally as "Galoosh."

Most of the Coolidges were buried along the lower curve of the ridge, several members of the family often sharing the same stone. John Coolidge, the President's father, lay with his two wives, the date of his death—as one could tell by the freshness of the incised lettering—cut long after his name and birth date, a not uncommon practice in thrifty New England. It was cheaper to have all the family names, living as well as dead, carved on a tombstone when it was ordered. The death dates could always be added with the event. Another Coolidge, the son of Sally N. Coolidge (Billings) who died in Quindaro, Kansas, was buried here at his last doggerel request, expressed in the inscription:

> Carry me back to old Vermont
> Where the rills trickle down the hills,
> There is where I want to lie when I die.

There is a thin path to Calvin Coolidge's grave. The simple stone is of white marble, rather than the prevailing granite or antique slate. It bears nothing but his name and the dates, July 4, 1872—January 5, 1933. Carved above is the Great Seal of the United States. Near him is a smaller marble stone similar in design but without the Great Seal, marking the grave of his son Calvin who died in his sixteenth year and of whom he wrote in his autobiography, "When he went, the power and the glory of the Presidency went with him."

Blue periwinkle flowers were peering out of last year's leaves and there were patches of moss pink in atrocious shades of mauve and magenta among the graves. The flags anticipating Memorial Day that marked the buried soldiers were still bright and unweathered. One could trace the decline of

Plymouth there—the goodly scattering of Revolutionary graves, the numbers of red, white, and blue cotton rectangles to mark the men who had fought in the Civil War, Vermont Volunteers, and the soldiers of the First Vermont Regiment, then the handful of veterans of the First World War. Close by the State of Vermont had marked with a boulder the grave of Esther Sumner Damon, who had died in 1906, the last widow of a soldier of the American Revolution. Near the top of the ridge I found a solitary grave from World War II, that of Everett E. Blanchard, who was killed on the island of Guam and whose body was brought back after the war in one of those futile gestures that organized sentimentality makes toward the dead.

From his high grave I could see the sunlight bright against the marble of Calvin Coolidge's headstone flanked by dark yew shrubs on either side—the sunlight that even in the long days of summer faded here at four o'clock. Fate seemed a curious thing in the morning brightness, the power and the glory that had accrued to that sharp-faced Yankee with the harsh voice. Here in Plymouth he was born, here he lived—all the life that really mattered to him—here he lay under his Vermont hills. The cycle was complete. Even the Presidency had been merely an interlude.

Arty Crafty and the Beginnings of the Joyce Cult at Harvard

I entered Harvard from the shabby gentility of the Roxbury Latin School just before the Great Depression. In those days few American undergraduates had much interest in politics and government, even though they were not quite the materialists, the incipient stock jobbers, the fag-ends of the Scott Fitzgerald jazz era that the more socially conscious generation of the thirties supposed them to be. Of the thousand or so freshmen entering Harvard that autumn, fully a third were determined to make their way in the literary world, and many a young heart, whether from fashionable St. Mark's School or beyond-the-pale Walla Walla High, was quietly prededicated to the Great American Novel.

At that time the cult of Joyce was just beginning to extend itself in American academic circles from its rarefied beginnings among the overseas initiates. *Ulysses* became the fashion. The fact that it was difficult to come by was an added incentive. True, no one was quite sure what the book was about, at least not all of it, but one man's guess was as good as the next one's, and Mrs. Bloom's soliloquy, with its wealth of previously unpublished material, became almost a shibboleth of the Newer Freedom. S. Foster Damon, who had spent years tracing the turgid symbolism of Blake's prophetic books, now wrote his critical interpretation, "The

Odyssey in Dublin," for the short-lived *Hound and Horn.* It was reprinted as a special pamphlet, and its publication spread the vogue still further. Most of us secretly preferred the simple Wertherism of *A Portrait of the Artist as a Young Man* (readily available for seventy-five cents in the Modern Library edition) although we did not dare say so.

Joyce was the last word, like the tattersall waistcoats that were coming in then. None of us wanted to have an unfashionable mind. There were people of the old genteel tradition, such as kindly Dean Hurlburt, who still spoke with regret of Henry James' departure as if it had been America's fault and might have been avoided, who looked back to Emerson and felt that Joyce was a kind of antipope. But to the young Harvard instructors living on pittances in the back streets behind the Agassiz Museum, this cult was the means of challenging the polite academic world of which they were the least common denominator. In private conversations, in the little classes in short-story writing to which the literary-minded third flocked, these earnest, underpaid, embittered young men, whether they quite realized it or not, preached revolt—as is the way with serious young men in their twenties before they have established themselves.

Bernard DeVoto, still in his salad days and hack-writing boy-meets-girl stories with a college background for the *Saturday Evening Post,* was the foremost of the lay preachers. This was before he had published his study of Mark Twain and reached academic dignity himself. "Gentlemen," he used to say, pacing up and down the unventilated lecture room of Sever Hall, "Joyce is the master stylist of the English language. In him all the styles of the past coalesce. For anyone who wants to write today, *Ulysses* must be his Bible and his Koran. I know it is difficult. Speaking for myself, I had to lift myself by my very bootstraps to understand it, but finally I was able to!" In spite of one's seriousness, one had the irreverent mental image of the pudgy man with the tortoise-shell glasses, large feet in still larger galoshes, floating round the fly-specked ceiling of Sever holding the thick blue Shakespeare and Co. edition of *Ulysses* open in his hand.

Our intellectual background was meager. We were ignorant of scholastic logic, were unacquainted with Goethe's *Faust*, even in translation, had never heard of a *Walpurgisnacht*—and Stuart Gilbert had not yet arrived to enlighten us ex cathedra. Yet though we understood little, nevertheless we felt that we had been admitted to some secret society from which our elders were banned. Those of us who were poor used to read Joyce in the treasure-room of Widener Library, where, after signing preliminary forms, we sat at a designated desk under the sharp eye of a singularly withered spinster. Those of us who had money could buy the paper-covered Paris edition through the intellectual underground at The Kelmscott.

A small green-and-red swinging sign in front of a shop on one of the narrow side streets running off Harvard Square was painted in plain lettering THE KELMSCOTT. Not THE KELMSCOTT BOOK STORE or even the more anglicized KELMSCOTT BOOK SHOP, but simply THE KELMSCOTT. Its single chaste window displayed a judicious selection of the cultured interests of the moment, with nothing commercial to distract the eye. The sense of timing was good. A new book by a semi-somebody like Maxwell Bodenheim would stay in a side corner for a day or two, an edition of Lawrence's *Pansies* would be in a more prominent place for a month, and the driblets of Joyce's *Work in Progress* that came over the sea in thin, signed, fantastically expensive rice-paper editions, would hold the center of the window for the better part of the winter. The indigenous poets Aiken and Hillyer were good for two or three weeks, Robert Frost for longer; but the major prophets were of course Pound and Eliot. Occasionally there was a concession to the local scene, such as a brief display of Georgie Weller's *Not to Eat, Not for Love,* billed as the "first adult book about Harvard." The *Hound and Horn* and the *Criterion* were Gog and Magog; *transition's* lower-case shadow lay everywhere.

In its interior The Kelmscott was small and intimate, more a study than a shop. The side walls were lined with bookcases six feet high. On the righthand wall was a reproduction of a line drawing by Picasso of a clown; on the left a bright-colored Braque. There were armchairs and a deep sofa upholstered in red leather set against the back wall, above which was Brueghel's *Winter,* somewhat reduced in size (and fated to come down when the Brueghel vogue had become too generally popular). Heavy metal ash trays were placed hospitably on the arms of the chairs and the sofa. The books on the right were English first editions, the somewhat larger selection opposite, American. Those near the sofa were the special press and limited editions: the Ashendene Press, the Elston Press, Shakespeare Head, the Golden Cockerel, and others—elaborate reprints of Spenser, *Paradise Lost, The Flowers of Evil,* Rabelais, as well as of the moderns. It was a catholic collection: first editions from Mark Twain to Hart Crane, from Robert Bridges to the pirated edition of *Chamber Music,* and even—for the sake of history—authors like Kipling, Galsworthy, and A. E. Housman.

One could browse through the books for hours, sprawl on the leather sofa, smoke and read. More often than not there would be no one visible in the shop. It was a little difficult if one wanted to buy a book, for either the owner was not at hand or, if he happened to be there, he was so engrossed in doing something else that it seemed almost presumptuous to trouble him. The hours of business, according to a small notice on the door, were from 10 to 4:30 P.M.; often it was nearer eleven before the shop was unlocked, closer to four when it was locked up again, and there was a period of an hour and a half when it was closed for lunch. Not that anyone ever mentioned it, but it was generally understood that The Kelmscott would buy first editions and autographed volumes of current writers. Only, when one did sell some book, one had the uncomfortable feeling—in spite of the atmosphere—that one hadn't been given such a very good price for it. Still, the proprietor always had the air of being so indifferent to any transaction that it seemed of no moment whether he bought the book or not.

He was a tall, rather stooped man in his late thirties with a high forehead and thin, receding red hair, a long, somewhat bulbous nose, and almost absurdly small gold-rimmed spectacles that gave his eyes an indefinite expression as if he were never really looking at anything. I do not remember the rest of his features. There was nothing to distinguish them, anyway, except that he had a more florid complexion than is customary for Americans. His name I never knew. He always wore shaggy tweeds, tailored by J. Press, the Gentleman's Tailor, near the *Harvard Lampoon* building. English-country was what J. Press emphasized in his carefully restrained advertising. It wasn't really English, but the imitation wasn't bad. A gentleman bookseller this red-haired man might be called, as he sat in his leather armchair in the corner under the Braque, smoking a heavy-scented brand of tobacco from Leavitt & Peirce, the Harvard Square tobacconist, puffing out clouds of smoke from his blackened briar pipe and slowly turning the pages of some book that had just arrived in the morning post. We all assumed that he had a private income and ran The Kelmscott as a hobby. It seemed a pleasant intellectual pursuit, with plenty of time left to read (and write!) and at the same time fill a very definite cultural need in a place like Cambridge, where all the other bookshops were brisk and businesslike and of the "textbooks bought and sold" variety.

In Paris at that time, one could go to the rue de l'Odéon and buy the Shakespeare and Co. edition of *Ulysses* for 125 francs. There were difficulties in smuggling it through the customs, but no difficulty at all in buying it at The Kelmscott. One merely approached the gentleman bookseller as he sat in the corner smoking his pipe and said, "Have you still got a copy of *Ulysses*?" He would get up slowly, the expression on his face not changing, walk out into the back room, and emerge a few minutes later with the familiar blue paper-covered volume lettered in white, hand it over, and resume his seat and his pipe, still without speaking. The price was $30.

Some time after *Lady Chatterley's Lover* had been written up at length in one of the week-end reviews, The Kelmscott was able to obtain several copies, and the sale of one of these developed into a *cause célèbre* in which the gentleman bookseller became a martyr to freedom of thought in and around Boston.

An agent of the Watch and Ward Society, posing as a Harvard graduate student, managed to buy a copy of *Lady Chatterley* and then proceeded to have the seller arrested on the spot. The Watch and Ward Society was a singular institution, the purpose of which was to watch over public morals and ward off influences detrimental to them. Much of its time then was spent in a feud with the Old Howard, a burlesque theater that among other things had pioneered in introducing the striptease to the United States. The Old Howard advertised itself by lifesize photographic semi-nudes in front of the chapel-like exterior of what was once a Millerite Temple, and by its slogan "Always Something Doing, 1 to 11." Many celebrities passed through its doors, including Professor Kittredge, the bearded historian. Occasionally the Watch and Ward would succeed in having it closed for as much as thirty days. At other times the Society would turn its attack on literature. A few years previously it had had a run-in with H. L. Mencken about a story in his *American Mercury.* Now, because of some overheard rumors, the proprietor of The Kelmscott had been tricked into selling *Lady Chatterley.*

The intellectual world rallied to the gentleman bookseller's defense. A group of Harvard professors signed a manifesto on his behalf, a fund was raised, a well-known liberal lawyer who had aided in defending Sacco and Vanzetti volunteered his services gratis. The bookseller was found guilty, but, as I remember it, was let off with a fine.

Business boomed at The Kelmscott after the trial. The general feeling was that everyone ought to buy at least a few books there just to show his solidarity with the liberal tradition. But the gentleman bookseller continued to sit in his corner and blow his clouds of perfumed tobacco smoke, as indifferent to customers as ever. Finally he acquired an assistant and spent even less time in his shop.

The assistant was John DeQ. Murphy IV, a senior at Harvard, who cut a surprising figure at the college, although what was actually known about him was vague and conflicting. He never admitted it, but according to the official records he had entered Harvard, so to speak, through the back door, transferring from Tufts, where he had been known as plain John Murphy. The "DeQ." and the "IV" he acquired in transit, also an accent that at least on the hither side of the Atlantic could pass for English. There was a certain magnificence in the way he utilized his given drawbacks and turned them to advantages. The name Murphy, connoting in old Massachusetts Ireland and mass immigration, was considered no password by the remnants of *Mayflower* descendants and the New England plutocracy that still controlled the social side of Harvard. DeQ., as he was henceforth to be known, met the challenge squarely. He was not just Irish, he was Celtic; he was not merely a Catholic, he was a Papist; he was of the emigrant, the Wild-Geese Murphies whose heraldic crest he had cut in his signet ring. Assurance he never lacked. Fact and fiction tended to blur in some half-world of his mind beyond the ordinary run of truth, and I think that in the end he was not able to separate the imaginary from the real. Emotional truths became more vivid for him than actual ones. It was truer for him emotionally that he had been educated at Winchester than at Somerville High School, truer about the Wild Geese and the crest than that his mother ran a lodging-house. DeQ. had an air and he carried it off. He had little or no money, yet somehow he managed. One could never quite picture him taking an ordinary job in his spare time. The Kelmscott, of course, was different.

I had come to The Kelmscott one morning just before midday to order a history book. I used to buy all my textbooks there because I could not afford much else, yet felt it was my duty to support such an institution. There were two students sitting in the leather chairs but, as usual, no sign of anyone else. Then DeQ., whom I'd met some time before in DeVoto's class, suddenly came out of the back room.

"Oh, hello," he said in his undulating voice. "I'm just unpacking a lot of new books. Come on in, and when I've finished we can go somewhere and have luncheon." He usually ate at one of the cafeterias in Harvard Square, but was always careful to say "luncheon" and not "lunch."

It was the first time I had ever been in back. The room was close and dark, and the paint was peeling from the stained walls. It was lighted by one small dirty window barred on the outside. There were stacks of books on the floor, and a table piled high with more books. In the center of the room was a packing case with the lid pried off, a hammer and screwdriver lying on the floor beside it. Beyond, under a green-shaded overhead light hanging from the ceiling by a frayed cord, was an old-fashioned roll-top desk. It had been moved from the wall and partly turned away from me, and from that angle I could see it was a singular piece of furniture. The back had been cut away and shelves added to make it into a concealed bookcase. Its roll-top front was only a disguise to give it the appearance of a normal desk. DeQ. was moving books from the packing-case to vacancies on the makeshift shelves.

"This is our private stock," he said rather airily.

I picked up one of the books at random. It was called *The Sexual History of the World War*. Then I looked closer and saw that the whole back of the false desk was shelved with *erotica*. The classical facetiae were there: DeMusset's *Gamiani*, Beardsley's *Under the Hill* and his illustrations to *Lysistrata*, a reproduction of Hokusai's notebook, *Sodom, Justine*. Most of the books, however, listed neither author nor publisher. They were cheaply bound and poorly printed accounts of nearly every conceivable perversion. Some were illustrated, the nude figures drawn with blank, emotionless faces. There must have been several hundred books in the collection.

These thin little volumes that could at most have cost a dollar to produce were marked $15, $20, $30, $50. At first I was shocked. I had never seen such books before, scarcely heard of them. Then I was puzzled. "Do many people really buy these?" I asked lamely, trying to keep the tone of surprise from my voice.

"Oh, yes," DeQ. said, as he arranged the last of the new stock and pushed the desk back against the wall. "We have all kinds of customers. There's an Episcopal clergyman who collects books on whipping, and there's a relative of Longfellow's who gets all the ones on pederasty. I can't tell you their names, but there are even people on the Harvard faculty. And women too."

Slow as I was, the connection dawned on me. "So that's how old What's-His-Name really makes his living, selling *these* books."

DeQ. laughed his somewhat affected laugh. "Why, of course." And he pointed toward the front room where I could just catch a glimpse of Brueghel's *Winter* with the hawk flying over the cold barren landscape. "You didn't think he could make enough to live on from that stuff in front, did you? That's just his hobby. This is what keeps him going."

John The Bold: Boston's John F. "Honey Fitz" Fitzgerald

The three-act play runs a century: sixty years from the Great Hunger in Ireland to the election of John Francis Fitzgerald —"Honey Fitz" to Massachusetts—as Mayor of Boston; forty more years to see his namesake grandson, the twenty-nine-year-old John Fitzgerald Kennedy, elected to Congress from Honey Fitz's old district as the first planned step to the Presidency. Those three dates, cut so deeply in Boston's history, mark the beginning, middle, and end of a phenomenon as old as history itself—the superseding of one class by another. Seventy years before the Potato Famine the seaport peninsula had seen it all happen before when on a blustery March day in 1775, Admiral Lord Howe embarked the Boston garrison, and the provincial aristocracy sailed away with the redcoats into exile. Those proudly armigerous Brattles and Vassalls and Dudleys and Hutchinsons abandoned the town to the non-armigerous class below them.

As Boston resumed its pace after the Revolution, the old mansions had new faces in them. "Fellows who would have cleaned my shoes five years ago now ride in chariots," a disgruntled relative of General Joseph Warren observed. The emergents were the sober, hard-faced merchants, men who would never dream of giving up their new counting houses for moth-eaten loyalties. Inheriting the town by default, they

—within the limits of their bourgeois sobriety—came to adopt the behavior pattern of their predecessors. One can mark the two eras by comparing the Palladian sophistication of Governor Shirley's Roxbury mansion (1745) with the naivety of Bulfinch's State House (1795), just as one can mark the next emergence in the contrast of the brick Federalist town houses of Beacon Hill with the Hyannis compound.

It takes about three generations for a new class to consolidate itself, and it took the grandsons of the Federalist merchants to give Boston its literary flowering and its label of the Athens of North America. That moment of flowering was not so much fruition as the pause before the end. And the end came to the self-contained brick town with the waves of Irish immigrants fleeing the Famine.

Between 1846 and 1854 over a million and a half people left Ireland for North America. They were driven out, dispossessed, without hope. Because the Cunard Line terminus was then at Boston, most of them landed there. Sunk in their defeat, they came over like cattle. Five percent of them died aboard the "coffin ships" on the way. The stench of those ships brought back memories of the old slavers; the Boston Harbor Master could recognize the odor of an immigrant vessel when it was still off Deer Island. Often there would be thirty or forty deaths in the course of a voyage on a ship containing 500 to 600 passengers.

The immigrants' memory of that flight and that passage and the desolation of their arrival remained green and bitter for generations. Over half the immigrants were illiterate; three quarters had no trade. In Boston their life-span averaged fourteen years. An able-bodied Irish laborer in the city could not in the 1850s earn enough by himself to keep his family. During the first-year depression of the Civil War the newcomers in their Paddyvilles and Mick Alleys starved. With their arrival they became the solid core of the new urban proletariat, alien in temperament, tradition, and belief to that Yankee plutocracy for whom they were to furnish the cheap labor and from whom later—to the outraged astonishment and moral indignation of the latter—they were to take over Boston.

They were the base of the social pyramid, the unfailing source of exploitable labor: ditchdiggers, stevedores, hod carriers, and stableboys. Construction bosses from all over America sent to Boston for fresh supplies of Irish workers. The Paddies went as contract laborers in coaches with sealed doors, the curtains nailed across the windows. Along the Erie Canal and the new railroad lines they died like flies.

These unassimilable foreigners with their uncouth solidarity more than doubled the population of static Boston, turning it from a coherent and comprehensive town to an incoherent and incomprehensible metropolis. From the padded perspective of the welfare state, it is easy to condemn the callousness of the Yankee Bostonians toward the newcomers, but the tremendous forced migration had no precedent; there was no mechanism for dealing with it. Beacon Hill felt no sense of responsibility for what was happening in East Boston. Rather, the Yankee epigoni, appalled by the Celtic locust-swarm, withdrew to the Beacon Hill–Back Bay redoubt. Unlike their Tory predecessors they did not quit the fort. For decades yet they would manage to keep political control of what they felt was their city. Its financial structure was and would remain in their hands—the industries, the banks, the stores, the investment houses. It was in reaction to these untouchable newcomers that the tradition of Boston *hauteur* came into being, the proper Bostonian, the myth of the Brahmin—that term the kindly Dr. Oliver Wendell Holmes coined originally to mean no more than a bread-and-water intellectual asceticism and that would now come to mean a class-conscious membership in the Yankee State Street financial oligarchy.

Though exploitable, the Irish seemed to the newly proper Bostonians (in the words of Mayor Lyman) "a race that will never be infused with our own, but on the contrary will always remain distinct and hostile." In the harsh atmosphere of Boston, alienated from the common life of the community both by their background and their religion, the Irish formed a society within a society, an emerging Catholic political bloc of their own against the Protestant Yankee oligarchs. The younger immigrants formed gangs in the spirit of the old Irish Whiteboys. During the seventies and eighties, these gangs and barroom associations controlled the politics of their street and block, gradually spreading out, precinct by precinct, ward by ward, until it was clear that in a matter of time the Irish would capture the city. Politics came naturally to the temperament of the Celts, particularly when all other avenues of mobility were barred to them.

Following the pattern of almost all ethnic groups, the transplanted Irish began by electing their best. Hugh O'Brien was the first Irish immigrant to become mayor. With the support of dissident Yankee Democrats, he was elected in 1884 for the first of four one-year terms. Six years previously he had been chairman of the Board of Aldermen, and this date marks the first break in the Yankee political structure of the city, although the Irish position was not consolidated for another generation. Not until 1902 did Boston receive its second Irish-born mayor, Patrick Collins. Both O'Brien and Collins were outstanding men, able and honest, the type one might expect to find as Lord Mayor of Dublin or Cork or Limerick. Collins, whose widowed mother had brought him over as a child in the Famine years, started out in life as an upholsterer. After years of struggle he managed to enter the Harvard Law School and received his degree at twenty-seven. As first president of the American branch of the Irish Land League he became a friend of Parnell. In 1880 he was elected to Congress from the newly reapportioned and overwhelmingly Democratic district that included Boston's North and West Ends, and East and South Boston. He served three terms. In 1893 President Cleveland appointed him consul general in London.

Like his poet-friend John Boyle O'Reilly, Collins in his innate mobility tried to pretend away the caste barriers erected against the proletarian Irish. He denied that there was any such thing as an Irish vote, and declaimed passionately: "Americans we are; Americans we will remain." He hoped for the future of the Boston Irish in the light of his own development as a process of accommodation and acceptance, with the Irish conforming to the respectable pattern of their Yankee neighbors. But in the hard emergence of the Fitzgeralds and the Curleys and the Coakleys he saw this hopeful dream dissolve. In his later years, disillusioned, Collins turned to drink, even as O'Reilly in his disillusionment finally ended his own life.

Collins, on his return from England, was urged by Boston Democrats to help reunite the quarreling factions in the party by running for mayor. Reluctantly, he agreed. He was elected in 1901 and re-elected in 1903. Unbribably honest, he disliked the political atmosphere of City Hall. The practical necessities of patronage he detested. While managing to thwart the City Council's periodic raids on the treasury, he preached "caution, prudence and economy" to deaf-eared politicians. In 1905 he died in office. President Cleveland wrote of him: "In public life he was strictly honest and sincerely devoted to the responsibilities involved." With one almost accidental exception he was the last mayor of Boston for half a century of whom this could be said.

After him the practical men took over. The Irish-American politicians, more and more of them now second generation, felt no obligation to observe rules made by the Back Bay ascendancy who had exploited them. The way was open and the trough full. In the autumn of 1905, John F. Fitzgerald was elected Mayor of Boston.

Honey Fitz, he was called, for his mellifluous rendering of "Sweet Adeline" on the hustings and on all possible social occasions except funerals. The song became his trademark. The taking over of City Hall by this dynamic little political buccaneer was as decisive a date in the history of Boston as General Howe's evacuation of the town.

John Francis Fitzgerald was not born with a silver spoon in his mouth, but he was born with a spoon—and this was much in the Irish North End in 1863. His father Thomas had come from Wexford, and like most immigrant Irishmen had worked first as a laborer, but by the time his third son Johnny came into the world, he had become the proprietor of a North End grocery and liquor store. Four more sons were to follow.

A hundred years before, the North End had been a fashionable residential section with an eighteenth-century unsegregated mixture of stout artisan houses like Paul Revere's scattered between the mansions of the aristocracy. Governor Thomas Hutchinson had his elegant town house there, with the English Crown carved on the lintels, where he had written his history of Massachusetts until the house was sacked by the Stamp Act mob in 1765. Encroached on by the business district, the neighborhood had managed to preserve a faded respectability until it was overwhelmed by the Famine immigrants. These ragged illiterates swarmed up from the waterfront to pack the partitioned rooms of decayed mansions, to overflow into the hulls and gutters of the dock alleys and rot away in basement warrens. Copp's Hill with its ancient burying ground was renamed Connemara Hill, Donegal Square's earlier name was forgotten, and Kerry Village came into being. The North End became and stayed a slum.

The Fitzgeralds lived in a four-story, eight-family, red brick tenement near the Old North Church. Their flat had no bath, no modern gas lighting, but no other family shared the few rooms and there was always food on the table. By the standards of the Irish North End the Fitzgeralds were well off, and the boys did not think otherwise. Young Johnny came to love the narrow streets and never developed the bitter sense of alienation that his more savage rival, James Michael Curley did.

"Johnny Fitz" the gang called him. He was smaller than the other boys, quicker with his feet than his fists. The teeming streets, littered with horse droppings, crowded with pushcarts and hucksters, were all he at first knew. He tagged after the older boys in their games along the docks. Masts and spars were part of his horizon. On winter days fog would often blanket the North End. In the hot, breathless summer nights the boy, lying in bed with his brothers, listened to the long-drawn wail of steamship whistles, the clang of the East Boston ferry bell. Johnny Fitz felt the sea in his bones. He never forgot it. "My playgrounds," he said years later, "were the streets and wharves busy with ships from every part of the world."

Early he showed that somewhat officious enterprise that is the mark of the embryo politician. The Fitzgerald brood were of course regular attenders at the North End's St. Stephen's, and Johnny was equally regular in attending all the parish social functions. As he grew older he helped the priests run picnics, minstrel shows, suppers, fairs, and dances. At outings he usually won the sprints and always the potato race. So involved did he become in neighborhood affairs, so reliable was he in getting things done, that he was elected president of the Neptune Associates when most of the members were old enough to be his father. The club was the strongest social and athletic organization in the North End.

Yet no one could say that Johnny Fitz was Alger all the way. At a time when most North End boys were considered fitted for life with a grammar school diploma, he attended the Boston Latin School where, as a contemporary of Santayana and Berenson, he received a reasonably classical education. During those years he lost his mother. On graduating from Boston Latin he entered the Harvard Medical School, but at the end of his first year his father died, and he had to turn to and help keep the family together. He left Harvard—still a heretical institution to most of the Boston Irish—and took the examination for a job in the Custom House. "I had to take care of all six of my brothers," he liked to relate tremulously at political rallies in after years, neglecting to add that he was then eighteen and that two of his brothers were several years older. "I washed dishes, scrubbed floors, sifted ashes and brought up scuttles of coal and firewood, climbing three flights of creaky stairs. For some reason it was my trust to boss the family. I even washed the faces of the younger boys every day, and oftentimes dressed them."

He came out near the top of the list on his examination, and for the next three years served as a clerk in the Custom House, where he took the measure of the civil service. Then he resigned to set up an insurance office in the North End, specializing in fire insurance. In those willow years he joined every organization that came his way and made his way to others: The Massachusetts Order of Foresters, the Ancient Order of Hibernians, the Knights of St. Rose, the Red Berry Club, the Heptasophs, the Royal Arcanum, the Charitable Irish Society, the Dorchester Catholic Club, the St. Alphonsus Association, the Catholic Union of Boston, the Young Men's Catholic Association of Boston College, the Franklin Typographical Association, the Knights of Columbus, and still others. He was glib and persuasive in casual talk, he was noddingly acquainted with almost all the North End families, and he knew every voter by name. Although nothing like a generation before, the North End was still a slum. Johnny Fitz sentimentalized it even as he flattered its inhabitants. "Dear old North End" tripped so easily and so frequently from his tongue that his supporters there came to be known as "Dearos." To those who were not his supporters, young Johnny became Fitzblarney. When he was twenty-six he married Mary Josephine Hannon, a young woman whose good looks became one of the inherited characteristics of the Kennedy clan. She had been Johnny Fitz's "girl" for eight years. After their marriage some of the Fitzgerald brothers moved in with them.

Johnny Fitz, with his flourishing insurance business and his face amiably familiar from one end of the North End to the other, was now as ready for politics as a duckling for a pond. Outwardly he suggested more a bantam rooster than a duckling, diminutive and cocky. He was a bouncing, dapper man, so much so that one tended to overlook at first the narrow mouth, the eyes a little too close together, the ready voice pitched just a little too high.

Democratic Boston in the nineties had no consolidating and controlling Tammany Hall as in New York. Power was split among the ward bosses: in the West End, Martin Lomasney—the Ward 8 Mahatma—the most picturesque, the most notorious, yet also the best of the bosses; in East Boston, Patrick Joseph Kennedy, a genial saloon keeper (he would become the paternal grandfather of a future President); in the South End, at a later date, James Michael Curley.

Johnny Fitz now set out to make himself the boss of the

North End. In 1892 he got himself elected to the Boston Common Council. It is true there were seventy-four other members in this haphazardly disreputable assembly, but it was a beginning. He hired a secretary and turned over most of his insurance business to his brother Henry. The upstairs office became the Jefferson Club, where anyone in the North End was free to drop in at any time. He was at every dance and caper, expanding the Catholic socials, introducing the first "sunlight dances" to Boston. He kept a card index of everyone in his district who needed a job. At Thanksgiving and Christmas he was on hand with turkey baskets. No wedding took place in the North End without a prominently displayed present from him. Each morning he scanned the death notices in the *Globe*, and he never missed a wake. He had the actor's gift of easy tears. In the summer of 1892 he announced that he was running for the State Senate. The old-time leader of Ward 6 died at this time, leaving the young councilor undisputed boss. "The North End Napoleon," the reporters ticketed him, and Johnny Fitz delightedly began to read up on Napoleon and even adopted some of his mannerisms.

Lomasney's announcement from neighboring Ward 8 that he was supporting Fitzgerald made the latter's election certain. It was politician's luck that the Mahatma had an old grudge against Honey Fitz's opponent.

All the political, historical, and sociological strands that make up the Boston ward boss were to be seen in the career of Martin Lomasney. Yet of all the bosses, he profited least from his position. An orphan bootblack, he started out in manhood as a lamplighter. Eventually he managed to become a city health inspector, and then, as the first step to controlling his ward, he founded the Hendricks Club (named after Cleveland's Vice President, Thomas A. Hendricks, who had once made a speech defending the Irish). It did not take long before Lomasney was master of the West End. His formula was basic: know every family in the West End; help everyone who needs help. The Mahatma's iron paternalism came to dominate the narrow slum streets. There should be a place, he maintained, where a man could come when he was in trouble, no matter what he had done. That place was for Lomasney the Hendricks Club.

> From the standpoint of politics [Lomasney wrote], the great mass of people are interested in only three things—food, clothing and shelter. A politician in a district such as mine sees to it that his people get these things. If he does, he hasn't got to worry about their loyalty and support.

Lomasney's cohorts were on hand to meet each immigrant ship as it arrived. The newcomers were welcomed, given lodgings and jobs, and their names entered permanently in the Hendricks Club's files.

For Johnny Fitz and Jim Curley, being a ward boss was a somewhat slippery stepping stone to something else. For Lomasney it was an end in itself. Day after day he held court in the nondescript hall that was the Hendricks Club. His familiar place was behind a battered rolltop desk, a straw hat, yellow with age, tilted over the baldness of his long head. A drooping handlebar mustache framed the jutting eminence of his pugnacious jaw. One by one the supplicants came to him, and his appraising blue eyes measured them through narrow gold-rimmed spectacles. No one would ever have dared lie to the Mahatma.

Ward 8 was a clean ward in the sense that there was no vice, no gambling, no rough stuff, no trouble about votes. Lomasney, with his filing system, saw to that. The little streets voted to his order. So did former residents who returned in droves as overnight lodgers to vote in old Ward 8. In close elections the dead were known to rise from their graves to vote at the Mahatma's bidding. The Mahatma did not take graft. Money to run the Hendricks Club services came from two sources. Those who got jobs, although it was never mentioned, understood that something was expected in return. Lomasney also accepted donations from all concerns that did business in the West End. The firms made their donations voluntarily, even cheerfully, but they might have found reason to regret it if they had not. Whatever money Lomasney had personally he made in real estate. He was shrewd and he was strategically located. It often happened that when the City of Boston needed to acquire a parcel of land for a school or public building, Martin Lomasney was found to have title to that parcel.

There was surprise among the pols when the Mahatma decreed that he was backing Fitzgerald. "Johnny Fitz must have hypnotized Martin," was the ward-heeler's verdict, and indeed Lomasney would live to regret the leg-up he had given to the North End Napoleon. Fitzgerald was almost unanimously elected. He spent two unspectacular years in the Senate quietly building up his machine for the next leap forward, using his State House opportunities to settle relatives and strategic supporters in plush jobs. With exemplary patriotism he sponsored the April 19 anniversary of the Battle of Concord and Lexington as a local holiday, and with an eye to the Italians now appearing on the waterfront he wangled the same favor for Columbus' birthday in October.

In 1894, moving crabwise but with his eye permanently fixed on City Hall, Fitzgerald announced his candidacy for Congress. The congressional district was made up of the first nine wards of Boston, and was the only sure Democratic district in the state. Again Lomasney backed him, opposing Congressman Joseph O'Neil, who was supported by most of the other ward bosses. It was a rough election as the Irish wards knew elections, with slug fests, mattress voters, and sudden darkness in the occasional close-vote polling place as enthusiasts cut the gas pipes while others rushed in to stuff or steal the ballot boxes. But with the solid support of Wards 6 and 8 Johnny Fitz, "the boy candidate," was not to be beaten.

Three terms Fitzgerald served as congressman. In his first term he was the only Catholic in the House. He made no name for himself, achieving scarcely more than a whimsical reputation as a jack-in-the-box for his insistence on popping up in irrelevant debate. He did sponsor a bill to purchase the frigate *Constitution*, "Old Ironsides," then rotting away at a pier in Portsmouth, New Hampshire. He managed to get the Charlestown Navy Yard reopened, and helped obtain several million-dollar appropriations for Boston Harbor. His love for the sea and for Boston the seaport was real and would last him all his days, but he also knew how to turn this love to his own ends. His chief concern in Congress was to expand his political power. Brother Henry in the North End kept the machine oiled and saw that supplies of oil were forthcoming. Johnny, during the Washington years, bought a house in rural Concord, but he still kept his legal address in the dear old North End.

In the 1895 election the time was not yet for another Irish mayor. Boston's ward bosses had to go outside the city to Quincy for the Yankee Democrat necessary to defeat Republican Mayor Edwin U. Curtis. The man they picked and elected was Josiah Quincy, after whose ancestors the town had been named. Three bosses—no friends of Lomasney's—did the picking: Smiling Jim Donovan, the chairman of the Democratic City Committee; Judge Joseph J. Corbett, the election commissioner; and East Boston's Patrick "P. J." Kennedy. Impressed by the rise of Fitzgerald, they were willing—if he would turn his back on the Mahatma—to admit the congressman to their circle as the fourth mayor-maker. Honey Fitz was willing.

Then in 1901 the Big Four, still biding their time, managed to persuade the austerely respectable Patrick Collins to be their candidate. Collins was easily if reluctantly elected. He always found the job of mayor distasteful. Smiling Jim he made superintendent of streets, but he refused most other patronage demands. Johnny Fitz galled him.

Meanwhile Fitzgerald had bought a moribund neighborhood paper, *The Republic,* for five hundred dollars. This he turned into an Irish-American social weekly which he both edited and published. Nothing in it was of any great interest, nor did readers flock to it. Nevertheless department stores, public utilities, and contractors hurried to buy half- and full-page advertisements. Despite its small circulation and stiff rates, *The Republic* somehow seemed a desirable advertising medium. Soon it was netting its new publisher $25,000 a year.

In 1903 Fitzgerald moved back from Concord to dearer old Dorchester. The house he bought on Welles Avenue was an ornamental wooden château in beer-baronial style, with a scroll-work porch, blank plateglass windows, and a mansard turret. On the stair landing he had a stained-glass window installed with a Fitzgerald coat of arms and the Gaelic motto *Shawn A Boo* (John the Bold).

John the Bold, full of bounce and pugnacious confidence, knew that the municipal election year of 1905 was his year, that he was on the crest of his political wave, and that the tide was coming in. Every ward heeler and precinct worker sensed instinctively that Johnny Fitz would be a candidate, would be indeed *the* candidate for mayor. Collins had died that September, and the question for the bosses was: Whom should they run against this dynamic challenger they had built up so casually a decade before? Smiling Jim and Kennedy turned to the Mahatma, and the three of them decided on City Clerk Edward Donovan.

Impelled from the clerk's office to the hustings, Donovan scarcely knew what hit him. Johnny Fitz was off like a whirlwind on the most spectacular campaign Boston's twenty-four wards had ever seen. Vacant walls were pasted with his posters twice as fast as opponents could tear them down. Bigger, Better, Busier Boston was emblazoned under the smiling Fitzgerald phiz, retouched to benignity by the photographer. The city, long used to pre-election free-for-alls with brickbats and "alley roses" sailing past a speaker's platform, marveled at the roar of its first political motorcade. Honey Fitz toured the wards in a large red car followed by flying squads of what the reporters described as "Napoleon's lancers," to be met in each precinct by crowds of militant Dearos. Ward 8 itself was invaded and here a zealous Dearo at one point pulled a pistol on several Hendricks Clubbers. Secretly, Fitzgerald solicited the help of younger Democratic hopefuls, the bosses-yet-to-be —and secretly they gave help. Even James Michael Curley, soon to be Fitzgerald's most durable enemy, now planned to back him.

For weeks Johnny Fitz made ten speeches a night denouncing the bosses and the "machine," and on the evening before the primaries he reached the almost breathless climax of thirty. But for Lomasney he would have buried Donovan. Fitzgerald won the nomination, carrying twenty of the city's wards, although it took a dozen wards to make up for what happened to him in Ward 8.

The reform Republicans and the Good Government Association—a civic organization founded two years before by the Chamber of Commerce, the Merchants Association, the Associated Board of Trade, the Fruit and Produce Association, and the Bar Association—had succeeded in nominating the highly respected speaker of the Massachusetts House of Representatives, Louis Frothingham. Unreformed Republicans, with the concealed moral and financial encouragement of Fitzgerald, ran Judge Henry Dewey—already beaten by Frothingham in the primaries—as an independent Republican. The split Republican ticket made Fitzgerald's election a certainty, as wily old Martin Lomasney at once realized. Nevertheless the Mahatma preferred defeat with Frothingham. "That gun play," he remarked, "on top of all the stuff they had been springing on the stump, made me determine to fight."

Frothingham represented all the things that Fitzgerald could ring the sour changes on—Harvard, blue blood, inherited wealth. Honey Fitz also spread the rumor thickly (and unjustifiably) that his opponent was anti-Catholic and anti-Irish. He kept up his whirlwind campaign with variations, visiting department stores and glad-handing the salespeople, even inaugurating a "soda water campaign" with refreshments provided for women's groups in critical wards. Honey Fitz had always been—with prudent impartiality—a ladies' man, and women always thought more of him than did men. They were his most solid supporters, from the days when he used to waltz with the wallflowers at the Irish social clubs.

The battle cost Fitzgerald $120,000—twice as much as it did Frothingham. "But it was not money which won," George Kibbe Turner wrote in *Collier's*, 'it was action, ingenuity, and boundless, cheerful effrontery. For thirteen years Johnny Fitz had held Ward 6 obedient and cheerful by public jobs. He extended that one basic system of ward politics over all the city."

The new Mayor took possession of the gray mock-renaissance City Hall on School Street like a conqueror exacting the submission of a taken town. *Enrichissez-vous!* Perhaps Johnny Fitz had read the Napoleonic maxim. His cohorts did not need to read it. The Mayor himself kept control of all the city departments except the schools and the police. He replaced physicians on the board of health with saloon keepers, he appointed another saloon keeper Superintendent of Public Buildings, a whitewasher Superintendent of Sewers, a bartender who had been expelled from the legislature Superintendent of Streets. For deserving Dearos he created such new offices as that of City Dermatologist. Eight additional Deputy Sealers were added to the Department of Weights and Measures—a department soon to erupt in open scandal. The vestiges of civil service were circumvented by the invention of novel job categories—Tea Warmers, Tree Climbers, Wipers, Rubber-boot Repairers, watchmen to watch other watchmen. Brother Henry was given charge of patronage and payments. "See Henry!" was the edict from the Mayor's office.

During Johnny Fitz's first administration, graft was blatant in all departments. "Thieves in the House," John Cutler entitled the chapter on that period in his discreet Fitzgerald biography. During these two years the city lost $200,000 in dealings with a single coal company, whose manager later absconded. In subsequent investigations the Finance Commission discovered that Boston had been paying sixty cents a barrel more than the going price for cement—a $240,000 annual loss. "Bills and vouchers could not be found," Leslie Ainley wrote in his life of Lomasney. "City work was contracted and bids often accepted verbally." There were dozens of strange land deals where the city ended up paying three times more than anyone had imagined a given property was worth. The Finance Commission reported "a steady deterioration in the technical competency and moral strength of the heads of executive departments, until administrative business of this great city was, with few notable exceptions, in the hands either of men without education, training, experience, or technical qualifications of any sort, or of men who had become so demoralized by the conditions which surrounded them as to be unwilling to protest against the most obvious extravagance or graft, if favored by the Mayor. For the first time," the Commission went on to say, "a man was elected to the office of Mayor whose aim was not merely to use or perfect the political machine then in existence, but to become that machine itself."

Meanwhile *The Republic* continued to flourish and expand —its advertising rates were perhaps the highest in the nation in ratio to its circulation. The Boston Elevated Street Railway Company and the American Telephone and Telegraph Company bought up pages, as did the New England Telephone Company, Edison Electric, New England Gas and Coke, Boston Consolidated Gas, the Boston and Maine Railroad, and any number of contracting companies. A list of the paper's advertisers read like a summary of the Boston Stock Exchange. In one special issue the city's banks took fourteen pages.

For most of the time the accumulating scandals seemed secondary to the dynamic ubiquitousness of the little man in the mayor's chair, who might suddenly appear at his office in a black-and-brown checked suit, blue striped tie, and blue-stone scarf pin. During his first term, he is estimated to have attended 1200 dinners, 1500 dances, 200 picnics, and 1000 meetings; made 3000 speeches; and danced with 5000 girls. He thought up Old Home Week and applied it first to Boston—even though Beacon Street held aloof. With his entourage he liked to drop in for a sudden meal, amidst the flattering bustle of the staff, at the various city hotels—the Adams House and the Parker House, Young's, the Democratic politicians' eyrie of the Quincy House on the fringe of the North End, the Winter Palace, and the South End's naughtily Edwardian Woodcock. He excelled as a greeter, entertaining personally such varied visitors as Prince Wilhelm of Sweden and the magician Houdini. Between 1905 and 1907 Johnny Fitz made himself a city institution.

Two years of Fitzgerald, however, brought an inevitable reaction. There were still transplanted Irish in Boston who felt that Patrick Collins was a worthier representative than Johnny Fitz and his Dearos. They could still remember how Collins, as mayor, had welcomed the delegates of the National Municipal League and asked them to report to him if they found anything shady in his administration. What the delegates might have found in the Fitzgerald administration did not bear thinking about.

For the 1907 elections anti-Fitzgerald Democrats nominated Representative John Coulthurst. Coulthurst also had the backing of Hearst's *American* and of all the bosses except Lomasney, who this time returned to Johnny Fitz. The Republicans picked their own variety of boss, George A. Hibbard, the Boston Postmaster. Hibbard was a parrot-nosed, thrifty Yankee who announced he was running for one term only for the purpose of "cleaning up the mess." Fitzgerald conducted his usual bouncing, badgering campaign, adding such bizarreries as circulars in Yiddish to persuade the newly arrived Jewish voters. Most Jewish leaders as well as the more responsible Catholic leaders repudiated him. In a narrow election Coulthurst swung enough Democrats from Fitzgerald so that Hibbard was able to win with a plurality of the votes.

Mayor Hibbard, while looking after needy Republicans, did much of what he had promised. He cut down on municipal workers, halved the cost of street maintenance, and reduced the city's debt. Through departmental efficiencies he managed to save about a million dollars. Toward the end of his administration, and in the hope of more reform mayors to come, the Good Government Association maneuvered the adoption of a new city charter. According to its terms party designations were to be dropped from the municipal ballot. There were to be no more primaries, and nominations for mayor could be made by the petition of five thousand voters. A nine-member council would replace the thirteen aldermen and seventy-five councilors.

Electorates soon weary of reform interludes, and those who are barred from the trough weary even sooner. By 1909 it seemed that the wheel had turned and that the colorless Hibbard would be replaced by the pied Johnny Fitz. To avoid four entrenched Fitzgerald years, Republicans and reformers united on the bluest blood of Beacon Street, James Jackson Storrow. A predestined Harvard man, Storrow had been captain of a crew that had beaten Yale, and now, as New England's wealthiest banker, he was an overseer of Harvard College. With far more civic conscience than most of his kind, he had served as chairman of the Boston School Committee, had been a president of the Boy Scouts, had founded the West End Club for newsboys, and had given much for playgrounds and amenities in the slums. A lean, imposing figure, he was a poor speaker. This was offset, however, by his being that atavistic anomaly, a Yankee Democrat.

Smiling Jim Donovan threw in his lot early with Storrow, impressing on the banker the truism that political campaigns cost money. Storrow was impressed—to the extent of half a million dollars before he got through. Storrow money was loosely plentiful, and Smiling Jim understood its application. Curley, then the visibly rising boss of the South End's Ward 17, said later that he had refused $60,000 to side with Storrow. Fitzgerald knew that without the support of Curley and Lomasney he could not win. The three came to an agreement. The thirty-five-year-old Curley, as junior partner, was to take over Fitzgerald's old congressional seat and bide his time in Washington until the next municipal election. What Lomasney was offered remains a secret, but in spite of personal distaste he stuck with Johnny Fitz.

"Take Storrow's money, but vote for Fitzgerald," was the word the Dearos passed round. Storrow tried to argue about corruption and the issues of municipal government. Johnny Fitz simplified the election to a contest between an Irish-Catholic boy from the slums and a wealth-encrusted Harvard blueblood who was anti-Catholic, anti-labor, anti-Negro and anti anything else Fitzgerald could think of between speeches. He papered the walls with large photographs of City Hall on which was inscribed:

NOT FOR SALE MR. $TORROW

"Manhood against Money" was another Fitzgerald slogan that was used under a touchingly domestic photograph of Johnny Fitz, his wife, and their three boys and three girls. The Storrow forces countered with a photograph of Fitzgerald alone, the word GRAFTER lettered across his forehead. That stung enough to bring tears. Storrow even coined the term *Fitzgeraldism* to describe the antics of Johnny Fitz's administration, but when *Fitzgeraldism* appeared in newspaper advertisements, Fitzgerald countered by running parallel advertisements with slogans: "For Better Streets!" ... "For Better Schools!"

In a day when a political meeting was for many the most entertaining event of the year, when the catharsis of a campaign could purge the emotions, as in later years films and television never could, when partisans packed the hall for hours to wait for their chosen candidate, Johnny Fitz was a circus and a prophet combined. His campaign is said to have cost somebody, if not him, a quarter of a million dollars. During the frenzied weeks before the election, he led his motorcade through several thousand miles of back streets, shouting his tenor voice hoarse at halls and corners. Storrow, trying in his unfortunate Harvard accent to emulate him, was driven out of South Boston by a mob swinging torches and throwing chunks of ice. Fitzgerald even managed to persuade Hibbard, mortally stricken with tuberculosis of the throat, to run as a token candidate in order to draw votes from Storrow.

The Saturday night before the election Fitzgerald staged his biggest and most bumptious rally in Faneuil Hall in the dear old North End. As an added attraction he had hired a brass band, instructing the leader to play "The Star-Spangled Banner" at his entrance and follow it up with "The Wearing of the Green." The latter song concluded before Fitzgerald and his entourage could manage to hand-shake their way to the platform. Because it was a popular song of the moment, and with nothing more in mind, the band leader had his men strike up "Sweet Adeline." Everybody joined in the chorus. When it came time for the second verse, Johnny Fitz, with deft spontaneity, capered down the platform and sang it solo, then led the crowd again in the chorus. And in that bellowing moment of beaming fair faces, the Honey Fitz legend was born. Ever after that the tenor voice and the treacly song would be harmoniously linked, and whenever at a Democratic meeting the speeches began to run dry, the cry would go up for Honey Fitz to sing "Sweet Adeline."

It was generally admitted by politicians afterward that Honey Fitz's demonic gusto in the last few days of the campaign won him the election. On the final night he spoke at thirty-five rallies and topped it off by singing "Sweet Adeline" from the roof of a hack. Even so, in the largest vote in Boston's history, he barely squeaked through with 47,177 votes to 45,775 for Storrow. The ailing Hibbard, repudiated by the Republicans, received only 1,614 votes—but enough to have swung the election if they had gone to Storrow.

Not much could be said about Honey Fitz's second term as Mayor that was not said about his first, except that Boston grew accustomed to the shenanigans. After four more years of Fitzgerald in City Hall no Storrow would have a ghost of a chance of being elected mayor—or would want to take that ghost's chance. And there were the solid accomplishments, whatever their price tag. Honey Fitz built the City Hall Annex, the City Point Aquarium, numberless public convenience stations memorialized with his name, and the Franklin Park Zoo. He founded the High School of Commerce to prepare boys directly for the business world who could not go to college. One of his more original minor inspirations was the painting of white traffic lines, for which he was accused by proper Bostonians of disfiguring the city's historic streets. With appropriate regard for sentiment he established the local sanctity of Mother's Day and began the custom of having a Christmas tree on Boston Common. He also inaugurated the banned-in-Boston tradition by forbidding the Turkey Trot and the tango as immoral, the opera *Salomé* as sacrilegious, and the red flag in parades as both.

The Mayor's official car was now the *Sweet Adeline II.* In 1911, as he sailed for a tour of Europe on the *Franconia,* he sang his theme song from the bridge. For the voyage he had packed a supply of rockets and other fireworks to set off at the first sight of the Irish coast, with the result that the Irish Coast Guard finally signaled: "Do you need help?"

Greeting and entertaining were his official delight. He welcomed such assorted figures at City Hall as the French actress Gaby Deslys, New Jersey's Governor Woodrow Wilson, William Jennings Bryan, Theodore Roosevelt, Lady Gregory, and the lord mayors of Dublin and London. Sir Thomas Lipton relaxed in his company, visiting him not only in Dorchester but in the wooden-gingerbread ark of Fitzgerald's summer house in Hull, overlooking Boston Harbor. In 1914 Honey Fitz's oldest daughter, Rose, married a brash, up-and-coming young Harvard graduate, Joseph Patrick Kennedy, the son of East Boston's P. J.

Honey Fitz had made a bosses' agreement to leave City Hall at the end of his term. He toyed briefly with the quixotic notion of running for governor or even for United States senator, but as his pleasant and profitable months in the gray School Street building narrowed he began to feel that his earlier renunciation was premature. Meanwhile, Congressman Curley, rounding out his second term in Washington, was regarding the gilt eagle on top of City Hall with an increasingly calculating eye. "You are an old man," he told the fifty-year-old Mayor by way of a Curley-type hint. "Get your slippers and pipe and stretch out in your hammock and read *The Ladies' Home Journal.*"

The lone wolf of Ward 17 was the one opponent whom Honey Fitz feared. Unlike most politicians, Curley never developed a nickname. Even though he had begun by imitating the Ward-6 Napoleon, he had been brought up in a harder school. He had a more commanding presence and a more resonant voice, a crueler tongue, and a quicker fist. Honey Fitz may have been meaner, but Curley was tougher, and he had the instinct for the jugular.

In November, 1913, Curley let it be known, officially, that he would be a candidate for mayor in the January election. A few weeks later Honey Fitz came out with the announcement that he had decided to run for a third term. Next day the *Post* quoted Curley's comment: "Fitzgerald wants a licking, and he will get it." The two were now archenemies, and in spite of intermittent superficial political gestures of good will, they were to remain enemies the rest of their long lives.

A few days after Honey Fitz's announcement, Curley announced that he would give three public lectures, contrasting famous characters of history with John F. Fitzgerald. His first lecture, given at the Dorchester High School, was on "Graft in Ancient Times *vs.* Graft in Modern Times," with comparisons between the Rome of the Caesars and Boston of the Dearos. The title of the next lecture was advertised as "Great Lovers: from Cleopatra to Toodles"; but before it could be given, Honey Fitz—on the grounds of ill health—had withdrawn his candidacy.

Toodles Ryan was a cigarette girl at the Ferncroft Inn, one of Honey Fitz's ports of call along the Newburyport Turnpike. He had met her there at a large party some years before. A blur of talk followed about the Mayor and the shapely blonde, and their names became more permanently linked in an anonymous limerick. In later years Honey Fitz righteously insisted in a statement to the *Post* that he had never done more than kiss Toodles casually and publicly at the party, with his wife present. Those close to Honey Fitz have tried to argue away the Toodles stories as no more than malicious jokes. Curley insisted that they and similar Honey Fitz tales long current in Boston were true, and he always maintained that his threat to tell what he knew about Toodles drove Fitzgerald from public life.

After his withdrawal, Honey Fitz and the ward bosses—with the exception of Lomasney—united incongruously with the Good Government Association on an anti-Curley candidate, City Councilor Thomas J. Kenney, an honest but uninspired budget expert who had once served on the School Committee. At the last moment P. J. Kennedy shifted his support to Curley. In spite of the opposition of the rest of the bosses—whom Curley now swore to destroy—the young man from the South End was unbeatable.

Winning inspired no charitable thoughts in Curley. When at his inaugural he had to shake hands with his predecessor, he stared coldly away. Then, with Honey Fitz sitting a few feet from him, he attacked the ex-Mayor so bitingly that the latter's face twitched and reddened. Six hundred of Honey Fitz's supporters employed at City Hall had to walk out the back door the day Curley walked in the front.

With Curley's election, Honey Fitz's political career came to an end. Though he would live on for a third of a century, though he would several times be a candidate, he would never again occupy public office.

For some time he enjoyed his leisure. He could now indulge in his passion for long auto rides, for cruising in Boston Harbor, and for sporting events—baseball, football, and prize fights. With the approach of winter, he sunned himself in Florida. His social life buzzed much as ever. He dined and he danced, he spoke and sang. In 1915 he received an honorary doctorate of laws from Notre Dame University, and liked afterward to have himself referred to as Dr. Fitzgerald. But by 1916 he could feel the old political stirrings in his blood.

That year was the first in Massachusetts for direct election to the United States Senate, and Senator Henry Cabot Lodge, who had served three terms by vote of the Massachusetts Legislature, was now forced to take his chances with the electorate. The chill autocratic Yankee with the gray curls and the gray spade beard was not an endearing personality. Disaffected Republicans and old Roosevelt Bull Moosers would have no part of him. Harvard's President Lawrence Lowell was later to refer to him as "a degenerate son of the University." A Yankee Democrat, in the wake of Wilson's Presidential victory, could probably have defeated Lodge that year. Not, however, Honey Fitz. With Curley occupied at City Hall, Fitzgerald managed to grasp the brass ring of the Democratic nomination. Only his Celtic optimism kept him from seeing that the ring was worthless. *The New York Times* could not understand why Massachusetts Democrats had not put up a worthier candidate against the "gentleman from Massachusetts." From the perspective of New York, Honey Fitz was "an amiable kisser of the Blarney Stone, warbler of 'Sweet

Adeline,' rider of Florida sharks, butterfly flitting unconcerned around the solid men of Boston."

The following year brought with it another municipal election, but Honey Fitz had no intention of tangling with Curley again. He preferred to take a temporary step down the political ladder and run for Congress from his old district. The present congressman, Peter Tague, was under a cloud in Boston, or at least in Ward 8. Lomasney had originally given Tague the support that elected him, but turned furiously against him when Tague failed to propose in Congress that the entry of the United States into the war be contingent on England's granting Ireland independence. In spite of the Mahatma's backing, Fitzgerald won the nomination by only fifty votes in a contest memorable even in Boston for the numbers of false registrations, mattress voters, repeaters, burnt ballots, and stolen ballot boxes. Tague refused to accept the result and announced defiantly that he was running on stickers. To counter this, Honey Fitz had blocks of stickers printed without the gum on the back. On election day dozens of his supporters, pretending to be Tague workers, handed out these stickers at the polls. When the ballots were placed in the box the ungummed stickers fell off, leaving blank ballots. Fitzgerald won by 238 votes. At once Joseph Kane, Tague's tough professional manager, complained to Washington that the election was a fraud. A Congressional committee came to Boston to investigate Kane's charges. They found enough evidence of fraudulent voting and "padded returns of alleged residents in cheap lodging houses" to unseat Fitzgerald and replace him by Tague.

In January, 1922, Honey Fitz announced that he was again a candidate to oppose Lodge for the United States Senate. As a token of party unity he and Curley shook hands at the Elks Club and then, to prove their harmony, sang duets of "Sweet Adeline" and "Tammany." But when the Republicans took to quarreling among themselves like so many Democrats about a candidate for governor, Honey Fitz decided he would rather take advantage of their dissension than confront the frosty Lodge. Not for another decade would the Irish Democrats take over the state, and Honey Fitz's challenge to Republican Governor Channing Cox failed by 60,000 votes. Nevertheless, the *Post* paid tribute to Fitzgerald's coruscating effort: "Nothing like it has ever been seen in Massachusetts. He is the superman of campaigners, and he is greater in defeat than he ever was in victory."

Honey Fitz, now in his sixties, was grayer, plumper, his jowls deeper, his face puffier, but still with the old outrageous bounce. Late in 1925 he let it be known that he was once more a candidate for mayor. Then, four days later, he changed his mind, to the relief of his son-in-law Joe Kennedy, who was getting a little tired of the Toodles stories that were revived with each Honey Fitz candidacy. Instead of becoming a candidate, the ex-mayor celebrated his birthday by singing "Sweet Adeline" over the radio. The mayoralty contest boiled up with six others, but somehow a Boston campaign without Honey Fitz lost half its savor. A reporter wrote nostalgically: "Lovers of the spectacular may regret that this most colorful personality will not be seen charging up and down the municipal gridiron, going through for gains, being thrown for losses, smearing his opponents or being smeared. The battle will not be the same with the 'doctor' out."

Some time in the mid-twenties Fitzgerald sold the Dorchester château and moved to a rent-free suite in the Bellevue Hotel, the politicians' Valhalla beside the State House. The summer house in Hull he exchanged for one in Wareham on Cape Cod, near the Kennedy compound. For an antidote to restlessness he took long rides in his chauffeur-driven Locomobile. As he grew older, that mellowing process took over by which politicians and other wayward characters become fixtures, so that in the end even their old enemies are glad to see them. In 1927 when the Adams House with its memories of so many political figures closed it seemed fitting that Honey Fitz should ring down the curtain with "Sweet Adeline."

The year 1930 marked his last real political battle. He announced that he was a candidate for governor. Massachusetts Republicans were never to recover from that second Depression year. Boston had been a Democratic city for a generation, and now it was the turn of Massachusetts to become a Democratic state. If Honey Fitz had won the nomination that year, he would have been elected. But two weeks before the primaries he collapsed, and from his hospital bed he sent word that he was withdrawing from the contest. In one of the strange turnabouts of Boston politics, Curley, who had become his most impassioned supporter and speechmaker, refused to accept the withdrawal—not from any belated affection for Honey Fitz but out of blind hatred for the leading candidate, Yankee Democrat Joseph Ely.

In the 1932 Roosevelt year, Curley was the first Massachusetts politician to sense the swing of the tide and to shift his mercurial allegiance from Al Smith to Franklin Roosevelt, a shift so unpopular among local Democrats that he was dropped from the Ancient Order of Hibernians. Honey Fitz remained an Al Smith man right down to the Democratic Convention, even though his astute son-in-law had become a member of the strategy group, "the Silent Six," touring the country in Roosevelt's campaign train. Nevertheless, the old Dearo was granted the innocuous post-election honor of the presidency of the Massachusetts delegation to the Electoral College.

The mellowing process continued, but now to a point of isolation. P. J. Kennedy had died in 1929. Lomasney followed him shortly after Roosevelt's inauguration. Only the indestructable Curley remained, alternately winning and losing elections. In 1936 Honey Fitz became president of the Clover Club, a local Celtic variation of Washington's Gridiron Club, and took the chair for the first time, dressed as Napoleon. The next year, with wry pride, he saw his son-in-law appointed Ambassador to England. On Honey Fitz's seventy-fifth birthday, 750 guests attended a party for him at the Boston Chamber of Commerce, and he noted with content that the patrician ex-secretary of the navy, Charles Francis Adams, was among them. He was on hand to meet Roosevelt's train when it arrived in Boston in 1940, and the younger charmer greeted the old with: "Welcome, Dulce Adelina!"

One of the few Republican survivors of the 1936 landslide had been Henry Cabot Lodge, Jr., the grandson of the "gentleman from Massachusetts," who had managed to capitalize sufficiently on the accumulated resentments against Curley to defeat him in the contest for his grandfather's old senatorial seat. Senator Lodge came up for re-election in 1942, and Roosevelt picked Democratic Joseph Casey to run against him. Honey Fitz, though now eighty years old and in failing health, decided to have his last political fling by contesting the nomination. For a few weeks he staged a radio counter-campaign with ghost-written speeches and a ghostly voice signing off with "Sweet Adeline." Son-in-law Kennedy consulted with Tague's old secretary, Joe Kane, wise in the ways of pols. Kane was sure that Honey Fitz, in spite of his age, could, by spending a few hundred thousand dollars, beat Roosevelt's dictated candidate. Kennedy wanted to know if the old man could beat young Lodge in the election. Kane said that he could not. Kennedy reached for his hat. "I don't know where you're going," he told Kane, "but I'm going back to the Ritz."

Although no one admitted it openly, it was obvious by the forties that the last of the Dearos was slipping. On his eighty-first birthday party at the Parker House a congratulatory message came from the White House addressed to Boston's Number One Booster. Charles Francis Adams was again present. The climax of the party came just as Honey Fitz was singing "Sweet Adeline," when his grandson Jack—now Naval Lieutenant John Kennedy—whom he had not seen for over a year, suddenly walked into the room, lean and yellow but buoyantly alive after surviving the loss of his P.T. boat and an attack of malaria.

There were bewilderments and there was sadness as well in Honey Fitz's closing years. In the spring of 1944 gossip columns spread the report that his granddaughter Kathleen Kennedy, then in London with the American Red Cross, was about to marry the Marquess of Hartington, the eldest son of the Duke of Devonshire. "Impossible," her grandfather told reporters at the Bellevue. "No grandchild of mine would ever marry outside the Catholic Church." But a few days later Kathleen Kennedy and Lord Hartington, a captain in the Grenadier Guards, were married at a registry office. The best man was Kathleen's brother Joseph, then serving in England as a Navy pilot. Young Joe was to die that August when his plane blew up over the Channel on a bombing mission. Lord Hartington was killed in action a month later. If he and his wife had lived, she would have become the first duchess of England, but she herself died in the crash of a private plane in 1948.

Jack Kennedy, after his discharge from the Navy, came to Boston, took an apartment round the corner from the Bellevue to establish his legal residence, and let it be known that in 1946 he would run for Congress from his grandfather's old district. He set up headquarters in the Bellevue and began to build his organization. Ironically, his chief strategist became that same hard professional, Joe Kane, who had unseated Honey Fitz twenty-seven years before. Grandfather and grandson spent hours together, the Dearo retelling his old political sagas, giving his shrewd old advice. But Jack, with his wealth and his Harvard background and his clipped speech, represented a new breed of Irish-Americans for whom the Dearos and the Smiling Jims and the Mahatmas had become crudely and quaintly obsolete, like gas lighting. The young supporters and strategists who gathered around Jack Kennedy in the Bellevue were Democrats in the liberal New Deal image: lean young men, college educated, most of them ex-officers, many from private schools, with only their surnames to show kinship with the old.

Ten candidates filed for the Democratic nomination—equivalent in that district to the election. Joe Kane saw to it that there were enough to fragment the vote. He paid one candidate $7500 "to stay in or get out," whichever Kane might decide was more useful. When one Joseph Russo threatened to monopolize the Italian vote, Kane dug up a second Joseph Russo to run against him. Kennedy won easily with 43 percent of the vote.

At the Bellevue, Honey Fitz danced a jig on top of a table

to celebrate his grandson's victory and followed it with a quavering "Sweet Adeline." Then, with the pride of a grandfather, and perhaps with the prescience of an old pol, he predicted that Jack would be President of the United States.

Honey Fitz lived long enough to celebrate his diamond wedding and to see Jack overwhelmingly renominated for Congress, but not quite long enough to see him triumph over Senator Henry Cabot Lodge, Jr., the grandson of his old Brahmin adversary.

I remember first seeing grandson Jack, Congressman Kennedy, in 1952 when he was running against Senator Lodge. He was on the plaform at Springfield, with the members of the Democratic State Committee, welcoming Adlai Stevenson to Massachusetts. Those assembled machine politicians were of the second generation: heavy-jowled, heavy-paunched Neanderthal types. The shoulders of their suits were vast and padded, their ties were handpainted in rainbow tints, and their eyes had that curiously beady look that one finds only in politicians, undertakers, and professional baseball players. Stevenson, the mutely dressed academic Hamlet, and the third-generation congressman in his narrow-shouldered suit and regimental-striped tie seemed from another world. Kennedy looked like what indeed he was, the youngest member of the Harvard Board of Overseers. Curiously enough, he had come to look much as Harvard overseers had always looked in their younger days. Watching him, I suddenly realized that, in this young man moving rather elegantly among the slobs, the consolidation of a new class had—reached its conclusion.

The Last of the Bosses

For the first half of this century and beyond, James Michael Curley was the most flamboyant and durable figure on Boston's political scene. Mayor off and on for a total of sixteen years, he spent four terms in Congress and two in jail, and for two Depression years he was Governor of Massachusetts. At his death he lay in state for two days in the State House Hall of Flags, the fourth person in the history of the Commonwealth to be so honored. His seventeen-room neo-Georgian mansion on Jamaicaway, with shamrocks cut in its shutters, was both a landmark of the rise of the immigrant Irish and a nose-thumbing in the direction of Yankee Beacon Hill. He was hated by Proper Bostonians with a proper and ultimate hatred, and held in mindless affection by the slums. His Irish-American political associates alternately embraced and knifed him. Counted out a score of times, he always bounced back. On several occasions and long before his death, he received the last rites of the Catholic Church.

Like his old enemy Honey Fitz, Curley was a transitional figure, a symbol of the emergence of the famine Irish from their proletarian status to political dominance. His father, Michael, came to Boston from Galway in 1865 at the age of fourteen. Sarah Clancy, his mother, arrived that same year—a meager-boned Connemara girl of the type the Irish wit Dr. Gogarty called Firbolg. She was twelve years old and worked first as a maid on Beacon Hill. Michael Curley became a hod carrier at ten cents an hour by the grace of Patrick "Pea-

Jacket" Maguire, boss of Ward 17, where Galway men clustered. Michael Curley was good-looking in a stumpy, plodding, impassive way. At twenty-one he married Sarah and took her to a tiny flat in one of the rotting three-deckers off Northampton Street. Along Roxbury Neck there were hundreds of those fetid wooden tenements that had been run up by jerry-builders for the shanty Irish. Beyond Northampton Street lay the North Bay, and at low tide the marsh gas sifting in across the mud mixed with the sour permanent stench of the Southampton Street dump. It was said that in Ward 17 children came into the world with clenched fists. In that Roxbury flat James Michael Curley, the second son, was born in 1874.

The boy's horizon was the waterfront slum. By the time he was five he ran with an urchin gang, pilfering, dodging the cops, wandering along the edge of the Roxbury flats while the herring gulls wheeled overhead, scaling stones at the wharf rats that scuttled across the dumps, selling old whisky bottles they found there to Jakie the Junkie. Daily they would see the cargo schooners coming up the Fort Hill channel from far-off places like Maine or Nova Scotia. In the summer they played about the old Roxbury canal or swam in the murky South Bay. Evenings they could hear the bullfrogs croaking from the marshes. Sometimes, though rarely, they wandered outside the ward. Only a little over a mile to the north was the newly filled area of the Back Bay with its wide avenues and brownstone-front town houses. To tenement boys, these opulent mansions with their turrets and gablings seemed like castles.

By the time Jim reached grammar school he was peddling papers. Afternoons he worked as a delivery boy at the Washington Market. When he was ten his father died. Mike Curley had always been proud of his strength. A workman challenged him to lift a 400-pound edgestone onto a wagon. He managed to raise it but then collapsed. Three days later he was dead.

The Curleys were then living in an alley tenement in Fellows Court. Pea-Jacket Maguire's point of view was limited—no votes, no help. And there was no help for the Curleys.

Sarah kept the family together by scrubbing floors in a downtown office building. Jim and his brother John, two years older, wrapped bundles and served customers at the Washington Market in their free time until the end of grammar school. At twelve, Jim was working in a drugstore an hour and a half before he went to school, and from half past four until eleven after school.

Reared in poverty, corroded with hatred of the Beacon Hill Brahmins, young Jim Curley formed his hard, unwavering, egocentric determination to succeed. Success, the road up from the Fellows Court flat to the imagined great house, was through politics. He knew that when he was still in short trousers. There was no other road for an Irish slum boy. Politics, then, was a game he would play as he found it, not to change the game or reform it, but to win. In the harshness of his own few years he grasped instinctively Boss Martin Lomasney's neoplatonic axiom, that, politically speaking, the mass of people are interested mainly in food, clothing, and shelter. For these they would barter their votes.

At fifteen, after a series of small jobs, he settled for the next eight years as a deliveryman, driving a wagon for C. S. Johnson, Grocers. He was strong like his father, wily and wiry, and except for his somewhat vulpine nose, handsome. He had a resonant voice and soon learned to modify the harshness of his gutter speech. From time to time he would drop in at Curran's livery stable, where the wardheelers gathered, or at One-Armed Peter Whalen's tobacco store, another political hangout of the district.

Meanwhile, he attended the Boston Evening High School two nights a week. In the public library he read Dickens and Thackeray and Shakespeare, and the Boston *Transcript*. He taught Sunday school, ushered and passed the plate at St. Philip's on Harrison Avenue, and joined the Ancient Order of Hibernians. He became chairman of committees for picnics, outings, minstrel shows, and church supper dances. For his straight purpose, games and girls and conviviality had no meaning. Time was too short; life too dear.

He knew the families on his grocery route as if they were

his own family; he talked with people—after church, at the Hibernians, at Whalen's, on committees. Always he was obliging and always available. By the time he reached his majority he showed the indefinable air of future success that a sixth-sense pol like One-armed Peter Whalen could spot at once. In 1898 Whalen tipped him to run for the Boston Common Council against Pea-Jacket's organization, and staked him to his first contribution. Curley won by several hundred votes, but by the time Pea-Jacket's henchmen had finished with the ballot boxes, he found himself counted out. The next year he organized his own strong-arms, and after weeks of pre-election gang fights and corner brawls, he won—too handily for Pea-Jacket to challenge him. So at twenty-six he formally entered political life as one of the three council members from Ward 17.

With his defeat of the aging Pea-Jacket, Curley consolidated himself as the new boss, organizing Ward 17 on the Tammany model of tribute and social services, and even calling his organization the Tammany Club. There was, however, this difference: Curley's organization was personal rather than self-perpetuating. In politics he would always be a lone wolf.

From that time on Curley never lacked for money. Merchants and others who did business in Ward 17 now paid to him on a more regulated basis what they had paid to Pea-Jacket. But from the ordinary people of the ward, deserving and otherwise, whose needs and requests Curley took care of quickly and efficiently, he expected nothing in gratitude but their votes.

The core of his support would always come from the slums. There he was given an allegiance that the Pea-Jackets could never command. But Curley never had a political philosophy beyond that of taking care of himself and his own. With equal ease he would at various times support Al Smith, Franklin Roosevelt, Mussolini, Father Coughlin, and Senator McCarthy. If he had had the vision, he might have become to Boston and Massachusetts what Al Smith was to New York. But his vision was limited to his own drive for power.

With Ward 17 in his pocket, Curley moved on to the Massachusetts Legislature, where he spent one term, more as an observer of the political passing show than as a participant. He was still learning. At the Staley College of the Spoken Word he took elocution lessons, modifying his speech still further to its final form. The Curley accent was unique, with grandiloquent overtones, impressive and at once identifiable, yet underneath synthetic. It achieved the desired effect, but it never rang wholly true. And in an election pinch, it could always be dropped for something more primitive.

In 1903 Curley met his first reverse. He was caught impersonating one of his less talented ward workers at a Civil Service examination and sentenced to sixty days in the Charles Street Jail. Yet, far from being disconcerted by this lapse, he capitalized on it. In later years he often planted stooges in his audience to get up and ask: "How about the time you went to jail?" Curley then liked to draw himself up and announce floridly: "I did it for a friend." Ward 17 understood. While in jail, where he spent a not unpleasant two months reading all the books in the library, he was elected to the Board of Aldermen, the upper chamber of Boston's city government.

Curley remained an alderman until 1909, when he became a member of the new City Council. And all the time he was laying his lines carefully toward his own clear though unexpressed goal—to be mayor and boss of Boston. His retentive mind had the city and its departments catalogued for future use. No one would ever be able to fool Curley.

Established in his thirty-second year, he now found time to marry Mary Herlihy, whom he had met at a St. Philip's minstrel show. With a background much like his own, she was a woman of grace and character, and she became a permanently steadying influence on him. It was a happy marriage for them both and a fortunate one for him. The boys in the back room might make up limericks about Honey Fitz and Toodles Ryan, but no enemy could ever touch Jim Curley that way. His private life was always beyond reproach, though it was to end sadly—only two of his nine children survived him.

In 1880, Mayor Frederick O. Prince had said: "No allegation of municipal corruption has ever been made against any Boston official." By Honey Fitz's time such a remark could be considered a flat, cynical joke. When Honey Fitz was elected to his four-year term in 1909, Curley, willing to wait for the next round, let himself be persuaded to run for Congress by the district incumbent, Bill McNary, who counted on insuring his own re-election by having Curley split his opponent's vote. For the first time Curley stumped outside Ward 17. In a day when political rallies were still a prime source of entertainment, Curley put on a campaign that was a combination of vaudeville, Chautauqua, and the prize ring. No one, his opponents realized too late, could equal him as a showman; no one could talk him down. There was the usual torchlight parade with the bands blaring "Tammany" to celebrate his victory.

He spent two undistinguished terms in the House and his weekends back in Roxbury. In Washington he and his wife mixed in a more sophisticated society than they had known before. They took instruction in etiquette, and this became a source of later jokes in Boston. In his autobiography, Curley maintained that he liked Washington. But Boston—the hard core of the city, the massed wards of the South End—these were his roots, and he never really functioned outside them. Before his second term was up, he resigned to enter the 1913 mayoralty contest.

Young Jim Curley—back from Washington, aggressive and dominating—was like a tidal wave. Honey Fitz, recognizing both the wave and the tide, retreated from the beach. He and the ward bosses finally produced a nonentity as token opposition to the Curley flood.

Curley's campaign for mayor dwarfed his congressional campaign four years before. He stormed the autumn city in racoon coat, "iron mike" on his head, and the gilded voice booming. He promised to clean out City Hall and give it back to the people—whatever that might mean. He savaged the ward bosses and invited the voters to call on him personally at City Hall. He promised more schools and playgrounds and beaches and parks and jobs. Politicians can hear the grass grow, and there was the underground feeling that he was unbeatable.

Incongruous as it might seem in later years, or even months, the newly elected Curley was at first hailed as a reform mayor. Hundreds of Honey Fitz's officeholders were ousted. True to his promise, Curley opened up City Hall. Those who wanted to see him about jobs, favors, or assistance, he received without appointment. A squad of secretaries catalogued each visitor before he was taken to the mayor. Decisions were made on the spot. If a request could not be granted, Curley said so and why. He was the superboss. Ward bosses became obsolete: Curley had destroyed their power, even in Ward 17. He talked to an average of 200 persons a day.

The financial and business community's satisfaction with the new mayor was brutally short-lived. Curley, they soon discovered, had lost none of his old resentments. Assessments were raised all round. A vast construction program such as Boston had never seen before was begun. Streets were ripped up, transit lines extended, beaches and playgrounds laid out, hospitals built, and services expanded. There was a job for every jobless man in the city. Here lay Curley's basic formula, then and in all his administrations: a juggler's act of public works without regard for cost. When the city treasury was empty he would borrow. The outraged Yankees could pay for it all through taxes.

Yet, much of what he did needed to be done. The cost would be excessive, the payrolls padded, a percentage of the contractors' fees would always find its way into Curley's pocket —but without him most of these projects would never have been undertaken. By the end of his first term he had altered the face of the city; by the end of his fourth term the tax rate had quintupled.

Though with him money went as easily as it came, though he liked to be known as the mayor of the poor, he enjoyed lush living. Midway in his first term he built himself the house overlooking Jamaica Pond that would be known as the House with the Shamrock Shutters. It was better than anything on Beacon Street. Some of the trimmings, including the mahogany-paneled dining room and the winding staircase, came from the recently demolished Fairhaven house of Henry H. Rogers, the Standard Oil executive. The Finance Commission and others were to ask in vain how anyone could build a $60,000 house on a $15,000 lot on a salary of $10,000 a year. Such questions never bothered Curley. In his autobiography he maintained—archly and without expecting to be believed—that he had made the money for his house on a stock market tip. Almost everyone in Boston knew that the house had been a donation from a contractor. The Curley wards felt he deserved it.

In 1917, when Curley ran for re-election, a curious amalgam of businessmen and bosses took the field against him. Martin Lomasney, the only ward boss to survive unscathed, entered two congressmen with Celtic names as pseudo-candidates to cut into Curley's Irish-Democratic vote. It was an old gambit, used many times by Curley himself, and it worked well enough to defeat Curley.

After several ludicrously unfortunate business ventures—in such matters Curley would always be both gullible and inept—he became president of the Hibernia National Bank, within wistful sight of City Hall. But this was for him only an interlude. His real life was always politics.

The 1921 mayoralty campaign was one of the closest and meanest in the history of Boston, and Curley fought alone. No political pro in the city was for him, and the betting against him ran over two to one. But his opponent, a respected Catholic lawyer named John R. Murphy, was not prepared for what he now had to face. It was said commiseratingly of him afterward that he was too much of a gentleman. Among other things, Curley sent some of his workers to Charlestown dressed in clerical black and carrying prayer books. There they let it be known that turncoat Murphy had joined the Masons and that he was divorcing his wife to marry a sixteen-year-old girl. Other Curley supporters rang doorbells through Catholic South Boston, posing as members of the Hawes Baptist Club and soliciting votes for John R. Murphy. Curley even gave a Ku-Klux Klan organizer known as the Black Pope $2000 to campaign against him.

Against all odds and predictions Curley won, with 74,200 votes to Murphy's 71,180. For the first time in a Boston election women could vote, and it was generally felt that Mary

Curley's "Personal Appeal to Women Voters," an open letter circulated at the last minute, gave her husband the extra votes that elected him.

Before anyone quite knew what was happening—anyone except Curley—there were 24 million dollars' worth of building projects under way. Several times the city treasury gave out. Curley merely borrowed more money against future taxes. If a banker showed reluctance to lend, Curley would threaten to start a run on his bank "a mile long." Taxes and assessments, as well as buildings, went up.

During Curley's second administration, and with Curley pointedly in mind, the Republican State Legislature passed a law that no mayor of Boston might succeed himself. Instead, in 1924 Curley ran as Democratic candidate for governor against Alvan T. Fuller, who would later become widely known in connection with the Sacco-Vanzetti case. It was a Republican year, and in any case, Massachusetts would not be ready for Curley until after the transvaluations of the Depression. Curley tried to make an issue of the Ku-Klux Klan and his own opposition to it. Wherever he spoke in the rural sections of the state, fiery crosses would suddenly blaze out on nearby hills just in time for him to point to them and say, voice resonant with emotion: "There it burns, the cross of hatred upon which Our Lord, Jesus Christ, was crucified." Later he admitted that the crosses had been touched off by his boys. Fuller won—but the size of Curley's vote gave the state party leaders, whose enthusiasm for Curley was at best limited, something to think about.

In the Presidential election of 1928 the Commonwealth of Massachusetts was one of the eight states carried by Al Smith. To the Irish Democrats of the Commonwealth, Smith was the most creditable man from Irish ranks who had yet appeared in politics. Before the national convention the Massachusetts leaders were solidly for Smith. All of them were at odds with Curley, and they took care that the ex-mayor would have no part in the convention or in the subsequent Smith campaign. They reckoned, however, without Curley.

Shortly after Smith's nomination, Curley opened what he called his Bull Pen in the vacant Young's Hotel near City Hall. He had the walls plastered with Smith signs and photographs. There were loudspeakers in the windows blaring a raucous mixture of speeches and music. Every day was open house in the Bull Pen. Inside it was like an amateur night. Anyone who felt like walking in and speaking his piece about Smith was welcome to use the microphone. And when Al Smith arrived in Boston to ride through the city in a whirl of ticker tape, the excluded Curley was somehow there in the car beside him, to the chagrin of the official members of the party. In the election, when Smith was trailing Hoover by 83,000 votes outside Boston, and the city's roaring majority gave him the state by 17,000, it was Curley's desperate drumming up of the last few thousand votes that made the difference.

After the Hoover sweep, Curley was astute enough to realize that Smith would not have another chance, no matter what Massachusetts Democrats thought. Four years later Curley was the first and in fact the only politician in the state to come out for Franklin Roosevelt before the convention. Massachusetts Democrats, still solidly and emotionally for Smith, were shocked and furious. Curley was a traitor. The wilderness was where he belonged.

The Massachusetts delegation to the 1932 Democratic Convention was headed by Governor Joseph B. Ely, an old Curley enemy. Curley was not to be a delegate to this convention; in fact, if Ely had anything to say about it, he would not even be a spectator. But, as the event again showed, one had better not count Curley out too soon. For directly behind the Massachusetts delegation in the convention hall sat the Puerto Ricans with their chairman—none other than Alcalde Jaime Miguel Curleo. The Alcalde, in a familiarly florid accent, cast the six Puerto Rican votes for Roosevelt; though even after the Roosevelt stampede the Massachusetts delegation glumly and stubbornly held out to the end for Smith. Behind the scenes, Curley had helped arrange with Hearst and Garner the deal that finally gave Roosevelt the nomination.

Public opinion in Massachusetts veered quickly. The emotions that for four years had been bound up with the fortunes of Al Smith were transferred overnight to Roosevelt. Having left Boston as an outcast, Curley came back from Chicago a hero. He arrived in North Station to find that a crowd of 250,000 had turned out to meet him. Streets were jammed all the way to the Common. Inside the station twenty-one bands were blaring at one another. It took a hundred reserve policemen to clear a path for Curley to his car.

From that night until the election all Curley's efforts went into the campaign. He reopened his Bull Pen, this time decorating it with Roosevelt motifs. He mortgaged the House with the Shamrock Shutters. He traveled 10,000 miles through twenty-three western and midwestern states to deliver 140 speeches. For the election he spent a quarter of a million dollars of his own money. With James Roosevelt as an assistant, he was the Roosevelt ringmaster in Massachusetts.

All this activity had not been undertaken just for the Forgotten Man. What Curley now wanted was to set the seal of respectability on his career by becoming Secretary of the Navy. After all, it was a job held recently by a Boston Adams. Shortly after the election, Curley, with his daughter Mary, called on Roosevelt at Warm Springs. There, according to Curley, Roosevelt told him, "Well, Jim, if that's what you want, the job is yours." A few weeks later, however, at Calvin Coolidge's funeral in Northampton, James Roosevelt took Curley aside and told him that a cabinet post was not possible. James went on to tell him that he might instead become ambassador to France or Italy, and suggested that he drop in at the White House to talk it over.

On that visit the President mentioned Italy. Curley asked for a few days to think it over. Whether Roosevelt ever intended to send the boss of Boston to Rome, whether Boston's William Cardinal O'Connell vetoed the idea, or whether Curley was simply being given the Roosevelt run-around, will never be clear. In any event, at Curley's next interview, the smiling President said there were difficulties about Italy and offered him instead the post of ambassador to Poland, remarking that Poland was one of the most interesting places in the world. "If it is such a goddam interesting place," Curley is said to have replied, "why don't you resign the Presidency and take it yourself?" To the newsmen who crowded around him outside the White House, he used a quick term to describe Roosevelt that Truman later reserved for music critics. In Boston a witticism went the rounds that if he had accepted, he would have paved the Polish Corridor.

Between the two conventions Curley had been elected mayor for the third time by a clear majority, and once more with the odds against him. His principal opponent was another respectable Democratic lawyer, Frederick W. Mansfield, silently endorsed by Cardinal O'Connell himself, who had long felt that Curley was a discredit both to the Irish and his Church. The Cardinal, from a slum background similar to Curley's, was of the cast of a Renaissance prelate. He spoke Italian like an Italian, English like a cultivated Englishman. An urbane and aristocratic man, he wanted to see the emergent Irish become respectable and accepted. Politically, the Cardinal was an innocent.

Curley, in his inaugural address, attacked the Republican Good Government Association and the "select and exclusive body of social bounders in the Back Bay." His new administration began with the usual Curley public works projects, the need for which was accentuated now by the onset of the Depression.

Even before his election he knew that his wife was doomed by cancer. She died the following June. Mary Curley's influence on her husband had been stabilizing and restraining. Without her he seemed to lose his balance. He drank too much, he coarsened physically, he grew bombastic and careless, he had less control over his quick temper. Opposing Ely's nomination for governor, he got into a fist fight with the chairman of the Democratic State Committee at radio station WNAC.

The older, less careful Curley now made the political blunder of appointing his friend Edmund L. Dolan city treasurer. Dolan was the legal owner of Curley's 93-foot yacht, punningly named *Maicaway*. As Curley's understudy, Dolan headed the Mohawk Packing Company and the Legal Securities Corporation. Mohawk was organized to provide meat for city institutions—at a third above the usual cost. Through the Legal Securities Corporation, Dolan managed to sell bonds to the city and also buy them from the city to sell to brokers, collecting commissions at both ends. The state-appointed Finance Commission uncovered these and certain aspects of land-takings and other facts sufficient, so it seemed for a while, to send both Curley and Dolan to jail. The younger Curley would never have left himself so vulnerable.

Eventually Dolan was charged with the theft of more than $170,000 from the city. When the case came to trial, he was caught trying to bribe the jury and received two-and-a-half years in jail. At the same time a bill in equity was brought against Curley, and after three years and thirty-four continuances, he was ordered to pay back $42,629 to the city treasury.

Now that he had no more Washington ambitions he badgered Roosevelt for more aid and more money for Boston. He devised new projects for the Civil Works Administration. After all, a CWA was what he had been occupied with all his political life. With Governor Ely, still a disgruntled Smith man, retiring in 1934, Curley had little trouble in getting the Democratic nomination for governor. That election, the second New Deal wave, swept almost the complete Democratic state ticket into office. Boston had taken over Massachusetts at last. The crowd from City Hall moved up Beacon Hill to the State House.

Curley's two-year term as Governor marked both the height and depths of his career. No such turmoil had occurred on Beacon Hill since cynical, droop-eyed Ben Butler had been governor fifty years earlier. Curley would now use the greater resources of the Commonwealth as he had previously used those of the city, but this time with a recklessness and an arrogance he had not shown before. Work there was, projects useful and otherwise, feverishly undertaken from the Berkshires to Cape Cod, and where there was no work there were at least jobs. The State House offices bulged with idle incompetents, the Governor's anterooms swarmed with old City Hall petitioners. When the Finance Commission again threatened to dig up old Curley City Hall scandals, its members were bribed or dismissed. Curley rode roughshod over the Governor's Council, courts, and department heads, his energy as boundless as his activities were unregulated.

Insolence of office trailed him through the state as he scorched the roads in his limousine with its S-1 license plates, preceded by state police motorcycle escorts with sirens wailing, and followed by carloads of his military aides, bright in incongruous blue-and-gold-braid uniforms. S-1 was in a series of accidents. One state trooper was killed, another badly injured. Curley moved across the Massachusetts landscape like a Latin dictator. For the 1936 Harvard Tercentenary, he arrived at the Yard escorted by scarlet-coated National Lancers, drums beating and trumpets sounding, to move ostentatiously past a stony-faced President Roosevelt, while a few Harvard die-hards booed.

Just before he took the oath of office, Curley had swung a parting punch at Governor Ely. That outrageous brawl within the State House became symbolic of his administration. The inauguration ball, held at the Commonwealth Armory, was a monstrous affair to which 14,000 people were invited. During his first year in office the Governor spent $85,206 for taxis, flowers, dinners, luncheons, cigars, refreshments, and trips for himself, his guests, and secretaries. The following winter he moved his entire staff to Florida. In those Depression times his daughter Mary's wedding to Edward C. Donnelly, Jr., of the Donnelly Advertising Company, was the gaudiest ever held in Massachusetts. The bride's trousseau cost $10,000—paid for, and not donated, as anti-Curleyites had hinted. At the packed Cathedral of the Holy Cross, under the dismayed eyes of Cardinal O'Connell, many of those present stood on the pews as the bride and her father came down the aisle. There were 2,300 guests at the Copley Plaza reception afterward. They downed two tons of lobster at thirteen dollars a plate.

Financially buttressed at the end of his Governor's term, Curley determined to revenge himself on Roosevelt. The President had not liked him as Governor, and he would like still less to find him in the United States Senate. For Governor Curley the senatorial nomination was easy to manipulate; the election seemed equally so. His Republican opponent was Henry Cabot Lodge, Jr., the grandson of the old anti-League senator, whose political experience was contained in two terms in the Massachusetts Legislature. Curley liked to refer to him as "Little Boy Blue." Yet in the New Deal landslide of 1936, when every other major Democratic candidate in the Commonwealth was overwhelmingly elected, Curley lost to Lodge by 136,000 votes. All the states except Maine and Vermont went for Roosevelt, but Massachusetts had had enough of James Michael Curley.

In a sense, however, Curley had the last word, for on that day when the cannon boomed across the Common to announce a new governor, he stole the whole show by marrying again. His second wife, Gertrude Casey Dennis, was a widow, a quiet woman without political or social ambitions, who would give him again the domestic stability he had found with his first wife.

The following year he again ran for mayor. He found himself opposed by a "reform" candidate, Maurice Tobin, a handsome and hardy young Democrat from his own district, who in the wheel-spins of politics would twice become mayor, then governor, and finally figurehead Secretary of Labor in Truman's Cabinet. Curley accurately described him as "a protégé of mine who learned too fast." It was to Curley's mind an easy election, but on election morning there appeared on the masthead of the Boston *Post,* whose editorials generally reflected the views of the archdiocese, a brief notice to the voters of Boston that read:

> Cardinal O'Connell, in speaking to the Catholic Alumni Association, said, "The walls are raised against honest men in civic life." You can break down these walls by voting for an honest, clean, competent young man, Maurice Tobin, today.

Thousands of copies of the *Post* were distributed free in front of all the churches. The quotation was from an address the Cardinal had made six years before, but few readers noticed that the quotation marks ended before Tobin was mentioned. To the faithful, it seemed that His Eminence had endorsed Curley's opponent. Curley furiously tried to get a retraction broadcast, but the Cardinal could not be reached. It was a maneuver worthy of Curley himself. Enough pious votes were swung to Tobin for him to win.

In 1938 Curley was strong enough to take the nomination away from the Democratic governor, but he was still unable to win the election. His opponent was the long-jawed speaker of the Massachusetts House of Representatives, Leverett Saltonstall, who as a Republican, a Harvard man, and a Brahmin combined the three things that Curley was best at excoriating. Yet Saltonstall was a new type of Old Yankee who represented a *rapprochement* with what Curley liked to call "the newer races." The growing numbers of middleclass Irish liked him. In later years, when he and young Senator Kennedy were colleagues in Washington, they became so friendly that Kennedy refused to endorse Saltonstall's next Democratic opponent. Saltonstall also had the advantage of owning one of the most agreeably ugly mugs in politics. Curley made the mistake of quipping that Saltonstall might have a South Boston face but he would never dare show it in South Boston. Of course Saltonstall walked through the South Boston streets the next day, talking with everyone he met and dropping in at the innumerable bars. He overwhelmed Curley at the polls.

By the time of Boston's next municipal election Mayor Tobin had built a tight political machine of his own. Curley ran against him nevertheless and suffered his fourth defeat in a row. At sixty-seven, after a generation in politics, it looked as if he had come to the end of the road. But that was not the way Curley saw it. He turned again to his solid core of supporters in the close wards of Roxbury, South Boston, and Charlestown. As if he were now going down the ladder he had once climbed, he asked them to send him back to Congress in 1942.

These days he was short of funds, and every week there was

the $500 installment on the $42,629 he had been ordered to pay the city. A few months before Pearl Harbor, unlucky as usual in his private ventures, he had run into a Washington promoter named James G. Fuller, who was organizing a five-percenter corporation to mediate between manufacturers looking for war contracts and the appropriate heads of government agencies. Fuller offered to make Curley president of this organization, to be known as the Engineers' Group, Inc. Later, Fuller was shown to be a confidence man and ex-convict. Curley, in spite of his title, had little to do with Fuller's corporation except to appear on its letterhead. Curley resigned from the company before being elected to Congress.

Two years later the Engineers' Group was one of the concerns investigated by the Truman Committee, and Curley was indicted because of his connection with it. He always maintained that the case against him was directed from the White House. His trial was postponed to allow him to run for mayor of Boston in November, 1945.

Tobin had moved on to become governor. The acting mayor was an obscurity, as were the other four candidates. Postwar Boston itself seemed derelict, a fading seaport as drab as the blackout paint that covered the gilt dome of the State House. So much needed doing, from street repairs to housing for veterans, and "Curley gets things done." That, at least, was the campaign slogan spread casually in public by his paid workers and taken up by others. Looking back to the prewar days, it seemed true enough. What if Curley was under indictment for some contract swindle? If he was guilty he hadn't done very much, no more than the rest of them. Anyhow, he got things done!

On election day Curley beat his closest opponent by two to one. For the fourth time he became Mayor of Boston, thirty-one years after his first inaugural. Two months later he was convicted by a Washington jury of using the mails to defraud.

His appeal to the Supreme Court was rejected in 1947. As the date neared for his sentencing he took to his bed. He received the last rites of the Church, and then unexpectedly his health picked up. Finally, the postponed but inevitable day came. He appeared in court in a wheelchair and wearing a collar a size too large. His lawyer produced a certified list of nine ailments from which he was suffering, any one of which might prove fatal. Unimpressed, the judge sentenced him to six to eighteen months at the Federal Correctional Institute at Danbury, Connecticut. "You are sentencing me to die," Curley croaked at him as they wheeled him away. Democratic House Leader John W. McCormack circulated a petition for Curley's release and it was signed by all the Massachusetts delegation in Washington except Senator Kennedy. After five months, President Truman pardoned Curley—because, as the President said later, "he was innocent."

Although it was not known at the time, Curley was shattered by his Danbury experience. There was nothing left of the young man who could shrug off a few months behind bars by reading all the books in the prison library. He now felt his age and a sense of failure, and for the first time he knew self-doubt. On his release, according to his daughter, he was hesitant about facing people again.

It warmed him to be met by a great milling crowd in front of the House with the Shamrock Shutters, welcoming him with "Hail to the Chief." Inside he found familiar faces and a huge cake inscribed "Happy Birthday to Our Beloved Boss." In a few days he was back at City Hall at his old desk, looking fifteen years younger and running the city in his old way.

Yet the city was not the same. His personal open-handedness as boss of old Ward 17, and in his many years as Mayor had now become a more impersonal function of government. Voters were no longer gratefully held in line by a job shoveling snow, by the odd ton of coal, by the perennial Thanksgiving turkey and Christmas basket. Social security and unemployment insurance and the psychiatric social worker had taken over. The Irish were becoming middle class. One couldn't even soak the rich any more. In an almost bankrupt city the tax rate could go no higher. What Boston mostly needed now was an efficient receiver.

In the 1949 election, Curley, to his derisive surprise, was

opposed by John B. Hynes, who had served as mayor while Curley was in prison. "A little city clerk," Curley called him contemptuously, but when the ballots were counted, Hynes, the administrator, had won by 15,000 votes. It was the end of Curley's political career.

The next year, by a twist of fate, his daughter Mary and his son Leo both died of cerebral hemorrhages on the same day. Mary, who had been closest to him, had led an unhappy life; her marriage had ended in divorce in 1943. Leo was, at the time of his death, a lieutenant in the Navy. In Curley's loss, even his enemies could feel pity for him.

After Curley got out of Danbury, he had complained to a Boston newspaperman, Joseph Dinneen, that the press had always been unfair to him. Dinneen thereupon offered to write Curley's life story honestly and objectively. Curley agreed, and with his collaboration *The Purple Shamrock* was written. It appeared in 1949. Curley was proud of the book and used to give away autographed copies to City Hall visitors.

The Purple Shamrock, the first attempt to put Curley's career in perspective, was the beginning of the Curley legend. What it told was true and often amazingly frank. Dinneen admitted that money was never a problem for Curley, although Curley could never quite explain where he got it, how his income skyrocketed when he was in office and shrank to a trickle when he was not, or how "there wasn't a contract awarded that did not have a cut for Curley." Yet Dinneen felt that even so, Curley's accomplishments justified the cuts.

Now that Curley was no longer to be feared politically, he began to seem a kind of institution. He had been around for so long. Even the Bostonians who had fought him hardest in the pugnacious City Hall days, now, in the nostalgia for their greener years, felt a certain left-handed affection for him. He in turn was pleased and flattered by the occasional courtesy from a Lowell or a Lodge. Every political figure from Senator Saltonstall to the last South Boston ward-heeler would drop in on the way past the House with the Shamrock Shutters. Curley in his old age could still charm the birds out of the trees.

When Edwin O'Connor's novel *The Last Hurrah* was scheduled to appear in 1956, it was carefully let out in advance that here was a novel about James Michael Curley. The editor of the *Globe* sent Curley a copy with the suggestion that he review it. The next day the book was returned with a note from Curley to the effect that he was consulting his lawyers.

Frank Skeffington, the politician-hero of the book, is undoubtedly Curley, even to his feud with the Cardinal, but he is a retouched Curley, less violent, more urbane. After Curley's first resentment had worn off, he began to see the Skeffington portrait as an asset. The book had toned down his ruthlessness, emphasized his benevolence. The various hints of fraud and peculation were, after all, no more than the admissions of *The Purple Shamrock.* For a while Curley took jokingly to calling and signing himself Skeffington. From originally intending to sue O'Connor, he ended up by congratulating him. As an aftermath he decided to write his autobiography, to out-Skeffington Skeffington by putting into a book what Dinneen had either not known or discreetly omitted.

In the final section of *The Last Hurrah,* when Skeffington is on his death bed, someone standing by the apparently unconscious figure remarks unctuously that if Skeffington had it all to do over again, he'd no doubt do it very differently. The dying man then manages to rouse himself and whisper: "The hell I would!" It was from this episode that Curley took the title of his own book, *I'd Do It Again.*

It is a rambling and uneven book, often dulled by the memory of obscure and forgotten ward-heelers, but on the other hand, enlivened by the brazen candor of Curley's admissions. Though actually written by Honey Fitz's biographer, John Cutler, after conversations with Curley, it preserves Curley's own style of the informal cliché. What runs through the pages as an undercurrent, sensed even when not visible, is the after-feeling of the Famine years, the old Celtic bitterness against the chill Yankee. *I'd Do It Again* is more reticent about Curley's financial background than is *The Purple Shamrock.* There is no mention of his income tax irregularities, and nothing is said of his connection with the Mishawum Manor blackmail scandal of the early twenties in which two district attorney friends of his were disbarred.

The summer after *The Last Hurrah* was published, Curley sold his Jamaicaway house to the Oblate Fathers. Those shamrock shutters, once a gesture of defiance, had become a familiar landmark. The massive furniture, the library, the Georgian silver, the Waterford glass and Crown Derby china, the jade and ivory *bibelots* and pious statuary had been purchased for the most part from auction rooms. Now to auction rooms they would return.

Curley moved to a small suburban-colonial house the other side of Jamaica Pond. He settled down there with his governor's chair and his mayor's chair and a selection of his smaller belongings. Governor Foster Furcolo appointed him to a sinecure job, for Curley was hard up again. The Boston papers always seemed to be printing little human-interest stories about him: photos of him fishing, or being shaved by Sal, the Huntington Avenue barber. Edward R. Murrow ran his Person-to-Person television show from the new house, and on it Curley announced that he was going to live to be 125 years old so that he could bury all his enemies.

Though Curley belittled it, from the time he moved his health began to fail. He was in and out of the hospital for checkups. His face grew gray and flabby. Yet his right hand had not forgotten its cunning. When Columbia Pictures was about to release its film version of *The Last Hurrah*, Curley, after he had viewed the picture privately, filed suit for "irreparable damage to a valuable property"—that is, his life story. Columbia paid $25,000 for the damage. Then it was discovered that the lawyer to whom the check was made out was nonexistent and that the stamp on the release form was that of a nonexistent notary. Curley claimed that his signature was a forgery. Officially, no one knows yet who got the money. When Curley renewed his threat of a suit, Columbia settled for an additional $15,000. The picture was running at a Boston theater when Curley died.

He entered the City Hospital for an intestinal operation on

November 4, 1958, election day. Just another campaign, he remarked. For the first few days he seemed to be mending. He was able to walk about and to talk of the great Democratic victory. A week later he had a relapse. The end came quickly.

He lay on a bier in the State House in the great hall where the battle flags of Massachusetts regiments are kept, and in two days 100,000 people filed past. Then, on a warm morning like an aftermath of September, he was buried from Holy Cross Cathedral. It was the largest funeral ever seen in Boston.

According to the Boston papers, Archbishop (later Cardinal) Richard J. Cushing had flown from Washington to deliver the eulogy. The late Cardinal O'Connell had spoken one when Curley's first wife died; the Archbishop himself had eulogized Mary and Leo eight years before. Now he sat silent and dominant in the sanctuary. The celebrant was Curley's youngest son, Father Francis Curley, S.J.

The coffin of polished mahogany glittered in the candlelight that was reflected again on the scabbards of the Knights of Columbus, Fourth Degree, who formed the guard of honor. They stood there, plump and middle-aged, in silk capes, their hands on their sword hilts, white plumes covering their heads. As the requiem mass reached its conclusion, the Archbishop approached the coffin. Then he prayed, in the grating, honest, South Boston voice that was his inheritance and that he was too proud to change. High overhead, suspended by a wire from the Reconstruction-Gothic dome and directly over the coffin, Cardinal O'Connell's red hat swung slightly in the air currents.

The prayer ended, and everyone watched the Archbishop's seamed face under its white miter, waiting for him to mount the steps to the pulpit. But the Archbishop did not move. There was no eulogy.

About the Author

Francis Russell has contributed historical and critical articles to such periodicals as *American Heritage, Horizon, The Yale Review, The Antioch Review, The Christian Science Monitor,* and abroad to *Irish Writing, The Observer, The Countryman, Time & Tide,* and others.

Born in Boston in 1910, he attended the Roxbury Latin School. Following several undergraduate years in France and Germany, he returned to New England and graduated from Bowdoin College in 1933. In 1937 he received an A.M. from Harvard University. During World War II he served in the Canadian Army as a captain in the Intelligence Corps. After the war he was a political intelligence officer with the British 30th Corps in Hildesheim, Germany. In 1955 his volume of critical essays on Joyce, Kafka, and Gertrude Stein was published in England as *Three Studies in 20th-Century Obscurity.* He is co-author of *The American Heritage Book of the Pioneer Spirit,* and author of *Tragedy in Dedham: The Story of the Sacco-Vanzetti Case.* He lives in Wellesley Hills, Massachusetts.